A Time to Dance

ANGELA BOMFORD

WESTBOW
PRESS
A DIVISION OF THOMAS NELSON

WestBow Press books may be ordered through booksellers or by contacting:

WestBow Press
A Division of Thomas Nelson
1663 Liberty Drive
Bloomington, IN 47403
www.westbowpress.com
1-(866) 928-1240

All Bible scriptures use the King James Version of the Bible.

Everything in the book is recalled as factually as possible

ISBN: 978-1-4908-0390-6 (sc)
ISBN: 978-1-4908-0389-0 (hc)
ISBN: 978-1-4908-0391-3 (e)

Library of Congress Control Number: 2013914061

Printed in the United States of America.
WestBow Press rev. date: 08/16/13

To my wonderful husband

DOUGLAS BOMFORD

After more than half a century,
still my sweetheart and best friend.

FOR OLIVE

The inspiration of my youth.

TABLE OF CONTENTS

With thanks to my very special friend JILL EATON BIBBY, without whose encouragement this book would never have been started and to LARRY ZUKERMAN, REV. RYAN KENNEDY, and HAL SMITH, without whom it would never have been finished. Thank you gentlemen for answering my frequent calls for help with my disobedient computer!

PROLOGUE

England 1937

THE SMALL GIRL gripped her big sister's hand with all the fierce love and trust only a three and a half year could muster. Olive was ten, and the young child felt an overwhelming assurance that as long as Olive was leading the way, her safety was assured. "Come on Angela!" Olive urged her small charge. "Hurry up, and whatever you do, don't trip over!"

There were few automobiles on the Streets of Wallasey in the nineteen-thirties. People could not afford such a luxury. Angela always enjoyed playing with her toys under the table -- the only space there was to play in the apartment over the little furniture store her father owned.

The radio was always on. The child knew the "Lullaby of Broadway" from the American Musical "42nd Street" and liked it when a singer called Bing Crosby sang "Pennies from Heaven".

But now, Angela's feet could hardly run fast enough. Her bright eyes danced at the thought of blowing bubbles with the new set Olive had just bought for her. However, when they reached home, mother had more important issues on her mind!

"For heaven's sake girl, you've got your knees all grubby again, and we have to leave soon," Mother scolded, lifting her younger daughter onto the draining board in the tiny kitchen.

The apartment was not adequate enough for the Steggles family. With three growing children, the mother thought longingly of a large house she had seen in a better part of town, as she began to soap the small, grubby knees.

A few weeks earlier, Olive had been rehearsing with a group to sing in a show at the local theatre. Angela, sitting on her father's lap, had been agitating to get up on the stage too, and have a bash at singing into a microphone like her sister.

Big brother Norman, a handsome seventeen year old, had needed someone to try out his home - made microphone, so he had taught the small child to sing a couple of songs into it. Angela had repeated them over and over for weeks, while Norman and his pal "fine tuned" the gadget at the end of the microphone wire outside.

Now, in a real theatre, the rehearsal over, the band began packing up their instruments. Angela's Dad took her up on the stage, and asked Jack Leigh, the conductor if he would let the three year old sing into the microphone for a minute.

The child began to sing.

After a few lines of "It's a Sin to Tell a Lie", the band started unpacking their instruments, and backing the small child up. After a second song, accompanied now by the whole band, the conductor spoke at length with Olive and Angela's father.

All over England, small towns were plans were being made to celebrate the Coronation of King George V1. His older brother had abdicated to marry a divorced American woman. Now the Duke of York, with his wife and two little girls, had been suddenly thrown into the world spotlight. It was particularly hard on the young Duke, as he was fighting to overcome a terrible speech impediment. Seventy-five years later, a movie that would sweep the Academy Awards would be made about him.

Towns all over Britain were having their own "Coronation Queens" and after Angela's impromptu performance, the producers decided it would be a novelty to have the young child crowned as the "Coronation Queen" of Wallasey, with her big sister Olive holding the long train.

So the knees had to be scrubbed to perfection, as it was May 12th 1937, Coronation day. They must leave for the theatre. "The Floral

Pavilion", New Brighton, would play a pivotal role throughout that small child's life.

Olive & Angela Steggles May 1937

Moving into 174 Wallasey Road in 1938 was like moving into heaven to the four year old. There was a good sized bedroom to share with her sister, and a lawn to run on in the yard. Thanks to thrifty parents who had saved for years, it surely looked as if Angela would never have to play under a table again.

But hardly a year had passed, when the Steggles family, along with the whole of Europe, was plunged into a life filled with bombs, air-raid shelters, and gas masks.

For World War Two had begun.

" *I said to the man who stood at the gate of the year, 'Give me a light that I may tread safely into the unknown'. He replied 'Go out into the darkness, and put your hand into the hand of God. That shall be to you, better than a light, and safer than a known way.*" (Author Unknown)

From the Christmas 1939 broadcast speech of King George VI

CHAPTER 1

A Time For War

"IF THAT HITLER thinks he's going to make me eat margarine instead of butter, he's got another think coming!" I heard a woman declare, as the parade of soldiers marched down Wallasey Road.

It was a hot summer day in 1939 when I first heard that name; a name that would forever depict evil and violence throughout the civilized world; violence which would cause the death of 60 million human beings.

Earlier that year, our parents had taken Olive and I to see a new Holiday Camp which was being built in Prestatyn, North Wales.

We walked over boards across the wet cement, peering in to what would be the chalets, similar to the later cabins on ships. With a swimming pool, skating rink, a huge ballroom and nightly shows offered, my parents booked us for two weeks in August. It was a wonderful vacation.

Olive and I had climbed the steps to the top of the camp tower, and looked thro the telescope. Beyond the beach and sand-hills, we could see a ship out in the Irish Sea.

There was no way for us to know that only six weeks later, barbed wire would be stretched across the beach, our chalets would be Military barracks, and where we were now standing, a soldier with his rifle would be on guard.

For on September 3 rd , 1939, the British Prime Minister Neville Chamberlain, after long months of appeasing Hitler, finally announced on the radio that as he had not received any assurance from Hitler that he would withdraw his troops from Poland, Great Britain was now at war with Germany.

For over two years, a Member of Parliament named Winston Churchill had been urging Britain to arm itself, and warning the country of what was to come. The press branded him a war -monger, and he was largely ignored. Barely two decades had passed since the First World War with Germany had claimed the lives of a whole generation. The nightmare had lasted four long years for Great Britain. The results of lost sight and limbs were still visible. Neither Parliament nor the British public would listen to talk of another war.

Months earlier, my father had flown into a rage while reading his newspaper. There had been a photograph of Prime Minister Chamberlain standing in front of a small airplane, smiling and waving a piece of paper in his hand. History would one day explain my father's rage. The paper had been the signed agreement between Adolf Hitler and the United Kingdom never to go to war again. "Peace in Our Time," had been the headlines.

The allies had not yet learned two valuable lessons my father knew. During the First World War, he had served in the trenches of France and knew that in order to stay safe, a country must be well armed, prepared at all times to defend itself, and *never ever,* attempt to appease a bully.

Norman, Olive & Angela Steggles 1940

My brother Norman, now nineteen years old, volunteered immediately for the Royal Air Force, while my dad started building a bomb shelter in the back yard. However, having dug down three neat steps, much to his annoyance, the next morning it was filled with water! That idea was abandoned, and a cupboard under the stairs was declared our 'air raid shelter' instead. A piece of string was attached to the outside knob, so that the door could be pulled inwards. Having no concept of explosion, I firmly believed I would be totally safe there.

Mothers put up black drapes, as not a chink of light was to be seen to aid any German bombers, as they sought out their targets.

All over England, wardens patrolled neighborhoods looking for a telltale chink of light. If that crime was detected, he shouted loud enough for the entire street to know who the culprit was. "Put that bloody light out!" became the standard cry.

Britain's skies were suddenly festooned with silver apparitions; the barrage balloons were to deter enemy planes from flying low enough to strafe the population. The idea was that the German aircraft would become entangled in all the wires that held the big gas filled balloons down to the ground. How our fighters got up there to shoot the German bombers down, without getting caught up in them themselves, I never did fathom.

Remembering the horrifying results of mustard gas during the previous war, everyone was issued with a gas mask. Mom took me to the Church hall where the Boy Scouts were assembling them. I remember how insulted I felt when the young scout handed me a mask with a Mickey Mouse face on it. Being well aware they were for children aged five and under, I told him that I was almost six years old for goodness sake, and wanted a grownup black one!

Your gas mask went everywhere with you. Anyone in a densely populated area, seen without a gas mask case over their shoulder, was likely to be stopped by a policeman or warden, and sent home for it! They could also demand to see our Identification Card. Children had Identity bracelets, which we never took off. Thankfully, at that time, people had the good sense to put the safety of their country before their demands to "rights of privacy".

Everyone was issued a Ration Card for meat, bacon, butter, margarine, tea, cereal and candy. We got 8 oz sugar, 2 pints of milk, 2 oz of cheese, & 1 egg a week. Canned and dried goods along with cigarettes were also rationed. Few people needed gas for their cars, as only people with special permission were allowed to drive one. Doctors and people using a vehicle to deliver goods, were among the few who had to make the strict gas ration stretch out. Everyone else owning a car had to put them in storage, as without the special ID, they were forbidden on the roads. Every gallon of fuel was needed for our planes and tanks. Transportation to work was by train, bus, bike or legs. I was the only kid in the class who had a car, as my dad used it to pull the trailer which was used to deliver the furniture from his shop, while he was still in business.

Rationing would last until I was 20 years of age. Even today my hips can attest to the fact that I find it impossible to see food thrown out, or leave anything on my plate!

The first six months after war was declared, nothing happened, and Great Britain was lulled into a false sense of security. History would call that period of time, "the phony war".

Then In July of 1940, the fate of England hung in the balance as she stood alone against Hitler & Nazism. .

Most people did not know that Hitler's planned invasion of Britain was already in place --- code named -----"Operation Sea-Lion". The Germans had already amassed invasion troops, barges & equipment on the coasts of France & Belgium. But Hitler's generals were worried about the damage the Royal Air Force could inflict on the German army during the invasion, so he agreed to postpone it until September 10th 1940, by which time Field Marshal Goering had promised Hitler, that his Luftwaffe would definitely have swept the skies clear over Britain. Thanks to the dove- like idiots who had called Churchill a war mongering old fool, England was totally unprepared. We had only 470 serviceable aircraft, and a very limited number of trained fighter pilots to fly them against 2,000 German aircraft. Our air fields were bombed, destroying most of what we had. Now the pilots slept in their gear, ready to get their planes off the ground the moment the wail of the siren sounded.

On the 15th of September 1940, at noon, Prime Minister Winston Churchill was in his war room. An hour later, every light on the panel was on, showing every available fighter was in the air engaging the enemy. Churchill asked the group controller, "What reserves do we have?" The answer came, "There are none."

A further wave of German bombers was reported crossing the coast. Churchill exclaimed, "Good Lord man, what do we do now?"

"Well sir, we just hope the Squadrons will refuel quickly and get up again," was the reply.

So those young men, whose average age was twenty-two, battle weary, after seeing their friends shot down, just refueled and took off up into the exploding skies again and again and again.

This would forever be known as "The Battle of Britain". It turned the tide of the war.

Winston Churchill later made his famous speech, saying, "Never in the field of human conflict, has so much been owed by so many, to so few." Today, I find it impossible to think about those young men, without crying.

It is interesting to note that the tracking of the enemy planes as they approached England's coast, and the record of where our Spitfires were, was done almost entirely by females; members of the Woman's Auxiliary Air Force. Lives depended on their total concentration and accuracy.

At the same time, a top -secret ongoing operation was taking place in a Victorian mansion in the Buckinghamshire countryside. It was called "Bletchley Park". Signing the Official Secrets Act, all of the brilliant young men and women kept their word decades after the war ended, even their parents eventually dying without ever knowing of their children's amazing contribution to, according to experts, shortening the war by two years. Their incredible mathematical brains had developed encryption techniques, which broke the enemy codes. In some instances, their work made it possible to misdirect the German bombers, so they dropped their lodes in fields, instead of on London. It would be over thirty years before husbands and children realized the incredible work that grandma had done to save lives, and indeed civilization in Europe. So much for women not being able to keep a secret! It was with great awe that sixty years after the war was over I walked through those huts where the impossibly difficult and tedious work had been carried out.

England's civilian population sustained over 23,000 deaths and 32,000 injured in air raids between July and December of 1940, but those numbers would have been far greater, without the men and women of Bletchley Park.

My brother Norman had been so disappointed when the Royal Air Force had passed him over for pilot training. Instead, he served as a wireless operator in Algiers, Sicily and Italy. If he had been a pilot in the battle of Britain, it is very doubtful that he would now be celebrating his ninety-third birthday.

It is interesting that the King of England called the country to prayer a number of times during those treacherous days. Miraculously, the date of Hitler's invasion of England was postponed three times, until mid -October when he finally called the whole thing off, and ordered his troops to attack Russia. According to all the military leaders of that time, and Winston Churchill himself, if Hitler had continued his efforts at that time, Britain would have definitely fallen to Nazism. Most historians agree that it would have been the end of civilization in Europe.

But now, the bombing of the industrial areas had just begun. My home town of Wallasey was part of Merseyside, near the shipbuilding of Birkenhead, and the major port of Liverpool – the Eastern end of the Trans-Atlantic lifeline of supplies to Britain.

By December 12th 1940, the area had suffered 300 raids, while 365 people were killed in three nights at Christmas time.

Night raids were all too frequent. I remember vividly the wailing sound of the air raid siren. At the first note, my father left for duty as he was in the Special Constabulary, a volunteer arm of the Police Department. Mom got fed up of running up to our bedroom and shooing my sister and I downstairs to the relative safety of the small cupboard under the stairs. Then Olive came up with a brilliant idea. "Put Angela's mattress in the cupboard and let her go to bed there straight away every night," she suggested. Thus it was that for the whole of my eighth year on earth, my bedroom was a small cupboard with a slanting ceiling. When the sirens sounded, Olive would scurry in, squatting down by my feet, while mom sat on a kitchen chair just inside the entrance, pulling the door closed with a piece of string hooked onto the outside latch. We felt very safe in our sophisticated bomb shelter! I was totally convinced that if Hitler's guys dropped a bomb onto our house, it would come through the attic, onto the top of the stairs above us, and bump down them to finally rest at the bottom in the hall. Perhaps Olive told me that, for I believed it totally. Fortunately, my seven year old mind had no concept whatsoever of explosion.

Some of the raids I slept through. Others were just too noisy. One night, a bomb dropped just up the road from our house. The explosion plus the racket of the anti-aircraft guns must have scared me, as I started to cry. My mother, in her usual gentle and loving way comforted me by shouting over the din, "Oh shut up and be quiet -- you're no worse off than anyone else!!" We didn't have school psychiatrists or grief counselors, in those days. But we did have those wonderful things called sensible mothers. I firmly believe that the typical no-nonsense attitude of my mother, equipped me for the knocks of life better than anything else could possibly have done. Contrary to popular belief, I never had any kind of nightmares about the bombing afterwards, and never met anyone my age who did either.

A few years ago, when visiting England, I went to the house at 174 Wallasey Road, opened the gate, walked up the pathway, and rang the bell.

The family living there had two teenage daughters. I explained who I was, and asked if I might please look in the cupboard under the stairs that had been my bedroom for over a year when I was a child. I explained the cupboard had been the air-raid shelter for my mom, my sister, and I. Those teenagers gave their mother a look that said, "Get this loony tune out of our house now!" The structure of the cupboard where they kept their coats and umbrellas, had not been altered in any way, and it seemed unimaginable that three human beings had spent so many nights in that tiny space.

Collecting pieces of shrapnel became a hobby with small boys. At breakfast one morning, we heard the front gate squeak open. Through the window, a lad about ten years of age could be seen picking something up from our front garden. Dad must have scared the kid more than the bombs, as he opened up the window and shouted with a huge booming voice, "Get out of here! That's our shrapnel. Go and find your own!" Olive and I got into trouble for bursting out laughing as father went red in the face with annoyance. Mother just frowned.

Boys and girls were educated in separate schools after the age of eleven, to be taught by members of their own sex. However, there was a desperate shortage of male school teachers, as most had been drafted, so boys were encouraged to leave school at fifteen and go out to work. In Liverpool, able- bodied males not in the Military, had to take their turn at "fire watching".

The man who would one day be my husband was sixteen years of age when he had to take his turn at 'fire-watching' in Liverpool. This consisted of Douglas going on the roof of a ware-house with another man, each with a sand-bag over their shoulders. Working in pairs, they would watch for an incendiary bomb to be dropped, then run across the roof, heaving their sand-bags onto the bomb before it could ignite and set the building on fire. Meanwhile, a few miles away, his future wife was hiding in a cupboard under the stairs

Those of us who lived through such times, should be forgiven if we become somewhat impatient with teen-agers who grumble if they can't have an upgraded Smartphone.

The idea of avoiding civilian casualties was not on Hitler's agenda. On the contrary, he believed that by *targeting* civilians, he could terrify the British into surrendering.

The nightly air-raids increased on the major cities of England. The subway became the bedroom of the Londoners. It was the only place that offered a modicum of safety during the blitz. The morning after a raid, they would pack up their sleeping- bags, and emerge onto the streets of rubble and burning buildings. If they found their homes still standing, they would set off for work. Sometimes the buses were not in service. This meant walking around rubble hoping that when they got to their destination, the building was still operational, and they still had a job!

Many people had "Anderson Shelters". These were made of corrugated iron, which were put down into deep holes dug into the ground of the family back yard. Mothers added bunk beds, flash lights, tinned food, and most important of all to any good Brit, a primus stove and a tea kettle. Hitler would not be allowed to deprive the British of their cuppatea, even in an air-raid! Families in London and the large industrial cities got into the habit of just going straight down to the shelter every night, before the sirens went off.

Some women had chosen to keep their children at home with them. But many had been evacuated. And so, with their husbands in harms way, their children also gone, they cared for their elderly parents while working in a shop or factory. Sometimes, they emerged from their shelter, only to see a hole in the roof of their dwelling place, their furniture and home in ruins. They would pick their way through the rubble in the streets, hoping to find a shop still open with food for sale. Sometimes the water mains were damaged. That meant walking with jugs and bowls, looking for a street that had not been effected, and standing in line to fill them from the water main which a warden had opened up.

The British "Tommy" fighting in North Africa or Burma, was just as likely to receive a telegram with the news that his family had been killed in an air-raid as *they* were to hear of *his* death. Thankfully this never happened to Americans.

Years later, I worked with a girl whose house had fallen on top of their Anderson shelter during a raid. She had been literally buried alive when she was nine years old, with her mom and her two month old baby brother. She told me she would never forget the welcome voice of the air-raid warden, and the firefighters shouting "don't worry missus --- we'll get you out!" They did of course. But I met her brother when he was 14 years of age. He had never heard or spoken a word in his life, as the explosion had permanently damaged his baby ear-drums. He was a cheery chap though, chattering with his sister in very fast sign language. It is something that I always remember, as I ask God to forgive me when I am tempted to moan that we are going through "tough times" today.

CHAPTER 2

A Time To Uproot

OVER THE COURSE of the war, some two million children in England were evacuated from their city homes to live with total strangers in safer, rural areas. Newspapers showed pitiful photographs of little ones, some only five years old, a small suitcase clutched in their tiny hands, and a string round their necks with their names on. Their tear stained faces were matched only by the tears of anguish from their mother's, as they watched the train carry their precious human cargo away from everything they had ever known.

Female teachers were also evacuated, and many city schools closed down, affording little education for any children left behind.

No doubt some children wondered what they had done wrong to have mummy send them away like this. How could they understand that she had made the heartbreaking decision to save them from the bombs they feared would rain down on their homes? There was no way for the Government to know that this precaution was being put into place far too early, some children being moved from their homes before the actual declaration of war. Due to there being no attacks on England during the first six months after the war officially began, many of the children returned home. Although later, after the bombing began thousands did evacuate, ten percent of the fatalities in London due to bombing would be children.

Those living in the safer country areas received unexpected visits from Government inspectors, for if there was an unoccupied bedroom, like it or not, that family would be assigned evacuees.

At the end of November in 1940, my brother Norman came home on leave. I thought he looked very handsome in his R.A.F. uniform, but he looked very serious, and didn't laugh a lot. His train had passed through the city of Coventry, which had been attacked by five hundred enemy aircraft a few days before, destroying 4,300 homes that one night, along with the beautiful Fourteenth Century Cathedral. Mass burials took place during that week.

Norman believed that Merseyside would suffer the same treatment by Hitler's Luftwaffe, and urged our father to get mother, Olive and I away from Merseyside. We were far too close to the shipbuilding and repair areas, and the Port of Liverpool, where England's life saving supplies arrived from across the Atlantic Ocean.

The next day, dad piled us all into the car, drove to North Wales, and rented a bungalow, declaring he would commute at week-ends from his furniture shop in Wallasey. The forty-five miles between Wallasey and Rhyl made a huge difference to our safety. There was no way the enemy would waste bombs on a seaside resort. In fact, it was regarded as so safe, even carrying the wretched gas masks was not enforced there.

Our bungalow on "Sandy Cove Estate" was only steps from the beach. However, we had to negotiate our way through special openings in the barbed wire, (which by this time was stretched around most of the Welsh and English coast) and scramble over a lot of stones before we could play on the sand.

One of the things I liked best were the pretty white chain- link fences round the little lawns. They were strictly for decoration, and made the whole estate look very attractive. However, every piece of metal not doing essential work was needed for the war effort, so one day, a huge truck came round and hauled them all off for the war effort. So my pretty fences probably wound up as part of a ship or aircraft.

My father worked in his furniture shop as usual, spending Saturday evening to Monday morning with us. The gas ration would not stretch to a daily commute!

So many people evacuated from Wallasey, it was becoming a ghost town. Customers were few, and finally when the shop was badly damaged in an air-raid, dad closed down his business. He put the car on blocks in the garage, boarded up the house, found an office job in Rhyl, and bought a second –hand bike to get there. The reduction in the family income was horrendous, but we all had to adapt.

Olive left school having passed the legal school-leaving age, and took a secretarial course. A year later she was working for an insurance company.

The owner, Mr. Gunn, knew she was not yet sixteen, but she was very bright, had a super personality, and with her hair up, high heels, and a smart black suit on, she looked easily eighteen years old. All his staff had been drafted so he hired her.

A few months later, Olive was left in charge of the one girl office, while the owner went away for a week. Welsh farmers came in about the insurance on their farming stock. When Mr. Gunn returned, he was delighted to find she had only made one mistake. Olive had typed in the form that the farmer was insuring his "mayor" instead of his "mare"!

There is no doubt that while even today, some fifteen year olds may be trusted to run a business for a week without supervision, it seems that too many have a problem even getting themselves out of bed in the morning without parental guidance!

The days were gone when Olive poured over movie magazines, showing me the photographs of Shirley Temple and Vivien Leigh. I still remembered a scene in a movie, with Lana Turner (who was then the epitome of glamour) in a bath, totally covered with big bubbles while talking on a white telephone, brought to her by a maid. Could such luxuries *really* exist we wondered?

Olive was able to sing exactly like Judy Garland, and did an excellent impersonation of Bette Davis too. Acting in a movie must surely be the most wonderful, incredible experience in the world!

Two words always conjured up dreams of glamour and wealth. "America" and "Hollywood". To a little girl in war -torn Britain, they were both totally impossible to reach.

We had only lived in Rhyl a few months, when my father said something that, to my mind, was absolutely ridiculous. He said that one day, we would be able to sit in the living room looking at a box, and be able to see people miles away singing and dancing! I really thought the pressure of the war had caused my dad to loose his marbles. It was either that, or my dad was making fun of me again. I was eight years old for goodness sake, and far too sophisticated to be fooled by fairy tales like that!

The loss of my parent's furniture business meant my private school education was "out", and the local Government school was "in". Thus far, I had been educated by gentlewomen who taught me good manners, along with the three "R"s, plus poetry and music. So having to attend the local Government School, landed me with a bad case of culture shock, for I was suddenly thrust into the receiving end of a cauldron of simmering childhood hatred. While a few of the children sounded like me, most of the evacuees were what we would now term "underprivileged children" from the worst areas of Liverpool and Manchester, who tortured the English language.

They picked on me unmercifully. Thanks to a mother who was determined her two daughters would not be handicapped by speaking poor English grammar, she had devoted a shilling a week from her housekeeping money for Olive and I to have elocution lessons. Speaking correct English and having no sign of a Merseyside dialect, I was a source of aggravation to many of my classmates. My long curly hair also became an instrument of torture, as when we answered a question, we always had to stand up at our desks. I shot up the first time and yelled in agony as the boy behind had tied my

15

hair to the back of my chair. His name was Derek. I have never liked that name since!

The Welsh children naturally resented the intrusion of all of us 'foreign kids' into their peaceful lives. This mixture could have been a receipt for a disastrous education. However, the Welsh teacher with the loud voice handled all thirty-two third -graders beautifully. She walked up and down the aisles, carrying a ruler and not always just to measure things with either! It worked. We shut up, we listened, and we learned. Well, it was better than risking a smarting arm for the rest of the day! However, I never did catch on to the beautiful lilting Welsh language we were forced to study.

The biggest dread now was not the bombs going off near my cupboard but "playtime." That was when almost totally unsupervised recess took place in a huge playground, surrounded on three sides by iron railings. The fourth side looked like a prison wall. The whole school had been built when Queen Victoria was a young girl. There was no grass to be seen anywhere. Only concrete.

Sensing my total ignorance of the skill of fighting, I was the perfect child to be picked on by the bigger kids. I was constantly bullied. Large groups would swarm around me in a circle shouting "pinch, punch or join in the ring." Those were my choices. I could choose to be pinched or punched by this hoard of idiots, or join in the ring with them, to be dragged off, arms crossed with each other, to attack some other poor victim! Outnumbered and out-maneuvered, I always had to succumb to their demands, and spend the rest of the miserable recess being dragged around the playground. I was infinitely more scared of these occasions than I had been of anything in my life, and found myself fervently wishing myself back in my cupboard under the stairs, hiding from Hitler's bombs!

At no time did I ever complain to my parents or to a teacher, knowing it would get me nothing but the admonition to learn to stand up for myself. However, even from these many "underprivileged children", did I ever hear filthy language, nor was it in any of the dozens of movies I saw with Olive and mum.

A short walk from our rented bungalow to the barbed wire at the beach could be fun, as there were small concrete forts called "pill boxes" every few yards. These had narrow openings so that guns could be fired on any intruding enemy from the sea. They were just absolutely fantastic for playing hide and seek in, and the gun ports made *great* spy holes!!

One of the nicest surprises when we evacuated, happened when mother answered a knock at the door. On our doorstep stood Muriel Martin Jones, our wonderful dancing teacher from Wallasey! She had evacuated about six miles from us. A few months later, she opened a dancing school, with Olive as her chief assistant. Being back in dancing class was a dream come true! We put on wonderful shows during the next two years, raising money for the War Effort. We were proud indeed, the day we were informed that we had raised enough to buy a whole propeller for a Spitfire!

Costumes and scenery for the shows were a challenge, as only blackout material was in plentiful supply. For "The Skater's Waltz" we had skirts made of flour bags dyed red, with long rolls of white medical cotton (cotton wool to the British) sewn round the hem. White muffs and little hats were made the same way. Olive said I "looked the cats whiskers in it".

Anything pretty was a treasure, so every piece of pretty paper was carefully folded and stored to either use again, or be used for props and scenery in our shows. It still grates on me when people tear open their beautifully wrapped gifts, and I drive them mad as I still take forever to open mine!

Norman came to our new home in Rhyl for his embarkation leave. The end of those ten days was a sad time, not knowing when or if we would ever see him again. Although his letters would be frequent, they would arrive with heavy black inked out bits, sometimes with words cut out of them thanks to the censors. Any hint of where the letter was coming from had to be obliterated. Even a reference to it being "very hot here" got the censors chop!

In the spring of 1942, something wonderful happened. Handsome young men in gorgeous uniforms, smiling and chewing gum, appeared on the local streets . The American G.I.s had arrived, and England would never be the same again!

A U.S. Army camp was built only two miles from us. My parents, their own son serving somewhere overseas, welcomed many of these young soldiers to our home. They were all delighted to be able to get into a real bath, with big fluffy bath towels, and get a home cooked meal, while my mom was delighted with the tea, sugar, butter and sometimes, *real* coffee they brought with them. I became devoted to Americans forever, as they brought me treasured bars of chocolate and candy. Some Brits coined the phrase "they are over- paid, oversexed, and over here!" But those we knew were very young, well mannered, and a long way from home. They were training for that special day when the allies would invade the continent, and drive the Germans out of the occupied countries. My mom and dad just hoped someone, somewhere, was being kind to our Norman, now a twenty-two year old R.A.F. Sergeant. We had no clue where he was serving.

Some of the Americans had guitars. They taught me the hit song, "Mares Eat Oats and Does Eat Oats and Little Lambs Eat ivy". I loved their easygoing manner, and their kindly ways.

Because Rhyl had always been a sea-side holiday resort, there were two great fair -grounds, and a whole slew of amusement arcades. It was deemed totally safe to allow children to roam around them during the daytime.

Olive and I particularly favored the machine that had a metal handle, which when flicked down, sent a tiny silver ball up and across six little holes. The game was to get the ball *into* one of them, causing two pennies to drop out of the machine, in place of the one that had been put in. Usually however, the wretched ball would bounce around from one edge of a hole to another for many breathtaking seconds, finally popping itself down the "Loose' gulley, thus leaving us stony broke.

One day, after just such an experience, Olive and I were about to walk away somewhat disgruntled, when a G.I. in uniform, handed me another penny. I automatically looked up at Olive, to see if it was alright to accept it. She didn't indicate anything to the contrary, so

I took the penny from him, and promptly lost it to the machine. If there were any bad incidents that happened, we never heard of them, and in the 1940s there was certainly no question of being frightened of a kind stranger if one had a big sister around! The kind American soldier just kept giving me more coins, apparently enjoying himself as much as us when I finally won a couple of pennies back.

We were all laughing. Suddenly, he looked down at me and said, "I've got a kid your age back home in the States." Then he touched my hair gently with his hand, and was gone.

Now, seventy years later, I have never forgotten the kindness of that American.

Many times I have wondered if he was fortunate enough to get home safely to his family, or if he was one of the thousands who never returned from the terror of war.

There was no way of my knowing the Lord planned that I should one day live in that soldier's homeland and become, like him, a very proud American.

At 16, Olive was tall very lovely, and extremely talented. As well as being a superb singer, dancer and actress, she had developed an uncanny ability to mimic some of the current stars. She studied them, wrote a script, added music, and soon had her own act impersonating British stars, as well as Judy Garland, Sazu Pitts, and Carmen Miranda.

I had developed something of a singing voice, and our proud father was always on the lookout for opportunities for us to perform.

One day my dad saw a poster on the front of a Methodist Church in Rhyl announcing " Free Refreshments and Entertainment will follow the Evening Service". At that time in Wales, absolutely nothing was open on a Sunday. No cinemas, no theatres, and no shops or restaurants. American soldiers roamed the streets in total boredom. So an enterprising Pastor had seized on a golden opportunity to increase his congregation. The front door of the Church hall was locked up, so the only way in to the entertainment was from the Sanctuary itself. Thus the price of admission was attendance at the Evening Service

Like many others lured by that poster, my father suddenly decided that his family should go to Church. I was nine years old, but that was the very first time I had ever been taken inside a place of worship.

The general public, including the soldiers, flocked in, and within weeks my father was Master of Ceremonies for the weekly entertainment. Olive and I were often included in the cast, which meant regular attendance at Church of course, plus a lot of rehearsing with new songs. Soon we were being asked to entertain at various functions to raise money for the War Effort, and Olive in particular, became something of a celebrity with her act as an impersonator, and received accolades in our local newspapers.

In Britain, Sunday school was for children only, and was held every Sunday afternoon. One day I asked my mother's permission to go to one near our bungalow in Sandy Cove.

After Sunday School, a teacher gave me a little text card with a pretty blue and gold cross on it. I read the words on the way home. It said "The wages of sin is death". I got so scared, I fell over and cut my knee, trying to run home as fast as I could. Terrified out of my wits, I determined never ever go to Sunday School again!

It was so sad that only half the text was on the card, for the rest of Romans 6 verse 23 has the glorious good news.
"For the wages of sin is death, But the gift of God is eternal life through Jesus Christ our Lord."

It would be some years before I understood that Jesus was the reason why I would never have to pay that price for sin, for He had already paid it for me, on a cross at Calvary. There was no reason to be afraid, He was my Savior. I just didn't know it yet.

Shortly after that incident however, I became aware of something more than just the physical things around me. There was a dear old lady who lived next door to us, who gave me a Children's Prayer book, which was beautiful. I loved the colored photographs and prayers, and still have it to this day.

Tiny seeds of faith were being planted.

Muriel and Olive's dancing school thrived, and added "Ballroom Dancing" classes for adults. I watched them teach the American military how to Quickstep and Foxtrot. Their partners were the local girls, many of whom were in the Women's Land Army. Dancing with handsome Americans was definitely a welcome break from driving a tractor, or picking potatoes!

Months turned into years, and soon I was begging my mother to allow me to accompany Olive and her friends to an afternoon tea dance at the Queen's Ballroom in Rhyl. Finally one day she said "yes". While the age of consent was still twenty-one, fourteen was the school-leaving age in England at that time, and many young boys and girls were working and bringing home wages to their parents, to contribute to their keep. As I was very tall, dressed in clothes Olive lent me, I looked all of that magic age. Nobody could have guessed I had not yet had my eleventh birthday!

The music was marvelous, and I loved the fantastic new dance the G.I.s threw themselves into with such gusto. It was called "The Jive" or the "Boogie-Woogie". Apart from the glorious Church music and Hymns my husband and I have sung together in choirs for thirty years, my favorite melodies which we still dance to, are those of Glenn Miller.

CHAPTER 3

A Time To Plant

BY EARLY 1944, Hitler needed his bombers for his attack on Russia, so as air raids were greatly reduced, it was deemed safe to return home to Wallasey. The evacuation we thought would last a few months had turned into three years.

Mom dusted off the cobwebs of a house that still had cracked walls from bomb blasts, and dad went to work for a furniture store in Liverpool. But there was still a long way to go to end the war.

British women could volunteer for their choice of military or other war work at the age of seventeen and a half or be drafted at eighteen. Olive didn't fancy the A.T.S. (Women's Army) uniform. It was a dull khaki and as *nothing* about my sister was ever dull, she volunteered for the W.R.N.S (the Woman's Royal Navy), as they wore smart Navy blue skirts and jackets with gold buttons. When Olive left for boot camp, we still had no clue where Norman was serving, as all his letters were still being censored. I missed both my big brother and sister dreadfully.

Then the great day came for Olive's first leave. She looked very smart in her uniform with the cheeky sailor hat. She said that three years in the bunk bed over me in our small bungalow in Rhyl had been good training for her life in a hut with 12 other girls. The recruits were from all over Britain, and Olive had us in pleats of laughter as she impersonated their different dialects. Her Scottish and Welsh accents were perfect. The week went too fast, and once again my wonderful big sister was gone from me.

On the evening of June 6th 1944, I was being sworn in to the Girl Guides, known as Girl Scouts in the United States.

At that same moment, the man who would one day be my husband, was nineteen years of age, and landing on a beach in Normandy in what History would forever call "D-Day". He was one of 120,000 men who sailed across the English Channel, as part of the largest armada in history, thus starting a year of bloody land battles that finally rid Europe of Nazism.

No person should be allowed to graduate from High School without seeing the movie "The Longest Day".. It is one of the finest educational tools available to teach about this vital part of American and European history. For June 6th1944 proved to be the beginning of the end of a war in which over 60,000,000 (sixty million) human beings died. All started by one evil man, and those who listened and followed him. We would do well to heed the warning given us long ago, that history must be learned by each new generation, or we will be condemned to repeat it. It is pathetic when the subject is brought up to folks in their twenties, to hear ignorance covered by a smile and the comment "I was never much into history."

Hitler now began a new reign of terror on Londoners with pilotless jet bombs we called, "Doodle-Bugs". Launched like rockets in the day- time from Germany, they could be heard screaming across the skies of London, an enormous red flame in their wake. There would be a sickening silence, when they turned downwards, and those below knew there was no escape. There was just an explosion. Many of the anti-aircraft guns were manned by the woman's army, A.T.S. women, located in Holland and Belgium in the path of the doodle-bugs. They did their best to shoot the flying bombs down before they got over the channel. But too many got through to England. My cousin was with her husband, who was on embarkation leave. They were rowing on the lake of a London park one afternoon, when she saw a red fiery tail in the blue sky above. "Fortunately, as we looked up, it didn't cut out and drop on us, but just kept on going," she told me.

At the age of 11, all British children had to sit for the dreaded "Scholarship". This was a set of examinations in Math, English, General Knowledge and Comprehension, each one and a half hours in length. A child's entire future rested on passing these examinations, as failure would mean being siphoned off to a school that would fail to provide any chance of learning the classics, a second language, or go to college – although only a very small percentage of young people achieved the last. Most families needed children by the age of sixteen to bring home money to contribute to the household expenses.

I will forever be grateful to Miss Ellis. She was a total disciplinarian. Holding a ruler in her hand at all times, her loud voice drilled the facts into us every day, and we faithfully repeated all she said, just as loudly. Fifty was the normal class size in sixth grade then, as there was a shortage of teachers with men in the military. Buildings were often makeshift too, many having been destroyed in the bombing. Miss Ellis got fifty out of the fifty-two of us through the scholarship examinations, so we went on to wonderful schools. Without her, my life would have been much the poorer in every sense of the word.

One day, in early May, my dad shouted out the magic words, "It's over! The war is over!!" Germany had signed the unconditional surrender, and we jumped for joy.

It would be another four tragic months before Emperor Hirohito of Japan finally capitulated to the allies, bringing an end to hostilities in the Pacific.

But right now, the war was over for us. We could hardly believe it! No more air-raid sirens, black-outs, or bombs! However, rationing became even worse, as Britain now had to feed the starving people of Europe including her former enemies, the starving Berliners and the other areas the British occupied. But the fear was gone; the terror was over. Great Britain had been at war for a grueling five and a half years.

A short time later, a large envelope arrived from Rome. It was from Norman. He enclosed a photograph of himself with a pretty Italian girl on his arm wearing a corsage, and as they were standing on the steps of St. Peters, it looked exactly like a wedding picture. It wasn't, but I thought my mother was going to faint at the idea of a daughter-in-law coming from a country that had supported Germany in the war on us. However, she read the letter and discovering Norman had been in Africa, then through the dangerous fighting in Sicily and up through Italy, I think she was just thankful her son was alive, with a pretty girl on his arm.

It was some years later that he met a super girl. . Patsy Haigh had been a well known theatrical child artist before joining the woman's army, the A.T.S. during the war. She had been to school with Olive. With three fine sons still living close by them in Wallasey, Patsy and Norman have now celebrated sixty-three years of marriage.

But now it was after midnight when I heard a cab door slam.

Norman had finally arrived home. I will never forget it. I heard my dad shouting out "You made it son, you made it!" Soon Norman threw open my bedroom door, and I jumped into his big arms. I remember the tickle of his unfamiliar mustache, and the sheer joy that welled up through my whole eleven year old body. My big brother was home! Three long years had passed since I had seen him.

I loved my new all-girls school. The constant competition between boys and girls to impress each other is taken out of the equation in one sex education.

The Oldershaw High School uniform of navy blue skirts and white blouses kept both parents and students from the worry of "what to wear" each day. A couple of years later when I balked at the boring, plain uniform, my mother's explanation was perfect. "We could afford nice clothes for you, but how do you think a girl would feel whose parents couldn't afford them? The uniform solves that problem." It made perfect good sense to me, and I never complained about it again.

Instead of 52 in the class of mixed boys and girls, there were now only 32 girls. Though we were only 12 years of age, the teachers called us "ladies", and as Eliza Doolittle pointed out in "My Fair Lady," when one is *treated* like a lady, one is more inclined to *act* like a lady. I found my confidence and self-respect growing under the tutelage of these wonderful women.

The assembly hall had a big stage, curtain, and tip-up seats. It looked like a real theatre! This was the icing on the cake of my joy at attending Oldershaw High School – an establishment where one began serious studies at the age of twelve.

I was raised on radio, and never missed listening to the "Children's Hour" from five to six o'clock every day. They had super, exciting plays on, some in serial form. Listening to those wonderful child actors, I knew exactly what I wanted to do with my life.

I was determined to be one of them. I wanted to be on a stage, or in a studio, entertaining people, and acting was a fine way to do it.

Norman had joined dad as a partner in "The British Furnishing Company" which sported a large sign announcing "A. Steggles and Son Ltd." Now the old typewriter dad had kept from before the war, was sitting in the back-kitchen. One day, using two fingers, I typed up a letter to the British Broadcasting Corporation. I told them about my years of elocution lessons, and the competitions I had won. Not knowing the address I just put "B.B.C. Manchester" on the envelope.

I had not told my parents, so it was a surprise when a very official letter arrived from them addressed to me. It said that the minimum age to audition to be cast in radio plays for the British Broadcasting Corporation, was twelve. I was still only eleven years old.

The day after my next birthday, I sent another letter and got an appointment. Being a Government run Corporation, they had to give an audition to everyone who applied, therefore a huge number of children were auditioning. My mother took me to the studio in Manchester. They only needed 4 boys and 4 girls for special training, so the competition was fierce.

Every day, I watched the mail dropping through our letter –box and onto the mat in the hall.

I was about to give up, when one day a long brown envelope addressed to my parents, arrived. It was from the B.B.C. I had been chosen as one of the four girls for special training in Broadcasting. It was the greatest thrill of my young life! At the end of the training, I would be in their "pool" of actors, to be called on when they needed me for a part.

The journey to Manchester involved riding on two buses and two trains. My mom took me on my first day of training, then having been drilled carefully on what station to change at, I travelled every day on my own.

I worked from 10.00 in the morning to 4.00 in the afternoon, in a large room with no windows, every day of my summer vacation. I could not have cared less that the sun was shining outside. I was in a broadcasting studio! The place where actors transported people into scenes of drama and excitement! I was in heaven!

At lunch- time, I stood in line at the canteen with actors I had listened to with my mom on "Saturday Night Theatre" or "Wednesday Matinee". I had no idea that the training I was getting at the age of twelve would be used in a studio forty years later, on the other side of the world.

Many of the plays were adventure stories, and often entailed the characters being trapped in a cave or some other weird place. In order to get the right "echo' sound for this, we had to run from one studio to another, and get there in time for our cue which was a brief flicker of a blue light. Total concentration was required, and no waste of time was tolerated. This special studio was on the next floor up. During a live broadcast, I would race up the stairs into the studio with the special 'sound booth", and hope I wasn't too late for the blue "cue" light to flick once, giving me the cue to speak. It was a strain sometimes, trying to sound as if I had walked into a cave, and not like I had run along two corridors and up a flight of stairs! The job required self control and unswerving focus. None of us were over fourteen years of age, but we were learning the self-discipline and concentration that being an actor requires.

Although the war was technically over, Olive was still in the W.R.N.S. waiting her turn to be "demobbed". The last in, would be the last out of uniform, so she had a long wait. While serving in the military, Olive had been cast in a play that toured the military camps. She always said this was the happiest time of her life.

Olive had spent many months stationed in Carlisle, near the Scottish border. She said that the only way to get warm that winter was to walk through the snow to the ablution block, take a hot shower, then walk back to her hut. Whenever she was on leave, she seemed to have a bad cold and cough. But she said the Medical Officer had told her to "work it off".

I was now part of the "reserve team" of young actors for the B.B.C. Children's hour. They would phone me when I was cast in a play. After the verbal commitment they would then send me the script, along with a contract that a parent and I would sign.

I could never wait for those working days in the Manchester studios to come along.

At ten o'clock in the morning, we had a read-through sitting at a big table in the conference room, then we would rehearse the whole thing through with half an hour for lunch, then broadcast live at five o'clock. By the following year, some of the work I did was being recorded. It would be fourteen years before tape-recorders were available to the public, so it was very exciting the first time I got home after a recording session at the studio, to sit in my living room with my parents, hearing my own voice coming from the radio. My dream of being a radio actor had come true.

Finally Olive was back in "Civvy Street". She had great dress sense, and with her cheerful, friendly personality, secured a job in sales at one of Liverpool's best stores. The stories she told over the dinner table each night, about the oversized women trying on small sized dresses, made me laugh till the tears rolled down my face. Years later, there was a British hit comedy series on television, called "Are You Being Served" (my voice actually introduced it from Miami on P.B.S.) which I always thought could have been written by Olive.

Every Christmas in England, we have huge musicals written around what American's would call, children's "Mother Goose" stories. In England they are called, "Pantomimes" and every town had a professional company presenting at least one every Christmas season. I belonged to a young people's amateur group called "The Chrysanthemums Pantomime Society." I was fourteen years old, when a girl called Carol Gatley and I were chosen to play the two leading roles in "Babes in the Wood". We were performing at "The Floral Pavilion" -- the same theatre I had been crowned "Coronation Queen" in ten years before.

As young teen-age girls do, I had developed a huge crush. The object of my affection was the handsome Director of the show. He was a grown man of twenty-three, and like my brother, was newly demobilized from the Royal Air Force. He was obviously interested in a nineteen year old from the senior girls dance team, as he took her home every night . Doreen lived on the same bus route as I did, and I remember sitting behind them one night, envying her as they talked together, his arm around her shoulders across the back of the seat.

My friend Jean Hobson who was playing the part of the Fairy Queen, told me that Mr. Bomford was leaving Wallasey to live in South America. "Why? What has he done wrong?" I asked. In every movie I had ever seen, criminals always wound up trying to get to South America. I didn't know the word "extradition", but just knew if the baddies could get there, they would be safe and never go to prison. I was pleased to hear however, that the object of my teen-age crush was just going to work there!

On the last night of the show, after the finale when we were all saying our goodbyes, I walked up the aisle of the theatre and asked for my heart-throb's autograph. We were standing just inside the entrance of the auditorium of the "Floral Pavilion," when he wrote in my album "To Angela - My charming leading lady, with love from Doug Bomford".

CHAPTER 4

A Grain Of Mustard Seed

I F THERE HAD been a prize for the very worst sports student in school, I would have won it.

While some may have found being the very last to be chosen for any sports team a humiliating experience, it didn't bother me one wit. My goal in hockey was to run as far away from the disgustingly hard little white ball as possible. I was always in rehearsal for a show or an acting competition, and there was no living way I was going to risk being hit across the head by a hockey stick! If the wretched ball came anywhere near me, I ducked out the other way.

I had long skinny legs, and my last name was "Steggles". More than once, a frustrated team captain, seeing I was the only one left, howled, "Oh no! We are stuck with Stegs the Legs." I wanted to skip the whole rotten business of running around a field, and get to the assembly hall to rehearse duets on the grand pianos with my friend Valerie Evans. Val was almost as hopeless at games as I was, but she was a wiz on the piano and at English composition. I had no way of knowing that one day, she would report my wedding in the local newspaper, and we would be life-long friends.

I tried my very best to play tennis. However, the ball and my racquet just never did see eye to eye, and very seldom met. The only redeeming feature I could see in a game of "Rounders", (kind of like baseball played with a soft ball) was that if one was fielding, one had a good view of the boys playing cricket. The only other time we ever clapped eyes on them, was in morning assembly Monday and

Wednesdays. The boys school was totally separate from ours. Some of the girls met the boys walking home after school, and stories of "who liked who" sometimes circulated. However, in the six years I was at Oldershaw High School, not one boy ever spoke one word to me. I was just ugly I guess. Their total disinterest never bothered me. I used to smile, realizing that they never saw me in my long gown, with high heels and make-up on, performing my impersonations. They never heard my applause either.

Sharing a room with my sister meant the fun of waking up when she came in from a date and chatting for awhile. Although Olive was almost twenty-one years old, our parents had very strict rules, and no female was ever out of the house after eleven o'clock at night. For Norman it was different. He had to walk the girl home then walk himself home, as our dad went to his club every night in the car, so there was no question of Norman being able to borrow it for a date. I heard him come in soon after midnight at times. Something that would not have been tolerated by our parents one moment if a daughter had done that! In England, throughout the fifties and sixties, young men as well as women, lived at home paying for food and rent to their parents till they married. They couldn't afford to do anything else!

One night, I was woken up not by Olive coming in from a date, but by her coughing.

I was still fourteen years old when one day I joined a small crowd of people gathered in front of a shop that sold radios. In the window was a twelve inch square box, with a lady talking on it. I was seeing my very first television set.

My father's predictions when I was eight years old had apparently come true. I could see someone many miles away, talking right to me! I went inside so I could hear the lady better. Sylvia Peters was natural and charming as she announced the upcoming programs.

"How wonderful it would be if I could do that one day," I thought. "Announce things on television!" I felt an indescribable thrill as a new ambition was born in my heart.

One Sunday afternoon, a friend from school came up the pathway and rang the door bell. She asked me if I would like to go to the evening Service with her at Claremount Road Methodist Church. It was an invitation that would change my life forever.

Soon I became a "regular" at the evening services, sitting with the rest of the young people. They were a friendly, fun loving group, and I looked forward to the long walks we took after Church. There was always a lot of teasing and repartee going on, as we walked along the sea front of New Brighton, watching the late summer sun setting.

The Pastor of the church held a weekly discussion group for the youth. I thought myself far too sophisticated to believe all the Church twaddle. How anyone with a wit of sense could believe there was a God, was beyond me. I had seen enough of war, and the horrible results of it, to believe in a loving God. It was all rubbish. What amazed me was that I could actually voice my thoughts to this patient and kindly gentleman, and not be ridiculed. At home, if I gave voice to my ideas at the dinner table about anything, the voice of a parent would cut in. "You be quiet. When we want your opinion, we'll ask for it". Which of course I knew would never happen. But my Pastor answered all my questions in a way that made sense. For the very first time in my life, a bona fide grown-up was *listening* to me.

One night, instead of the usual Youth Evening, Pastor suggested that we should all go to Central hall, Liverpool, where the famous Japanese Christian, Dr. Kagowa would be speaking. This incredible gentleman had come from a wealthy family, and could have lived in luxury, but he had devoted fourteen years to ministering to the very poorest people in his country, living in the worst slums with them, and ministering to them while preaching the Gospel of Jesus Christ.

The idea of hearing someone speak whose very identity would have struck terror into my heart only a few years earlier, intrigued me.

Our little group of teen-agers sat high up on the seats of Central Hall. I have forgotten much of what this gentle, diminutive man had to say, but I remember his smile. He seemed to look straight at me as he quoted the words of Jesus from the Gospel of Matthew Chapter 11: verse 28 thro 30

"Come unto me all ye that labor and are heavy laden, and I will give you rest. Take my yoke upon you and learn of me; for I am meek and lowly in heart; and ye shall find rest unto your souls. For my yoke is easy, and my burden is light.

I was an apparently carefree young girl, materially more than well cared for, and nobody knowing me then, would have believed these words of Christ could strike a chord in my heart.

But they did.

Moments later, Dr. Kagowa quoted from Matthew 6, verse 28

"Consider the lilies of the fields, how they grow; they toil not neither do they spin. And yet I say unto you, that even Solomon in all his glory was not arrayed like one of these."

It didn't happen suddenly, and there was no invitation to respond to publicly. It was something I could not fully understand, but by the time I reached my front door that evening, I knew I belonged to Jesus. He would be in my heart, and guide me throughout my life.

Less than a year before this experience, a Bedouin shepherd with his cousin and a friend, had made the greatest archeological find in history. Ancient Hebrew scrolls, dating to before AD 68 had been found in a cave in Qumran, near the Dead Sea. Later whole libraries of ancient manuscripts were found there. Every book from the Old Testament was discovered, with the exception of the Book of Esther. Copies of texts of Genesis, Deuteronomy and Isaiah were also found in the fourth cave. Strangely, the text was identical to that used in the King James Version of the Bible, which had been written from manuscripts dating from only 1,100 AD. For generations, Christians had just trusted by faith, the Word of God as they read it in the King James Version. Now, the scholars all agreed that it was indeed correct, as it was word for word exactly the same as the ancient Dead Sea scrolls, written so soon after Jesus had walked the earth.

However, it would be forty-four years before more than only twenty-five percent of the scrolls translations were released, and in 1991 "The Crucified Messiah Scroll," was fnally made public.

It would be some years before I understood that the evidence from the Old Testament prophecies telling of the coming of the Messiah, was fulfilled in the Gospels, some in amazing detail.

But for now, the tiny mustard seed of faith, planted by a caring next-door neighbor, with her gifts of Christian books when I was a nine year old "evacuee", was taking root.

A "Twenty-First Birthday" was a huge deal in those days, as it marked the day when one could finally be allowed to vote, marry without parental consent, and be accepted finally, as a real "adult". In England, anyone who could possibly afford it threw a very special party for their child, and plans for Olive's twenty-first were well under way. My father had booked the Church hall, my mother had ordered the cake, and the invitations were sent out.

Olive had dated many nice young men, and had been engaged briefly at one point. But right now there was nobody special in her life.

It was a great party. Aunts and uncles and cousins were all there. I wrote a special song for Olive and played it on the piano just before she blew the candles out on her cake.

But Olive's usual bright and fun loving nature had changed. She was coming home from her job in the Liverpool store every evening, extremely tired. She had been off her food for some time, and had lost weight. The constant worry about her older daughter made mother fractious and bad tempered with us all.

In those days, doctors came to the house. I was there and saw Olive slumped in an armchair. I heard the Doctor's pronouncement that she was "Like a lot of the young ones these days, she is just lazy." He prescribed a tonic. The same doctor had saved my father's life a few years before, so naturally, my mother trusted him. Finally an x-ray of the lungs was ordered. A few weeks after her twenty-first birthday, Olive was diagnosed with tuberculosis and was taken to the hospital.

Telephones for patients are a rarity in British Hospitals now, and were unheard of then. I was too young to be allowed into a T.B. ward, so except for waving to her through the hospital window, it would be a year before I saw or spoke to my beloved sister again.

Sometimes, if my parents were taking me somewhere after visiting Olive, I would drive with them, and while they went in to see her, I would stand outside on the hospital grounds, looking up at the ward I knew she was in. Olive was too ill to get out of bed and come to the window, so I passed the time by singing the Hymns I enjoyed in school at every morning assembly. My sister couldn't hear me through the thick walls of the Victorian structure, and the window was very high up. So sometimes I just cried.

CHAPTER 5

Paris!

THE TIME TO graduate from High School was drawing near. The "School Certificate" was never given out as a matter of routine, and at that time only a minority of students were presented with it. Indeed, having one's "School Cert" was considered the mark of a very clever student. Hence the reason why nobody expected *me* to get it.

However, I had managed to extract a promise from my parents, that if I *did* manage to pass my examinations and actually get the treasured Certificate, I would be allowed to follow a career as a professional actor. This ensured my diligence at school and on my homework, for the entire year.

At the end of each semester, report cards were given out. The name of the girl who had the highest marks was read out first, and on downwards. *Nobody* wanted to be identified as the worst student in the class, thus providing a huge incentive to everyone with any sense to work hard. Fortunately, the idiotic idea that a student coming bottom of the class would be traumatized for life, had not yet taken root. The school was doing a great job of preparing us for the competition of real life, and it was where we learnt that giving anything less than one's best was not good enough – lessons all too often forgotten in many schools in the U.S. and Britain today. Our competitors overseas however, are still teaching it, and benefiting from the effect.

About this time, Oldershaw High School announced plans to take part in a student exchange program. Girls fifteen and over, would have the opportunity to improve their French by going to Paris! I could hardly wait to take the notice home to my parents and hugged them profusely when they agreed I should go.

We were to spend three nights in a Paris hotel, along with the three teachers who would accompany us, then we would be placed in a family that had a girl of our age. They in turn, would come to stay with us in England for the summer.

The fortunate few who were going counted the days and hours until we finally stood together on the platform of Lime Street railway station, looking for our sleeping- berths on the Liverpool-London train.

Travelling in those days, was an opportunity to look smart, not to wear cut-off shorts and show as many bra straps as possible The teachers had only seen us in our uniforms of navy blue skirts and white blouses, and were astonished when they saw their students in make-up and "new look" dresses. After years of war time material being in short supply, Christian Dior had made a hit with feminine calf- length skirts. All the stores had copied them, and we girls all wore them.

The first three days in Paris were fantastic. We were free to roam the City of Light during the day in twos and threes, but at night we dressed in our best silky summer dresses, and accompanied by our three teachers, were taken to the theatre. Of course it was all in French, but the productions were bigger than anything our war weary eyes had ever seen, and my eyes boggled at the lavish costumes and scenery. We experienced opera, ballet, and musical comedy.

The fun was over however, when we were all split up and had to go with our French families, to face over two weeks without a word of English. Why didn't anyone warn me that five years of conjugating verbs didn't qualify me for the speed of real conversational French? I couldn't understand a blooming word! It was hopeless. Foreign languages were not my bag! The people were kind, but after three days I just wanted to go home to England.

A desperate homesickness for my own country overwhelmed me. I yearned to see a bright red English telephone booth, or Mail Box. Even the dogs in Paris seemed to bark differently! I hated every minute of it. I was a Brit, and would always be a Brit. I didn't need any other country or language. I swore with all the fervor of my fifteen years that I would *never, ever, ever,* leave England again as long as I lived.

Fortunately, the Lord is gracious to us, lifting the veil of the future one moment at a time!

By now, Olive had been in hospital almost eighteen months, sharing a ward with ten other young women. Most of them had served in the armed forces during the war and, like Olive, had been diagnosed with tuberculosis after their demobilization.

Instead of getting better, Olive's condition was deteriorating.

After my fifteenth birthday, I had been allowed to go into the ward and visit my beloved sister. The National Health Service had recently become law in Great Britain. It was during one of my visits with my mother, that I heard one of the patients call out to a passing Nurse that she was in pain. "What do you expect when you just had your body cut open? You *are* getting all this treatment for nothing you know" was the retort, as, without stopping to check on the patient, she swished through the ward and out of the door. As soon as was humanly possible, my parents signed Olive out of the hospital, and brought her home.

Our living room was turned into a hospital room, and although it was wonderful to see my sister again, it was distressing to see her legs so thin and weak from disuse.

Olive had been given a chest x-ray when she enlisted. The Government admitted neglect as she had not been x-rayed again when she was demobilized. If they had, the disease would have been found in its early stages. Instead, during the ensuing year, the disease had spread to both lungs. Olive received a 100% "sorry we messed up" Pension from the British Government for the princely sum of two pound ten shillings a week. The buying power today of roughly $35

I longed to hug my wonderful big sister, however I was warned by the doctor to stay physically away from Olive as much as possible. But there were times when, alone in the house, I had to take care of her needs. Usually I would sit on a big chair across the room from Olive's bed, and talk about what was going on at school or at my acting classes, embroidering the incidents making them as comical as possible, in the hope of seeing her smile.

During that summer, I was able to take Olive out a few times in a wheel-chair. There was nothing actually wrong with Olive's legs except for the weakness in the muscles from lack of use, and her lungs no longer worked well enough for her to be able to walk more than a few steps. Olive told me her ambition was to be able to wear out a pair of shoes, and one day she told me she wanted to go up to the shoe shop and try on a pair. Mom helped Olive into the wheel chair, and we set out up the road to the local shops. It was a perfect English summer day.

In the 1950s, it was perfectly safe to leave an infant outside the local stores, securely strapped into big baby carriage, while their mothers went inside to shop. Sometimes the baby carriages were parked three deep outside Woolworths. Beautiful babies would gurgle and giggle at those of us who would stop, bounce the carriage a bit, and talk with them. There was never a problem with this nationwide custom until the 1960's when the free-wheeling life styles resulting in the trashing of high moral standards, made it necessary to not only discontinue the custom of leaving babies outside shops, but to make it illegal.

So now, Olive's sense of humor not wavering, she told me to park the wheel-chair outside the shoe store. "I want to see peoples faces when I get up and walk in without any help" she said, mischief showing in her large grin. Slowly she stood up. In her smart brown pantsuit, looking tall and dignified, she strolled slowly inside the shoe store. "I bet they are saying what a horror I must be, making my poor little sister wheel me around town," she giggled.

The one thing that *did* annoy Olive, was the habit people had of talking over her head, something many folks are guilty of when they are dealing with wheel-chair bound folks.

We passed the Floral Pavilion, remembering the times we had performed there, and approached the New Brighton Pier. I presented the entrance fee to the man on duty.

There was a turnstile which we could not negotiate with a wheel-chair, so he had to come out and open a gate for us. Totally ignoring Olive, he said to me over her head in a loud voice, "What's wrong with your sister?" Before I could react to his lack of tact, Olive shouted up at him, "Dandruff. Let's go!" We sailed through the gate, onto the pier at maximum speed.

Over the years, I had studied and passed all the acting examinations set by the "London Academy of Music and Dramatic Art" and now I was back-stage waiting to perform in my finals for the judges.

Another student told me she was auditioning the next day for a movie starring Alec Guiness. I didn't have the nerve to ask her for the details of the audition and anyway, my parents were expecting me back on the evening train.

I passed my finals with flying colors, but would always regret not following up on that audition. For if I *had* been cast as one of the school- girls in "The Lavender Hill Mob," I would have worked with a young unknown actress who, as the British would say, "Didn't do too badly" in the acting profession. Her name was Audrey Hepburn.

CHAPTER 6

New Beginnings

I PASSED MY FINALS and became one of the youngest students to gain the silver and gold medals plus the coveted Diploma from the Drama department of L.A.M.D.A. stating that I was now "Qualified and capable of appearing on stage in any West End production". Silly me firmly believed I would soon be earning a living as a bona fide actor. For that is what it said didn't it?

With high hopes and much prayer for guidance, I boarded the train to London, and started my trek round the Theatrical Agents who specialized in casting actors both in London and around the country.

As everyone who has ever sought employment in an overcrowded profession knows, the trick is to get past the receptionist and actually get to see the decision- maker in the room behind. Never an easy task. All receptionists were females, and I never managed to persuade even one of them to read my resume. Without at least two years acting experience in professional repertory, one was dead in the water.

I was verbally shoved aside with remarks which all added up to the same thing - "Too young and too inexperienced". One receptionist although seated, managed to look *down* her half spectacles at me as she announced in a loud voice "We are looking for mature people with experience ---- not *tennis girls!*" The last two words put me in a place with the cockroaches, which I had no doubt infested the decrepit floorboards of her miserable office. I crept past the other more "mature" actors in the waiting room, and crawled back down the four flights of stone steps to the pavement below. It was the 1950s, and the worship of youth had not yet begun.

There seemed to be a tacit agreement among the landlords of these old buildings, that all theatrical agents should be shoved into the top floor. By this time, most of the buildings that had survived the blitz in Central London, were over a hundred and forty years old, so an elevator was a rarity. As well as handling the repeated disappointments by the end of a few days, I was physically exhausted. My meager savings were shrinking at an alarming speed. Walking and climbing were only tiring, but the constant rejection bit into my soul.

One day, having tried to get in for the umpteenth time to see the last agent on my list I was walking aimlessly along the crowded sidewalk in Leicester Square. My head was bowed in depression. Convinced I was in the Lord's will in my pursuits of a career in acting, the job He had given me the gift for, I had prayed and prayed for a "break". But it hadn't come. My bright ambitions had hit a brick wall, and a large tear slipped down my cheek. There was positively *nothing* I wanted to do with my life, but be an actor.

A passing man spoke in a cheery Cockney accent, "Cheer up love ! It can't be as bad as all that," he remarked. I felt ashamed as I remembered what he and thousands like him had endured just a few years before in the blitz. My father had told me about his customers during the war saying "If the bombing would just stop, I swear Mr. Steggles, I would never grumble about anything again as long as I lived!" But of course they did. We all did.

Now the sun was shining, no "doodlebugs" threatened, and I was just having a pity party.

I packed up that night and went home, determined to find another way into my chosen profession.

The "Liverpool Playhouse" was considered one of the top four Repertory Companies outside London, and many famous actors had started there. More stars since then have emerged from that wonderful theatre. I have always wondered how they ever managed that, as I couldn't even get past the doorman!

I had to think of something else.

There were industrial towns dotted across the North of England, each one had their own "legitimate" theatre presenting a different play every week. Small black and white television sets were only just on the market, and the social highlight of the week was still a visit to see a play at the local Rep. If they were lucky enough to have a second theatre in their town, tickets for the Variety Show as well. My idea was to get to these small towns, where hard working, discerning people, supported quality live entertainment.

If an agent wouldn't act on my behalf, and send me out for auditions, I would just have to go and get my own!

Cars were still a luxury in England, and virtually nobody my age drove one, so I planned to ask father if he would take me round some of the smaller rep theatres in his car, so I could try and meet the Managers and Directors in person. I held little hope of my father agreeing to this plan, and was amazed when he readily acquiesced. I was unaware of the fact that Olive's Doctor had advised my parents to get me out of the house if possible. Still only a teenager, I had been helping to nurse a patient with active tuberculosis for over a year and although tests showed I had a high resistance, the Doctor warned them that their second daughter could be in danger of contracting the contagious disease.

So early one morning, with an overnight bag stowed on the back seat of the car, my mother waved dad and I off on my job hunting expedition.

There were no expressways at that time, and the ride round narrow roads to our first stop fifty miles away took forever. We drove over the hills and dales of Lancashire, where I tried my luck, with negative results. Then we pressed on travelling through tiny villages and narrow streets, through the beautiful Yorkshire dales.

Welcoming fields opened up their green hands to us, while wisps of chimney smoke came out of solitary cottages set in the undulating hills. I relived this experience thirty years later, when viewing the opening scene of the B.B.C. Television series "All Creatures Great and Small".

My father and I developed a routine. Dad would drop me in front of the repertory theatre then drive round the corner where he would read his paper, while I tackled the problem of getting myself a job.

The billboards trumpeted the name of the current play for that week, and showed the photographs of the cast. Only a small percentage of professional actors are ever actually working at any given time, the unemployment rate being among the highest of any trade or profession. But I would look at pictures of fortunate actors who had a job. I looked at the black and white photographs with envy, then, shoring up my courage, I would try walking through the stage door.

If it wasn't locked, there would be someone inside who would shoo me away.

After a few negative experiences, over two days of touring round like this, I finally struck oil! The producer at "The Theatre Royal" in Huddersfield would take me on as an "Assistant Stage Manager." I would not be seen on the stage for a while, but finally I had my foot in the only door I was interested in – the door to the magical world of acting !

The Theatre Manager had recommended a lodging house for me. It would cost me all of my wages, but as I was still not quite eighteen years old, my father agreed to subsidize my pitiful income until I got my first raise.

I could hardly wait to get home and give Olive and my mom the great news!.

A few days later I said goodbye to my family, and along with my brand new suitcase, took a train to Huddersfield, and my first real job in "the theatre".

In keeping with most repertory companies at that time, we presented a different play every week, twice nightly, with matinees on Wednesdays and Saturdays; fourteen performances a week, with only Sundays off.

Part of the job of an Assistant Stage Manager, was being the first to arrive, sweeping the stage, and having the tea made before the ten o'clock rehearsal. I had the script in my hand at all times as I was the "prompter", and marked the lighting and curtain cues, as I was also responsible for them throughout the show. It was also my job to be sure the actors were in the wings ahead of their entrance time.

While the actors went home for lunch and spend time studying their scripts, I spent the afternoon finding the "props" for the new production. First I was told to check out the large area under the stage, which was known as "the prop room". If I couldn't find all I needed there, I was to scour the shops in town and talk the proprietors into lending them to us for the week. Free passes for two for the Monday night performances always helped to smooth the way.

On my first day, the rehearsal was over and everyone went home. Then to my amazement, I was entrusted with the key and told to "lock up" when I left. At seventeen, I wasn't thrilled at being alone in a place that had been built in 1881, but I descended the rickety wooden ladder, peered through the gloom, and finally located the light switch. I turned it on. There were sofas, easy chairs, and side tables galore, all representing styles from the turn of the century onwards. There were large framed pictures, a variety of lamps, and, sitting on top of one, a large cat. It took only another moment to realize that it was not a cat, but an enormous rat! I ran up the wooden steps faster than an Olympic star, slammed the door, and ran all the way back to my "digs".

I soon located the antique stores, the furniture stores and the "knick knack" shops that would loan us what the set needed for the following weeks production, and carried everything but the furniture myself. When we did "A Christmas Carol" I located the chains for

Marley's ghost. I had to drag the wretched things up the high street. At the end of the week, everything had to be slammed into reverse, as all the props had to be returned as well.

One week, the production called for a poodle dog.

The kennels were miles outside town, and meant having to catch a bus and fetch "Fifi" every day in her cage, then return her after the final curtain every night. It was eleven thirty by the time I had caught the last bus back into town, and walked up the hill to my digs.

One day, the Producer gave me one hundred pounds in cash, (the buying power today around $600) to buy a new carpet for the stage. There was no question of my having to sign for the money, it was just given to me in my hand. I had only worked there a couple of months, and as my pay barely covered my rent, he was a trusting soul for there was nothing to have stopped me from taking the cash and catching a train home to Wallasey!

I took the bus through the Yorkshire dales, chose the carpet for the set, arranged delivery, and rode back to Huddersfield with some change for the producer. He seemed very pleased when he saw the carpet, but I didn't get a raise.

The Stage Manager was responsible for "the big stuff", like seeing the sets were correctly built on time and put up safely, and making sure the lighting was working alright. As his assistant, I had to fire-proof the new carpet, and any new material furnishings, and put a film of Vaseline across any mirrors on the set to prevent "reflection glare" into the eyes of the audience from the strong lights. Helping the females in the cast with any quick-changes was another duty, along with checking that the props were in the correct place both on and off the set, and making sure every actor had any "personal props" they needed. If they didn't have the gun, dagger, or letter they needed on them for a performance, I would get the blame. I made sure it never happened. It taught me to be organized, and somewhat nit-picking, a trait I know I have sometimes been resented for.

One morning, the manager of the company came to me in a big hurry. Rehearsal was about to begin, and I was "on the book" ready to prompt the cast through act three. "Quick!" he whispered in my ear, "Choose a stage name." I must have looked at him strangely, as he hurried on " You have a part in the next play, and we can't print your real name, "Steggles" on a program, it would look ghastly!" He continues, " I need to know what to put you down as in the cast, right now." Trying to listen to the actors, and dream up a stage-name at the same time, just wasn't working I had always admired Danny Kaye. I whispered loudly, "I'll be Angela Kaye." So for the next eleven years, I was.

Every actor's contract contained the clause that they be in the theatre at least thirty minutes before the commencement of any performance. We had no "stage door-man" to check them in as the bigger theatres had, and there was no back-stage sound system for announcements, so I had to go to each dressing room, knock on the door and shout "half an hour please", and wait for an answer from each cast member. Actors may be notoriously late for most appointments, but for auditions or performances, they are always early. I repeated my rounds of the dressing rooms at the quarter hour, then "first act in position please", after which I perched on a stool in the wings, the script in my hand, ready to cue the "House lights down" and "Curtain up" .

When I had an appearance early in the play, then I would have to race to my place in the wings for my entrance. Too bad I f anyone messed up on their lines when I was onstage-- there was nobody to "prompt them". These amazing professional actors learned huge long parts in a few days. They were performing fourteen times a week, plus learning next weeks, and taking a peek at the script for the week after, all at the same time, yet it was a rarity that I ever had to give any of them a "prompt". I smile when I see the politicians turning their heads to read their teleprompters today. But of course, most of them are pretty good actors anyway.

Every Thursday afternoon, the cast list was put on the bulletin board, and the scripts given out, for the show the week *after next*. Finally my parts got bigger, I got a raise, and was declared a true cast member of the company. So they had to hire a new Assistant Stage Manager.

One night, after the show was over, I sat on a rickety chair in my tiny dressing room with the bare light bulb, creaming off my make-up. I prayed a prayer of thanksgiving to the Lord for bringing me to the "Theatre Royal, Huddersfield" for I had never been so happy in my life.

CHAPTER 7

From Drama To Musicals

A s THE PARTS grew larger, so did my pay packet. It was good to be financially independent. But that happy situation was to be short-lived.

A strange phenomena began to take place.

Our audiences started to dwindle in direct proportion to the number of television antenna that sprouted up on roofs across town. People had discovered they could see wonderful British dramas without paying either a baby-sitter or a box-office. Nor did they have to battle the elements of wind and rain in order to be entertained.

By the end of November, the announcement was official. Huddersfield Repertory Company was closing down. We were all out of work.

The theatre management chose to close its' doors with a comedy. It was hard trying to make people laugh while the future looked so bleak. The close-knit little band of players said goodbye to each other, and went looking for employment.

While big cities still have their own "Playhouses", the fantastic training ground and source of income for actors and writers known as "Weekly Rep", would never exist again in the small towns of England.

"Dear Lord" I prayed, "What now?"

The answer to my prayer came in the form of the memory of Jean Hobson who had been in the show with me at the Floral Pavilion when we were both fourteen years of age, and I had had a crush on the handsome Director. It was Jean who had told me that Douglas Bomford was going to live in South America. Carol Gatley had been in that same show, and all three of us had gone into the theatre professionally.

Now, remembering that Jean was contracted to play a leading role in a production of the Christmas show "Cinderella", I wrote telling her of my plight. She must have given a glowing recommendation of me to the Director, as within a week a contract arrived in the mail at home. After all my training and experience in drama, I was going to be a chorus girl - for a few winter months anyway. It was employment! It was show biz! I was thrilled!

While my parents were not jumping for joy at the turn my career had taken, Olive thought it was a great lark. She looked up at me from her bed, her eyes glowing. It was then I realized how much she wished she could go with me on my new venture, instead of lying in bed, looking every day at the same walls. She was only living her life through me.

Our parents had done everything possible to get the finest treatment available for my sister, but Olive's condition was getting worse. Mom had little patience with anything or anybody, including me when I was home, her face in a permanent frown.

Months of watching her precious daughter trapped in a sick bed, had turned into years. It was taking a heavy toll on our mother.

My father was at the shop all day, affording him an opportunity to take his mind off the situation somewhat, and he rarely missed an evening out to play snooker with friends at his club. But mom rarely escaped the permanent reminder of Olive's condition.

Some friends thought I should give up what I was trying to do, and stay home to help my mother nurse Olive. But again, the doctor's warning rang true. I have often thought since, what a miracle it was that I did not contract the dreaded disease myself. Our beds had only been only inches apart when I shared a room with Olive during my early teens, when she was coughing so much before the diagnosis. "Why her and not me Lord?" I still ask.

I was at the house when three specialists in the field of tuberculosis consulted together in our living room. After examining Olive and viewing her most recent x-rays, they decided to try a new medicine on her. "I know they are using me as a guinea -pig," she remarked after they left. "They really have no idea how much they should be giving me of the stuff." Isolated only a few years before, streptomycin was still in the experimental stage. However, Olive was devising a plan of her own to improve her chances for recovery.

Jean Hobson met me at the railway station in the beautiful historic city of York, where the company would rehearse and perform before going on tour.

"You're sharing my digs!" She shouted over the noise of the steam blowing from the loudly departing train. We walked from the station, through the narrow streets steeped in two thousand years of history. The black and white Tudor facades intrigued me.

We turned a corner, and suddenly there in front of me was one of the most beautiful buildings I had ever seen. The famous "York Minster." I lowered my suitcase to the ground, and just looked and looked. While the first small wooden place of worship was built on the site in the seventh century, now this magnificent edifice, one of the largest Gothic buildings in Europe, still stood to the glory of God. Parts of the original stone work placed in the twelfth century could still be seen.

"Come on Angela, we can't stand gawking all day, the landlady will have our tea ready," Jean exclaimed as she hurried me along the street to her lodgings.

Three other girls from the cast of the show were staying there. One of them was already sharing with Jean, and I was to be "squeezed in". Jean showed me to the room, which only had one double bed in it. (Europeans must be friendly folk, because the King Size has never caught on there.) We were to sleep 'heads and tails", which meant one in the middle slept with her head at the bottom of the bed, and two either side right side up.

I didn't sleep a wink the first night, the slightest movement of the other girls nearly pushing me off the edge on to the cold linoleum floor beneath.

After ten days rehearsal, the show opened in York, before touring England travelling by train every Sunday, sleeping in new "digs" each week.

The leading lady was a superb "Cinderella". I stood in the wings every moment I could, studying her showmanship and timing. She carried the whole audience with her, from the crying waif in scene one when the ugly sisters go to the ball and she is left behind, to the transformation scene when her rags turn into a beautiful ball gown. Another ambition was born in my heart!

(In fact the following year, I auditioned to play the title role in "Cinderella" with another company, and played that part each Christmas six different seasons. The thrill of hearing the "oooos" and "aaaas" of children as two beautiful white ponies drew me on-stage in a crystal coach, is indescribable. Then again, in the ballroom scene, walking down the steps, dressed in a froth of tulle and diamante into the arms of "Prince Charming" the children's reaction thrilled my heart. One blustery, cold morning, I had the opportunity to visit a large orphanage with "The Prince" both of us dressed in our "ballroom scene" finery. It is an experience I have never forgotten. Surely lighting up the eyes of a child must be one of God's greatest gifts to us on this earth.)

Worshipping at a different Church every Sunday evening was an interesting, and unique experience. I always invited some of the girls to come with me, but with limited success. They just thought I was "weird", and as far as the chorus girls were concerned, I was mostly shunned from their conversations and social activities.

The end of the run of the pantomime with Jean was looming, when I was suddenly contacted by my old boss, the former Manager of the Huddersfield Rep.

He was forming a company to take a comedy on the road with two big stars of the time, Claude Hulbert and Enid Trevor. We were to play at the bigger theatres all over England, and he needed an Assistant Stage Manager , (an easy task this time as it was the same play every time) and to understudy the Leading Lady.

In all the movies I ever saw, the lead player gets sick, or has an accident, and the understudy "gets her big chance". I am thankful to report I honestly never did pray for the lady to get sick. She remained in robust health for the entire run of the play. The only person who fell down back-stage and got such a badly sprained ankle that they had to miss performances, was me!

Olive had read in the paper that the Member of Parliament for our home town had made a great recovery from tuberculosis after spending some months at a sanatorium in Switzerland. Olive was convinced that if she could just get to that same place, she too, would be cured.

Olive's Doctors told our parents it would be no use. That it would be a waste of money. This would be private medicine, to be paid by my father. But after five years of illness, Olive finally had a spark of hope in her eyes. To their great credit, mom and dad contacted the M.P. for Wallasey who gave them advice about the Schatzalp Sanitarium in Davos, Switzerland, and helped them to get the ball rolling to get Olive there.

Jet flights were not yet available, and travelling across Europe in 1952 was not easy. My sister would be many miles away from home, and the cost for the specialized medical treatment would be tremendous. The family income was not large, but again my parent's thrift was making it possible to grant an opportunity they would otherwise have had to refuse their child.

Arrangements were made for a Nurse to accompany Olive and mother by ambulance to the airport, and on a flight to Zurich, then across Switzerland to the sanitarium. It was situated high on a mountain outside the town of Davos. Mom stay a week, then had to leave Olive and come home. Fortunately, the furniture shop was doing well, thanks in a large part, to the talent and hard work of my brother Norman, who now had a son of his own.

For almost four years I had been praying for a cure for my wonderful sister. Surely now, with the clean, clear air of Switzerland high in the mountains, in a facility which specialized in her disease, she *must* begin to improve.

Meanwhile, as a job in any of the performing arts, rarely lasts very long. The five month tour of "For the Love of Mike" was about to end, and once again I was facing unemployment.

CHAPTER 8

A Time For Change

THE EARLY FIFTIES, overseas travel and cruises had not yet evolved, and the Brits took vacations at their many seaside resorts. My parents had never missed a summer season program at "The Floral Pavilion", and by my early teens I was familiar with the format. Every cast member had four different solo acts, as the programs would rotate each week for a month.

While Olive was confined to bed in Wallasey, she had re-written her impersonations act for me and encouraged me to perform it at local talent competitions. I always came in the top three. That was how I earned my pocket money. Probably in fear of my becoming an obnoxious big head, my mother constantly cut me down to size. Once I asked her before going on stage to line up with all the competitors, if I looked O.K. She said, "What makes you think anyone is going to look at you if there is anyone else on the stage?" That shut me up fast!

Bringing the script and characters up –to- date yet again, I rehearsed hard and long, then answered every ad in the trade paper, "The Stage" looking for Concert Party artistes, describing myself as a "Comedienne/Impersonator".

About this time, my father was in charge of organizing his Lodge "Ladies Night", and had to engage a couple of acts for the entertainment, so dad booked me along with a young Liverpool chap who sang and told jokes. A friend had seen his act, and said he was extremely funny.

Feeling well rehearsed and confident, I set out for the Victoria Hotel in New Brighton, having no clue that it would be *the* worst performing experience of my entire life!

The young man opening the entertainment started to sing in a wonderful light baritone voice. He had chosen what many male singers had performed for years in England, called "The Floral Dance". But with his bulging eyes, buck teeth and hair that stood on end plus a cheeky grin, within minutes he had every person in that room including me, holding our sides with laughter. His clean, original jokes that followed kept the formally attired gentlemen and the long gowned ladies, in pleats of laughter.

Encore after encore ensued. I thoroughly enjoyed every minute of it. Of course, it was impossible to follow that act. I did the best I could, but it was *hopeless*. It would be the only time in my life that I could not *wait* to get off the stage. It was like an old English saying; "After the Lord Mayor's show comes the muck cart." If only my father had put me on first!

There was no way for us to know that I had just tried to do the impossible; follow a young man who would become England's greatest comedy star. He would have records in the top ten, his own top rated television show, be honored by Her Majesty the Queen and have his statue placed in Liverpool Lime Street railway station. I had just followed the fabulous Ken Dodd!

Two years after that event, I stood in the street, reading the billboard of the Nottingham Empire. I was appearing at another theatre in that city, under my stage name, Angela Kaye. However, the star of this show was Harry Secombe, but reading down the list of supporting acts I saw, in small letters the name "Ken Dodd". I attended a matinee, and after the show, giving my real name "Angela Steggles" to the doorman, was soon ushered in to Ken's dressing room. He greeted me warmly, asked after my father, and recalled the night when we had appeared the same evening at the Victoria Hotel, New Brighton a couple of years before. His fiancee was there. She sat in the audience and would chart his jokes, measuring the laughs. His aim was to get at least seven laughs a minute. He certainly did.

That day, I was attending what would be a landmark date for that great comedy artist, for it was Ken Dodd's first professional theatre appearance. At this writing, he is still entertaining the British people, and still getting too many curtain calls to stop before midnight. He is eighty-seven years young.

After weeks of rehearsing and trying out my new act at Senior Citizen centers and charity functions, I was ready, and once again boarded a train to London

I was in the habit of praying each morning that the Lord would put me just where He wanted me to be, doing just what He wanted me to do, and that prayer was reiterated, as I walked nervously from the bustling city street, down a long flight of stone steps to a "cellar" below ground level, where the audition was to take place.

There was a piano on a raised platform, with two men seated in chairs directly in front of the stage. One of them wore a brightly colored waistcoat and a yellow bow tie - the typical "Concert Party" Comedian /Director.

For the first time in my life, I was auditioning as a professional act, with my own script and jokes, not as an actor given the lines to interpret. My script had to be good enough to entertain people

"Hello there!" the bright waistcoat called, "I am Bobby, and this is Harold, the Producer. Sit yourself down and enjoy the gang" he invited with a broad smile.

A magician auditioned. He was great. Then a couple of singers both with incredible voices performed, and then it was my turn. I was the youngest there. All the others were obviously very experienced, with totally polished acts. What was disconcerting to me was the fact that they stayed to watch each other audition. Usually auditions are "closed" and only seen by the people who are doing the hiring.

"O.K. Angela. Give the pianist your dots, and let's see what you have for us," Bobby invited. After explaining the music cues to the accompanist, I started. To my great relief, they all laughed in the right places, and applauded enthusiastically when I finished.

I sat down, expecting the usual "don't call us, we'll call you" routine. But Bobby was beaming at me as he said, "We will send you the contract at the end of the week. I take it you have three other acts with different material?" " I will have!" I chirruped. " Good," he continued. " We rehearse here for one week starting May first, then travel to Sheerness, opening the following week for a four month run."

The rest of the cast pumped my hand along with "Great having you with us" comments. They had apparently worked as a group for this gentleman before, and were just showing him their updated songs and acts. I was the only new kid on the block.

I felt myself grinning from ear to ear. Then I remembered I had to get music, write, rehearse, and costume three more acts in three weeks!

Olive, my great script- writer, teacher and confidence- builder, was in hospital on the top of a mountain in Switzerland. How could I possibly be ready in time? Then the Lord reminded me that Olive had written copious notes while she had been confined to bed the previous two years. I dug them out, and got to work.

The sea-side town of Sheerness in the lovely garden County of Kent was delightful. It sported a sandy beach, a fair-ground, delightful shops, and as I soon discovered, wonderful Christian folk. My landlady was a dear, and I soon settled in.

As well as having our own acts, we all took part in the many Production numbers and Comedy Sketches which are called "skits" in the U.S. Every member of the cast had to be very versatile and adaptable. I was in hog heaven! Making people laugh brought me more joy than I could ever have imagined. To me, the songs and dances we did as a group were an added bonus.

Although television was "in", this audience still got a kick out of hearing a great soprano or tenor sing, then witnessing the same people performing comedy later in the program.

I had spent all my teen-age summers envying the cast of the fabulous "Melody Inn" concert party back home at the "Floral Pavilion", and now I was doing what they had done – bringing laughter and entertainment into the lives of hard working people.

It was a lovely change to be able to attend Services at the same Church every week.

If only Olive had been fit and well at home, my life would have been perfect.

Realizing I was a young stranger in the town, one family insisted on taking me home with them after Church for what was England's biggest meal of the week, called "Sunday Dinner", eaten around one o'clock. They had three children near my age; two pretty daughters and one handsome son, which *really* made me look forward to Sundays! I worked six nights a week, so dating Frank was out. But that lovely Christian family taught me that love and joy had nothing whatsoever to do with one's income. The mother of the family cleaned other people's homes for a living, while the father was a window-cleaner. They had little, but they had everything. In the years following when I visited them, I continued to envy that family. The Lord had indeed, put me exactly where I needed to be at that time.

The perfect summer ended in September, and the specter of the unemployment line rose again.

Once again I scoured "The Stage" newspaper.

One day, I spotted an advertisement for a "Versatile soloist to tour with The Royal Kiltie Juniors".

It was a very well known girl's band featuring singing, dancing and comedy. They had performed for the Royal family at Windsor Castle years before, when Princess Margaret and her big sister, who was now Queen Elizabeth, were young girls. Hence they were permitted to use the prefix "Royal".

I sent my resume, and got an audition date.

The owner of the show was a ferret- faced little man, with a black lick of hair that fell across his forehead, making him look uncannily like the late Adolf Hitler. It wasn't his fault, and I did my best not to look at him while I sang and did the various impersonations.

After a stony silence, the ferret asked in a whining voice, "Don't you play an instrument ?" I played a couple of current songs on the piano. When I finished, there followed another minute of stony silence.

Then the whiner asked "Can you dance ?" I rattled off enough steps to show him I could tap dance, and then did some ballet steps."

I was out of breath when, in a disappointed voice, he whined "Don't you do any acrobatics?" "No. I don't!" I almost shouted, as I gathered up my props and music, and left not caring a jot if I never heard from the nasty little man ever again.

I was contracted to play the title role in "Cinderella" for a nine week engagement. The cast routinely met at the theatre to "check our mail" by the Doorman's desk, then go out for coffee together.

One morning, there was a long, fat ,brown envelope in my mail slot. It was a contract for a year to tour with the "Royal Kiltie Juniors". I would average one day off a week. The tour of "Cinderella" was almost over, and unemployment was about to rear it's ugly head again. However, what really clinched my decision to sign on the dotted line was that I would be flown to join the show which was appearing at the Kongresshaus in Zurich, Switzerland, only a three hour round trip train ride from Davos---and my beloved Olive! The chances of getting work in a show so close to my sister were a thousand to one. The hand of the Lord was obvious in this.

The show was scheduled to move on after eight weeks in Zurich, but any thought of dread at having to spend a year overseas for the foxy little man from the grueling audition, was obliterated by the realization that the Lord had arranged for me to see my sister, albeit one day a week, for eight weeks, and get paid while doing it! This was before jet travel, and flying out of the U.K. was still unusual in 1953. It was an exciting adventure to fly to Zurich, watch the show, then perform in it the following night.

It was a fast paced show, with one act following another with only seconds for applause, giving time for the band to turn the page in the music! The audience used to say it "took their breath away" as an instrumental act quickly followed a lovely ballet routine, then on to a popular chorus number etcetera. Four of us did an "Al Jolson" selection, including my slipping on white gloves and a huge red bow tie, turning just in time to give a fast rendition of "Toot Toot Toosie Goodbye", before switching back to conducting again.

(Sixty years later, I would attend the wedding of Al Jolson's granddaughter, Katy Jolson. I would watch with her proud mother Victoria, as the bride and groom waltzed to the strains of the bride's famous grandfather, singing the words he had written to "The Wedding Song" from the sound track of "The Jolson Story".)

The next week, I was ordered to report for lessons on the xylophone, an instrument I had only ever seen from a theatre seat!

I rehearsed the "Trish Trash Polka" every morning with another girl called Pat Grey, who played the second xylophone. At the end of two weeks, the foxy man's wife, announced, "You are playing in the show tonight."

The two beautiful, sparkling xylophones stretched across the entire stage, each one three octaves long . "Trish Trash" was a fast, very showy piece. With the long chrome of the instruments shining in the spotlights, the two of us dressed in Scottish Kilts with lace cravats, we probably looked rather good. Anyway, we always got very loud applause when we finished the last credenza with a flourish.

However, some weeks later, there was a never-to-be- forgotten performance when something totally unrehearsed occurred. The xylophone number followed a very quick costume change for me, and one night, I shot onstage so fast that my body hit the six foot long instrument, and it started a slow "roll" downstage. I could do nothing to stop it. I watched in horror as it rolled right off the end of the stage, onto the empty few feet of space between the stage and the front row. The expression on the faces of the audience seated there was a study. The band had played on of course, but I was left standing holding the xylophone sticks in my hand, with nothing but empty air before me! Nipping smartly over to the other xylophone, I told Pat to "Shove up an octave". She did, and we finished the duet on one instrument. Making a dash for the wings en route to my next quick-change, I was followed by Old Foxy himself, screeching at me "Miss Steggles! Wallasey's own gift to show business! What the blue blazes did you do?"

The beautiful, expensive xylophone had fallen apart on the floor, wooden keys flopped across chrome. I was fairly sure the instrument was not broken. It had just come apart as we always broke it down to pack it. However, as a performer, it was definitely *not* my finest hour!

The show was an hour and a half long. We performed five shows a day, six days a week in a huge restaurant-auditorium. Every Sunday found me seated on the 6.30a.m. train from Zurich while it wound its way up the side of the mountain. I was awe- stricken by the spectacular scenery. With snow clad mountains on both sides it was like being transported into fairy-land. Alighting in Davos, a sleigh took me to the funicular which carried me up to "Schatszalp" sanitorium, and to my Olive. But the Sundays went too fast.

Spring arrived and Olive's bed was wheeled out onto her balcony, where we talked against a background of tinkling cow bells, the animals grazing on the hills below. One day, she got off the bed, and wearing a smart sweater and hat she had knitted herself, posed on the balcony for a photograph. After six hours together it would be time for me to catch the evening train back down to my little Pension in Zurich.

Olive at Davos, Switzerland

During one of my Sunday visits, Olive's doctor stopped me in the corridor and told me that her last hope would be major surgery. Reeling from the shock I journeyed back down the mountains. I had truly believed my sister was getting better in the wonderful clean air of the Swiss Alps. The show was about to leave Switzerland, and I was under contract to move with it, so I wrote telling my parents what Olive's Doctor had said.

The morning of my last Sunday in Zurich, I was in a deep sleep in the small Pension that had been my home for over two months. I was woken up by the running of water from the room next door. I looked at my clock. It was ten minutes past six. My alarm had failed me, and the train that would take me for my last visit with Olive would leave in twenty minutes. Snatching up the phone I ordered a cab, threw on my clothes, grabbed my purse, and ran down the stairs. I was on the train only moment before it left the station.

Many times I have thanked God for that person in the room next to mine running the faucet when they did. Without that running water, I would not have woken up, and I would never have seen my beloved sister again.

CHAPTER 9

A Time To Weep

THE WIFE OF the owner of "The Royal Kiltie Juniors" acted as Wardrobe Mistress and like her husband, had all the warmth and personality of an alligator.

I knew I should try to feel sorry for this lady who was obviously caught in a loveless marriage, but found it hard to keep charitable thoughts of her when, after rehearsing all morning then performing five shows till late at night, we would arrive the next day to find all our costumes thrown in a heap in the middle of the dressing room floor.

Mrs. Fox took a leaf from the military book of discipline. If one person had left something not hung up in the right place, we all had to be punished.

As all twenty girls wore the same uniform for the opening of the show, it took forever to locate every kilt, sporran, shoe, sock and lace cravat that belonged to us. They all *looked the same!* But picking up the wrong costume could mean either popping buttons or slipping skirts as we differed a lot in size However, the discipline worked, as even in the fastest of quick changes, we hung up our clothes or risked the wrath of the entire company!

The day came when we were to move from the big Kongresshaus of Zurich to start our tour across Europe. Mr. Fox had secured a contract for the show to perform for the American Military occupational forces in Germany, Austria, France and Italy. This would sometimes entail moving every day.

The G.I.s were a fantastic audience, cheering and whistling after every act. Sometimes we would perform on a makeshift stage in a Military camp, and the next night, five hours bus ride away in a boxing ring set up in an enormous aircraft hangar. The U.S. forces were still under canvas in France, and sometimes we performed in a huge tent, doing our quick-changes behind canvas screens.

We travelled on special buses or trains, packing everything ourselves after the last of the cheers had died down, and most of the troops had left. Whatever instrument you played, you were responsible for cleaning and packing. Sometimes, when dismantling and packing the two big xylophones, I wished I had taken up the violin!

We could breakdown the set, pack and be ready to go thirty minutes after the applause had stopped. There were always a few soldiers who would lag behind. Seeing young girls push and pull the instruments and costume skips, they would want to climb onto the stage to help us. However, their gallant offers were thwarted by the burly M.P.s who stood at the front in a protective semi-circle. There was a strict "no fraternization" rule, and if we were caught even talking to one of the soldiers, we were in under threat from "Old Man Foxy." Months later our beautiful crooner Fran, became engaged to an officer. Nobody ever worked out how she had managed it!

Some two years after leaving The Kilties I was listening to the Armed Forces Radio Network home in England, when I heard Fran's name. She was identified as the wife of one of the officers and sang "Stormy Weather" just as she had done with our band. A super singer, and obviously, a very clever girl!

Shortly after we had left Switzerland, I had notified my parents about the Doctor's advice regarding Olive's surgery, and arrangements had been made for Olive to be transferred to the hospital in Basle. I had emphasized how important I thought it was for our mother to come out to be with her. For the first time in my life, I was able to do something for my parents.

There was a very strict limit on the amount of money a person could take out of England at that time, and mom could only bring sixteen pounds, (forty dollars) to Switzerland with her. We had no idea how long she would have to stay in a hotel, and buy her food, so I arranged to have my weekly wages sent directly to her hotel in Swiss francs. My parents had never needed any help before, and I gave God thanks for putting me in a position where I could give back a little for the years my parents had paid for my elocution, voice, and drama classes. At nineteen, I had the tremendous satisfaction of seeing my work benefit my family at a very difficult time.

The on - stage band leader of the "Royal Kiltie Juniors" was a Yorkshire lass, who was an excellent versatile stage artist with great comedic timing. But after four years with the band, her contract was not being renewed.

Nobody could imagine doing the show without Molly.

There were two other gals who had conducted when Molly was doing a quick-change or performing, and it was obvious that one of them would be asked to take over the baton. It was just a question of which one.

It came as a genuine shock when without any warning of any kind, I was told to report to the Musical Director for lessons in conducting. I was to be Molly's replacement.

Being the youngest and newest member of the troupe, the resentment in the cast was palpable. I was in a very difficult situation. This happens in other jobs where you go home every night. But we all lived together twenty-four seven, and being treated as an outcast by the other hopefuls was a bit rough.

On the plus side, my prayer life got a good work-out, as I asked for the grace to forgive the slights and snide remarks that were thrown my way. My brother Norman had once warned me, that as soon as someone gets their head a little bit above the crowd, there would always be someone ready to shoot it down. Although his words were true, that bit of knowledge helped me not one iota.

Our Musical Director had been trained by Sir Malcolm Sergeant, famous Conductor of the Liverpool Philharmonic Orchestra. Of course we were just a show band, and although I read music well enough to "follow the dots," I was not a highly trained musician. However, my long stage experience had taught me the showmanship that was needed, and after all, as long as one stops wagging the stick when the band stops, who is to know the difference? (Apologies to all Musical Directors and Ministers of Music!)

Every member of the cast was richly talented. It was a thrill to me when before every performance I announced on the microphone, "Now for your entertainment, we are proud to present, "The Royal Kiltie Juniors!" and led the band into the opening number.

In May of 1953, we arrived in Germany at the beautiful city of Heidelberg. Goethe had waxed long about it, and Turner had made it a subject of his paintings. Winston Churchill had attended the University there, and the allies had been ordered to spare it from bombing. However, I do not have happy memories of that lovely city, for on my return from a brief morning shopping trip, the consierge at the desk handed me a telegram. My beautiful, laughing, talented sister, my mentor in all things about acting, about life, and about love, my precious Olive, after five years of illness, was dead at the age of 26.

There was no question of my missing a performance. Probably my solos could have been cut, but I was not given the option.

I recall that night very well.

One of my solos was a song made famous by Betty Hutton from the film of the musical hit of the time, "Annie Get Your Gun". Dressed in a bright red cowgirl outfit, silky white fringe dancing from my red skirt and cuffs, a Stetson hat tipped onto the back of my head, I sang "There's No Business Like Show Business".

I had performed it dozens of times, but that night there seemed to be something lacking in the band behind me. Later I discovered that the girls felt so sad for me they were choked up and were having a hard time blowing their instruments. Some of the words say "There's no people like show people they smile when they are low". I was being paid to help lift up the spirits of the guys in uniform, who were thousands of miles from home. The Lord lifted me up and over my sorrow, granting me an emotional anesthetic so I could do my job.

While the choking tears and mourning would come later I was fine all the way through to the end of the show. I just knew the Lord was with me, and that my precious Olive was watching me from the wings.

I had never believed my sister would die.

Why this vibrant, talented person only had twenty-six years of life on earth, I do not know. Many have less and some of us many more. I could only recall the words of the Apostle Paul in the first letter he wrote to the Corinthians in chapter thirteen, verse twelve.

"For now we see through a glass darkly; but then face to face; now I know in part; but then shall I know, even as also I am known"

At home, Olive had always teased me about my Church- going, and had accused me (along with my parents) of wanting to get out of the house on Sunday mornings just to get out of helping to cook the big traditional English Sunday dinner which was served at one o'clock.

I will be forever grateful to an unknown English Pastor in Davos, who used to visit Olive in the Sanitarium. I never met him, but on one of my last visits to Olive before the show moved on, she had told me that she realized the evidence was overwhelming that Jesus was indeed the promised Messiah of the Old Testament, the Savior of the world, her Savior and mine. That is why I know without a doubt that one day we will meet again, in that place we call, "Heaven".

CHAPTER 10

The Royal Kiltie Juniors

W E WERE ALL billeted Army fashion in barracks with about sixteen beds in each room. One night, I woke up to an acrid smell of smoke.

Jumping out of bed, I looked out of the window. Flames were belching out from the building next door. Only two of us were awake. We were not in any immediate danger as there was a large space between the buildings, but we shouted to the rest of them to get up. "Save the instruments," yelled one girl, "Just get out," I shouted back. But instruments were not only valuable, they were the way the girls earned their living. I was the only one not clutching an instrument case when we emerged from the billet, and feeling heartily glad the xylophones were stored in a special trailer behind the bus!

A crowd had gathered. I remember standing among the onlookers, suddenly feeling rather cold. Looking down, I saw there was a sprinkling of snow on the ground.

Getting out fast had been our primary concern. When packing and unpacking sometimes on a daily basis, one kept everything to a bare minimum – literally in this case, as none of us had packed a robe! We all stood shivering in the freezing cold, dressed in PJ's and slippers, much to our embarrassment and the distinct amusement of a number of American soldiers!

A few weeks later, the totally unexpected happened. We were told to be packed up and report to the bus at 0600 hours.

We supposed we would fall asleep again in our seats, our purses acting as pillows to face yet another long journey by road. However, it was only minutes before the bus slowed to a stop.

Looking out of the windows, we realized we were at the guardhouse of a Military Airfield. We were suddenly all very much awake! The bus was waved through and proceeded to move past a number of hangars and planes before stopping in front of a large Nissen hut. It was somewhat disconcerting when a large Sergeant handed each of us a parachute, showed us how to put it on, then gave us a three minute lesson on which piece of string to pull if the worst happened, and we had to bail out! That was one of the many times that I found myself wishing for the luxury of a camera to record the expressions on everybody's face. Once the Sergeant had made sure our parachutes were on right, all twenty-three of us walked across the tarmac. We looked a motley crew, some of the smaller, thin girls, almost buried under their parachutes.

We boarded the four engine prop job, and very carefully climbed over the big costume hampers and boxes of instruments, which were already tied to the floor down the middle of the fuselage. We sat on long canvas benches which stretched straight from the door to the pilot. I had seen this in the WW2 movies, when spies were preparing to be dropped behind enemy lines. I remember they would "hook on" to something above them before being given the green "Jump" light. I sincerely hoped no such fate would await me!!

Unfortunately, where I was sitting was in line with the tall, heavy wooden xylophone case. I will never forget taking off on that flight. My parachute was rammed against the fuselage of the plane, while my face was inches away from the huge crate. I could hear the ropes holding it down to the floor straining as if they would snap at any moment. As the nose of the plane sought an upward path to the sky, my body jammed against the girls on either side of me. I was infinitely more concerned about being crushed to death than trying to find the right string to pull after jumping out! I kept thanking God for a life that was full of adventure, but asked Him to please let me live long enough to play the wretched xylophone at least one more time before it crushed me to death!

Christmas had come and gone, but the mail had not caught up with us as we criss-crossed Europe. Now it was New Year's Eve. We had packed up after the show and been jostled around on a five hour bus ride, until we finally arrived at a hotel in Paris. We were all too exhausted to care *where* we were.

Mr. Fox informed us that if we wanted our mail, we could collect it the following day at the American Express Office near the Place de la Concorde, but we should remember they would be closing at noon. Totally exhausted, I just grabbed the key issued to me, hauled my suitcase into the rickety elevator, located my room, and fell into bed as soon as I could.

Waking early the next morning, not having received any letters for three weeks, my primary concern was getting the mail from home. I showered and then shot downstairs. None of the other girls seemed to be up yet, so when the doorman pointed along the road to the nearest subway, I set off for the American Express office without a backward glance.

The weather was unseasonably warm, and soon I was seated at an outdoor café in the heart of bustling Paris, sipping coffee and pouring over my Christmas cards and letters. I sat alone in the watery sunshine.

The loss of Olive was still very much on my mind, but I could not bring her back.

I tried to count my blessings. I was twenty years old and being paid to be in Paris. I was the leader of a wonderful musical show that brought a welcome distraction to lonely Americans troops far from home, as well as being a sort of "ambassador" with the rest of the cast, for Britain, and I had seen five different countries. My heart whispered a prayer of thanksgiving to God.

It had been five years since my school trip, but now I was all grown up, and answered to my stage name, Angela Kaye.

Angela Kaye in "The Royal Kiltie Juniors"

It was fun to revisit some of the highlights of my school trip once again, this time reveling in the fact that there was nobody to tell me when it was time to move on.

I explored the Louvre at my own pace, rode to the top of the Eiffel Tower, and after lunch at a sidewalk café (where I was stared at as the idea of a young lady being alone was not a common sight) explored the lovely department stores.

It was twilight when I decided to return back to the hotel. Then it struck me.

The previous night, in a state of total exhaustion, I had almost crawled into the lobby and got my key. This morning I had gone straight outside, and asked for the nearest subway. At no time had I noted the *name of the hotel, or the name of the subway station I started from!* My school French had deserted me, and after a full minute, I had to accept the fact that I was totally lost and alone in a foreign country!

I saw a Gendarme, and imagined how the conversation would go with my broken French.

Me: I am lost.

Gendarme: Where are you trying to get to?

Me: I don't know!

That was not going to fly.

That morning, when the doorman had pointed out the nearest subway, I had just run down the steps and hopped on the train standing there. It was quite hopeless. If cell phones had been invented, I could have contacted someone in the cast. But this was only the dawn of 1954

Berating myself for my idiocy, I did the only thing I could. I prayed for the Lord to guide me "home" to my hotel.

Suddenly an idea formed in my mind. The only way to get back to where I had come from was to attempt to retrace my steps back the way I had come. Returning to the Place de la Concorde I descended into the subway. Unfortunately, this particular train station had multiple intersecting lines.

The one thing I could remember was that at one point, about three stops before my destination, the train had emerged up onto ground level, and I had seen the Eiffel Tower on my left side. I systematically boarded one train, counted to five stations, and not coming up into the daylight, got off, crossed over to the other platform, and went back to the Concorde station, then started the same process over again from a different level.

On my third try I hit pay dirt! Joy flooded through me, as the train came up into the twilight, and there was the famous Paris landmark on my right hand side! I was on the correct train, going in the correct direction but to where? The train was once again underground, and I decided to get off at the third station.

Emerging into the now dark of night, I looked about me. There were five main streets branching off from the center circle, all packed with cars, and all with horns blaring. I slowly walked around the circle, praying all the time for something I might see that was familiar.

A metal plate on a hotel boasted that English was spoken there. I knew it wasn't my hotel, but I walked in and spoke to the receptionist. She didn't understand a word I said.

Not being an American, it had not dawned on me until now that their Embassy might be able to help me. I looked up the number in the small lobby pay phone, and praying they would still answer the phone at seven o'clock on New Year's Eve, dialed the number. I nearly dropped the phone in thankfulness to hear an American voice. I introduced myself, told her my predicament, and asked if she could tell me where they usually billeted the entertainers when they were in Paris. A moment later, I emerged from the phone booth, and showed the address to the hotel receptionist. It was the hotel immediately around the corner from where I was standing.

The Lord had guided this foolish, lost young girl, safely "home" through a city of forty square miles, with more than two hundred and sixty-seven thousand people. I wonder why we are so surprised when the Lord who made the Universe and put us in it, manages these little miracles?

Our next performances would be in Vienna, but once again entertaining U.S. troops.

At that time, Austria was split up into zones and the Capital was cut up into sectors. In order to get to the American sector of Vienna, we would have to travel through the area occupied by Communist Russia (known then as the U.S.S.R.) thus literally going behind the Iron Curtain, as it was then called. This was the stuff spy movies were made of, and I looked forward to the adventure.

We set out by specially designated buses, then a train. It seemed that Russian soldiers boarded and scrutinized our papers every few miles. I hung out of the train window as it passed slowly through small towns and villages, looking at the people standing at the railroad crossings, and it struck me how poor and tired the people looked.

Although I had been a child living in Britain during the war, I remembered some of the grown-ups looking a bit worried sometimes after an air-raid. But they still had their freedom of speech and thought. They kept their dignity and their incredible British sense of humor.

But these Austrians, their home towns occupied by Communists, were different. There was something infinitely sad about the inanimate faces that stared up at me. They clutched their old bicycles and baby carriages, watching our train go slowly by them. Never once did I see anyone smile or wave. In my soul, I knew I was looking at the faces of human beings in despair.

The wonderful world of equality which Marx and Lenin had promised with their redistribution of wealth, had bound the people with worse chains than the ones they had promised to remove. Communism had choked all ambition and freedom of thought out of these sad human beings. I knew then, that freedom would always be worth fighting for.

It was a thrill to perform at the Vienna Opera House.

The famous theatre was packed with G.I.s who gave their usual cheers, applause and whistles along with a standing ovation at the end of our fast-paced show.

I thought what a hoot it would be to be able to honestly say one day, that I had conducted and sung in that famous Theatre.

Forty-eight years later, while touring Europe with a group I had organized, the Tour Guide on the bus pointed out the "Vienna Opera House". My friend from Church was sitting on the seat ahead of me. I tapped her on the shoulder, and whispered to her that I had sung a solo there. She obviously didn't believe a word I said, especially when I confessed my song had been, "There's No Business Like Show Business" for the U.S. troops. Probably word went round Church that Angela Bomford was either senile or the most dreadful liar!

My memory also includes a forbidden date I kept on my night off in Vienna.

A new girl called Nora had joined the company the week before. Somehow, in spite of all the rules and regulations against fraternizing with the military, she had managed to make a date with a handsome U.S. Officer. He had asked her if she could get one of the other girls to make up a foursome with his friend, for dinner and dancing at a famous restaurant in the city. She asked me if I would like to go.

I was well aware of the rules laid down by Mr. Fox for the entire cast, no matter how old we were. Common sense ruled out wandering around a strange city alone after dark, so my choice was between spending the evening nattering once again with the girls in a hotel room, or break the rule and go on the blind date. I was twenty years old, worked very hard, and told myself I deserved a break from entertaining other people. I agreed to go.

The two young men looked very handsome in their uniforms, as they met us in our hotel lobby. We barely gave them time to catch a breath, as Nora performed the introductions, and we hastily trotted them out of the front door, fearful that old man "Foxy" might appear and embarrass us all!

The guys told us the restaurant was "just a couple of blocks away".

A block in my home town in England is a forty second walk. That was the first time I discovered just how long an American's idea of a city block can be! But it was a lovely evening and a relaxed camaraderie was quickly established.

We finally turned into the lobby of a large impressive building. The elevator stopped at the top floor, and we emerged into a large restaurant. Couples were dancing to a Rosemary Clooney song. It would be another seven years before her nephew George would be born.

After ordering our meals, the conversation turned to our show. Both men had obviously been impressed with our performances at the opera house the night before, and chatted amicably over delicious food we had not tasted in years. Then for the first time in my life, I actually danced the "jive" with a real live American. It had been ten years since I had watched Olive dancing with the visiting soldiers in Britain at a tea dance in the Queen's Hotel ballroom, Rhyl, where we had been evacuated.

I wished fervently that I could tell Olive about this lovely evening.

The four of us walked onto a balcony that appeared to run round the whole top floor. We were in the American sector of the city, but our new friends pointed out the French, the British and then the Russian sector. The last was easy to identify, as it was in total darkness. It was surrealistic to see all the bright lights, to the left and center, and then on the far right side, total blackness. Again I was reminded of my train journey a few days before. The "darkness" of the communist philosophy, was emphasized once again.

I checked my watch, and to my amazement, found it was close to midnight. I felt like a real Cinderella, knowing we must get back to the hotel as fast as possible. The guys took us back in a cab, and while Nora lingered behind, I made a fast exit from the taxi onto the pavement, thanking my partner for a lovely evening, and assuring him I could make it the few paces into the hotel alone .

I had never been allowed out after eleven o'clock at night at my parent's home, and anyway, I wanted to get away before any kissing began. While my partner had been a perfect gentleman all evening,

I wasn't going to take any chances on his being tempted to abandon his good behavior.

It was just a small "pension" hotel, and the lobby was pitch dark and quiet. I thought that Nora would be following close behind me, but it appeared I was alone.

Taking off my shoes, I tip-toed to the foot of the staircase, my eyes cast down, riveted to each step ahead of me, as with one hand on the banister, and one grasping my dancing shoes, I proceeded up the stairs as quietly as possible.

Suddenly I saw two lace-up men's shoes looking up at me from the next step!

Slowly I raised my eyes, and while it was too dark to make out a face, the voice of Old Foxy cut through the gloaming, putting shivers down my spine.

"Miss Steggles," he began, "And just where do you think you have been till this hour?"

Suddenly, the whole pressure of months of packing and unpacking, sitting for days at a time on buses, rehearsing new numbers at this man's whim, going without rest and loosing my precious Olive, all caved in on me.

I had two more months on my contract, but I suddenly hated the thought of it. "Oh, please, please, just let me go home!" I begged.

This was not what he expected. I had taken his only weapon from him by my request. The regular Musical Director had left for England the week before, and nobody else was trained enough to keep the changing tempos correct for the whole show.

So my punishment was not to be dismissed, but to be kept on!

Nora, however, was never seen again. When we piled onto the bus the next day, she was gone. Her room -mate never told me what happened, but I guess she was packed off home from the Vienna airport, her solos cut from the program.

Over the next few months, the young officer who had been my partner that evening followed the show around Europe. On arriving at a hotel, he would be grinning at me from a lobby sofa, and then from the audience, usually on the front row. I had no interest in him whatsoever. I have no clue how he managed to get the time off and travel as he did.

It had been a great experience, but I was very glad when my contract ended, and I was finally free of The Foxes, and "The Royal Kiltie Juniors."

Chapter 11

In A "Manor" Of Speaking

I N THE INDUSTRIAL North of England were some very nicely appointed clubs for the working men and their wives to socialize, dance and watch professional live entertainment. It was a great way to try out a new act, and I was glad when my agent booked me into some of them.

Angela Kaye- Comedienne/Impersonator/Instrumentalist

I had bought my own xylophone and incorporated it into my new act. My brother Norman had built a huge box for it which travelled on the train in the guards van. More than one railway employee suggested I might have a body in there, as it looked remarkably like a coffin!

There was a young singer on this same circuit. He was using the name "Gerry Dorsey". The audience loved him, but financially he was struggling. His agent suggested he should change his name. He did. He took the name of a German composer of the Nineteenth Century - Englebert Humperdink..

My savings dwindled horribly during the bleak weeks when there were no "show business" bookings. Over the years I had used some of my "home time" between bookings to learn Dictaphone typing, and was registered at a temporary Secretarial Agency, as well as taking a modeling course and registering with them also for temp work. I was never home for more than a week without working in some capacity to earn my keep.

In the fall, the modeling agency sent me on a job with the English Electric Company as a demonstrator of their latest kitchen appliances around the country.

Having been raised with sales talk from my father and brother, it proved to be a successful venture, and the company offered me a permanent job. It would have been the right financial decision to make, but I declined. My only true love was the theatre. I wanted nothing else but to entertain people.

Meanwhile, all my friends back home were getting married. I could not understand why anyone would want to settle for a ticket to total boredom. In fact I had a very nasty re-occurring nightmare about the subject.

In the dream, I would be sitting in a limo in a wedding gown, my father beside me, obviously en route to my wedding, when in a claustrophobic fit, I would scream to my dad that I wanted to get out of the car and go home! I would wake up in a cold sweat, relieved it had only been a dream, and that I still in fact, had my freedom!

The English Electric company had requested me at the Modeling Agency. They wanted me to work for them at the Kelvin Hall "Ideal Home Exhibition" for a month. My job was to demonstrate a very new machine which the company hoped would catch on. It was one of the very first tumbler clothes dryers. Something which today is classified as a necessity. Until then, British housewives had spent half their lives pegging the laundry outside on a clothes line, then racing back home from the shopping every time it started to rain to bring it all in again! With the British climate, this was one of *the* most frustrating things about housekeeping. However, on my last visit to the U.K. I still found that many homes have the washing hanging out in the garden.

Most mothers did not work outside the home, in the 1950s, as it was believed that any man not able to provide for his wife and children, was a failure. Wives were live- in maids who bore and raised children. Sticking babies with strangers while mother worked, was a definite no-no unless the mother had been widowed, or the husband was an invalid. Whatever the husband earned was what the family had to live on. If you didn't have the money to pay for something, you did without it.

Part of my job was to cut through that thinking, and encourage women to buy their freedom from drudgery, and if they couldn't afford the machine right now, to buy it on credit. This was not the norm and now perhaps one might question the wisdom of the change that has bankrupt people and nations around the world.

I took a train to Glasgow, and settled into the small, comfortable Guest House the company had booked for me.

Kelvin Hall was full of bright, shiny, new appliances and inventions. The person in charge of the English Electric exhibit was David Ward, a cheerful, efficient young man. The small group worked well together for the entire month. It was a very happy experience.

On hearing I would be playing the part of "Cinderella" in his home town of Sheffield that Christmas, David suggested that I should spend the holiday with his family instead of alone in my theatre lodgings. The invitation was attractive, and so was he!

We had spent a lot of time working together, so on the last day of the exhibition, David gave me a piece of paper with his address on it.

It was very short. It just said, "The Manor House, Sheffield". Laughing I said, "Is this all there is to it?" "Yes." He smiled. "I'll pick you up from the theatre after you finish rehearsing on Christmas Eve. Bring an overnight bag, so you can stay with my family, then I can drive you back to your digs Christmas night."

Pushing the paper into my purse, I thought no more about it, as just then the young Scottish man I had been dating during that month, arrived to take me out for a late dinner.

December came quickly, and true to his word, David Ward called me to finalize the arrangements.

We chatted easily as he drove to the outskirts of the city of Sheffield on that chilly Christmas Eve. He turned the car into a long driveway with tall, elegant trees on one side, and a lawn on the other. In the distance I could see an enormous house. Years later, when I watched an English program entitled "To the Manor Born" the opening shot always reminded me of it.

David pulled the car up on the wide white gravel driveway. A servant magically materialized, opened the car door for me, and carried my suitcase up the stone steps of "The Manor House". Coming as I had, from my small studio room near the theatre, I truly felt I was a real "Cinderella".

David's father was obviously not exactly thrilled at the idea of his son bringing an "actress" home for Christmas, or for any other time probably! But he was very courteous and David's mother was a perfect hostess.

She showed me up to my room. It was large and airy, with a superb view over the lawns. It also had the first private bathroom attached to a bedroom I had ever seen in my life.

That evening, after a sumptuous dinner, David's siblings and young friends arrived. We all went out carol singing to other large homes in the area. These privileged young men and women were great fun, and I was included in all the joking and laughter which accompanied our singing.

I remember being terribly impressed when I looked through the windows of one mansion house, seeing not only *one* television set, but through another bay window, I could see *a second television!* Having *two* televisions in any one normal house was unheard of in England at that time, but these were not the average homes of average people. They were homes of wealthy industrialists; people who had prospered through generations of hard work and ingenuity. These families over the years, had given employment and livelihoods to millions of people, and been key to building the enormous working middle- class of Great Britain.

I have never envied children of the wealthy, nor felt that life was unfair because I was not one of them. After all, one cannot ask a poor man for a job. Only successful people can provide the kind of employment that does not use tax- payers money. It is my custom, on seeing a Rolls Royce, or any high priced car, to give an inward cheer. For there goes someone who creates jobs for the rest of the population!

At eleven o'clock, we all trooped into a large Anglican Church. It was packed with worshippers, and it was a thrill to take part in the Lord's Supper just before midnight--I felt truly happy and blessed.

The small group of friends finally scattered to their homes, amid hearty Christmas wishes. It was after one o'clock Christmas morning by the time David and I arrived back at the Manor house. He let himself in with his key.

Everything was in darkness, as we tip-toed to the foot of a staircase which reminded me of the one Rhett Butler had carried Scarlett O'Hara up in, "Gone With the Wind". However, my experience was to be very different!

My companion motioned for me to take off my shoes. I did so, and started to climb the stairs with them firmly clutched in my hand, believing the point of this exercise was to be as quiet as possible, and not disturb the rest of the household. However, what followed was an embarrassment.

David stopped me silently, and motioned me to leave my shoes on the floor. I just couldn't understand what he meant. I continued to carry them up the next couple of steps. Finally, drawing level with me, he insisted on taking the shoes out of my hands. He proceeded to tippy - toe back down in his sock-clad feet, and left my shoes next to his on the floor at the bottom of the stairs. The perfect gentleman, David bade me goodnight, and went to his room, while I slid thankfully beneath the largest duvet I had ever seen before, or since!

It wasn't until the next morning, when I saw my shoes beautifully clean and polished outside my door, that I realized David had been trying to tell me to leave my shoes for the servants to clean! It was fortunate indeed perhaps, that I had no ambitions whatsoever of becoming, "The Lady of the Manor" for without a doubt, I had failed the test!

CHAPTER 12

"Trust And Obey"

THROUGHOUT THE 1950S, theatres still closed on Sundays in England, and opened on a Monday. That meant the cast of touring productions boarded trains crossing the country to the next engagement, on the Sabbath.

On arriving at my new "digs" on a Sunday afternoon, I would locate the nearest Church and check the time of the evening service. I soon learned that God's people invariably follow the advice of St. Paul in the letter he wrote to the Romans in Chapter 12, verse 13 to *" --- be given to hospitality."*

There are wonderfully kind and generous people everywhere, but none more than in God's house. It has always mystified me how the finger pointing public declares their excuse to stay away from Church is because there are hypocrites there. They are right. However there are hypocrites in the supermarkets too, but I have not noticed it stopping anyone from going there for food for the body ---- I need food for my soul too though.

Early in my career, I had joined the "Actor's Church Union". They coordinated with local Church Pastors in each town who volunteered to act as a Chaplain to the actors who passed through their local theatres each week. They usually made an appearance back-stage on the opening night.

The ACU sent out a list of inspected and recommended lodgings for every theatre town in the country where members could safely stay while on tour. Next to my Bible, it was the most important piece of reading material that I owned.

One week, I had forgotten to make reservations for accommodations early enough. There was a show with a very big cast playing at the other theatre in town, and every room in the ACU book was taken. None of us had cars, and wherever our lodgings were, had to be either on a good bus route, or within walking distance of the theatre.

Actors receive good compensation for their work when they *are* working. But living expenses have to be met during those many weary weeks and sometimes months between engagements. So although I was playing a leading role, paying to stay for a week in a real Hotel was out of the question, and the Guest Houses I had researched, were all full.

Telephoning the Actor's Church Union, I told them of my dilemma. They were sympathetic, said they were sorry, and hung up. "A lot of help *they* are," I grumbled.

That Sunday afternoon, I stepped off the train at Salford railway station into pouring rain. The January freeze bit through my coat. I pulled my hood up, and as the idea of wheels being put on cases had yet to be invented, picked up my big heavy case , and began the trek into town.

Like most industrial areas then in England, the buildings were all blackened with the soot of chimneys that had belched out smoke ever since the industrial revolution a hundred and twenty years earlier. A discouraging sight even in summer sunshine, but under these circumstances, it was positively depressing!

Praying for guidance to be shown where I should go, I went knocking on the few doors that had "Bed and Breakfast" signs outside. I prayed the rain would stop as well. But it just persisted.

One landlady admitted she had a room available, but announced with tremendous self-righteousness indignation, that she did not take in "theatricals" -- the last word sneered out as if it was the same as "criminals". She shut the door in my face, leaving my suitcase and I standing in puddles on her dripping door-step.

It was one of those "low moments" in my career as an actor. I felt the Lord had led me to where I was, so why was He letting me down like this?

I wasn't used to being cold, hungry, and homeless! But I should have known better than to doubt His Word.

With no alternative, I dragged myself to the theatre only to find that some of the chorus girls had already resigned themselves to sleeping on the floor of the dressing rooms. Memories of my encounter with the large rat in the prop room at my first job, did not endear me to the idea of putting my head anywhere near the floor, even in the "Star" dressing room. But there appeared to be no alternative.

Suddenly there was a knock on the stage door. There being no doorman on duty, I opened it.

A tall gentleman, in his mid- fifties, clad in a beautifully made winter coat, stood with rain pouring off a large black umbrella.

I invited him inside.

"Are you Angela Kaye?" he asked, using my stage name. "The Minister at our Church announced in the service this morning, that there was a lady from the cast of "Cinderella" without a home for the week. My wife and I would like to have you," he beamed. He gave me his Pastor's phone number to check up on what he had said, but I knew instinctively that this gentleman was all he appeared to be. Although today one would advise more caution, I gratefully handed him my suitcase and clambered into the passenger seat of his car.

He drove me to his lovely home, where his wife greeted me warmly. Brass fire-irons twinkled on the hearth, reflecting the tongs of fire leaping up the chimney. A hot cup of tea was placed in my hands, and I was "home" for the next two weeks.

Apparently the "Actor's Church Union" had contacted their appointed "Chaplain" in the town, and this had been the result.

Remembering my initial reaction to my phone call to them for help, I felt ashamed. Contrary to my belief that they were doing nothing to help me, they had cared enough to address my dilemma most efficiently.

During the week, the Pastor visited our company back-stage, and told me that the gentleman who, along with his wife had so graciously opened their home to me, was a deacon of the Church, and the manager of a large local Bank.

When the time came for the show to move on once again, my hosts refused any payment for my splendid accommodations, or accept any monetary contribution towards the sumptuous meals I had been served. I met this type of kindness from people in both rich and poorer circumstances, in all of the houses of Worship I attended. They were all "angels" to me in my walk with God and my chosen profession.

My wonderful sister Olive had been to me, the font of all knowledge and wisdom, particularly in my formative years. Therefore her opinion of the institution of marriage had made perfectly good sense to me.

"What in the world could any two people have to talk about after a couple of years together? Marriage must be *the most boring* existence imaginable" she would declare.

I had agreed.

Now years later, I was still having the nightmare of being on my way to my wedding, and still woke up in a cold sweat, heartily grateful it had only been a dream. The word "marriage" to me, meant to be trapped in a boring, daily grind. Why would anyone even entertain the idea of being just "a housewife"? I was living a life of travel and adventure, doing what I loved the most.

But as the years passed by, a strange new feeling began to haunt me. It was something that I finally recognized as loneliness.

While enjoying the camaraderie of both sexes in the cast of all the shows, I had studiously avoided any personal involvement with men. Friendships are transient in show business due to the nature of the job, and I had decided very early that it would be a disaster to become serious about any man in my profession. Family life was non-existent for the wife of an actor, as he was invariably "on the road" while she was stuck at home looking after the kids. Except for the small percentage of stars, financially the job was a disaster, with money for a few months, then zero income for weeks.

However, I knew that I would have nothing whatsoever in common with anyone *not* connected with the theatre. I would make the poor man miserable as he would never be able to understand me! I could *not* fathom how the Lord could possibly have anyone for me to spend my life with. Needing someone who would appreciate my love of performing, yet not be in the business - someone with a fantastic sense of humor who I actually fell in love with, meant I needed someone who didn't exist!

The young Scottish man I had dated while working in Glasgow had stayed in touch and over the months and years, our relationship had grown. He drove to and fro, transporting both me and my xylophone back and forth to theatres around the country at the beginning and end of the longer engagements.

My friends told me how lucky I was to have found such a wonderful man. I knew they were right. Common sense told me I should settle down near to his home, so we could pursue a real courtship. This meant giving up show business. So finally, I did.

After securing a job in a department store in Glasgow, I moved into lodgings close to where my young man lived with his elderly father. The pretty country village was just twelve miles from the city. One day, determined to be sensible and lead a "normal life," I agreed to become engaged.

But every time there was an offer of a good contract from my agent, off I went to do "just one more show."

Time went by, and I tried desperately hard to fall more in love with this wonderful man who would obviously be a superb husband. Being sensible was the best thing I could do. We set a wedding date for May 23rd, 1958.

But the Lord kept waking me up in the middle of the night in a cold sweat. Just the thought of not being able to call Wallasey home, the thought of permanently leaving my parents and my brother Norman and his family, to live miles away in Scotland, made me feel wretched. It was all wrong.

After weeks of prayer, I was finally convinced that this was not the path the Lord wanted me to follow. But I had worn this lovely man's ring for two years. How could I let him down? My soul and spirit were being ripped apart.

During a lunch break from the store one day, I walked into a Glasgow Church to think and pray, seeking answers and peace for my soul. The Lord sent me a real, live angel in the form of an elderly lady, in a voluminous old coat. She had grey hair and bright, smiling eyes, and sat in the pew near to me. Seeing my distress, she smiled and began to talk in her delightful Glasgow accent.

I tearfully bleated out my dilemma, and she shared with me her own story. "When I was young, I told all my boy friends I loved them," she confessed. "I didn't realize how much I was hurting them." She added. Then she told me anecdotes that put a smile on my tear stained face, and somehow, courage in my heart. "Just tell him the truth about how you *really* feel," she advised. "The Lord will help you through it all," she assured me. I have thanked the Lord many times since for sending me that "angel".

I broke off the engagement, packed, and took the train home, distraught at the realization that if I could not love such a wonderful man enough to give up the theatre, and spend my future with him, I was incapable of loving anyone!

"What," I worried, "is *wrong* with me?" I asked that question of my Pastor, and my Doctor. Neither could throw any light on my dilemma.

However, as soon as I got a contract in my hands for a new show, I was happy again.

Psalm 120 v1 "In my distress, I cried unto the Lord, and He heard me."

In the fall of 1961, I auditioned for the job of Television Announcer for a new Commercial station that was to open in the North of England. Twelve years had passed since I had seen my first television set in a store window, and decided that one day I would like to be an announcer.

All television was still transmitted "live". Sometimes the signal would go down so that the audience was getting either voice only with no picture, or the other way around! The audition included having signals sent to me that these things had "gone wrong" and I had to react accordingly.

The total lack of nervousness amazed me at the audition. It seemed to come naturally to "cover" and carry on, sometimes holding up the "Normal service will begin as soon as possible," card, or continuing to speak, knowing I could be heard, but the vision had gone down.

The audition over, the director asked, "You've done this before haven't you?" I hadn't, but he was smiling and obviously very pleased with me. I left the studio with high hopes.

It was a bitterly cold winter in England when, on December 31st, 1961, after two performances that day, I huddled beneath the large comforter in the small bedroom of my lodgings near Blackpool. The landlady had been particularly kind. With no central heating, rooms became like ice-boxes very quickly, so she had put a two bar electric fire against the wall telling me, with her huge Lancashire smile, to leave it on all night. I was glad to take her advice. There was snow on the ground, and the wind was whistling outside the old Victorian sash window.

The hands of the clock on the mantelpiece crept up to midnight. Soon it would be 1962. I had failed to get any of the cast members of the show to attend the Church Watch-night Service with me. I had let in every New Year that way for almost ten years. But now discouraged and alone, I had just gone back to my digs, had supper, and gone to bed. But sleep eluded me. My Doctor had told me to keep very mild sleeping pills on hand for those times when I found it particularly difficult to sleep in the constantly changing surroundings. It was something I rarely did, but now I lay awake, wondering if I should take one.

Five days earlier I had turned twenty-eight. I had decided to give up on ever finding anyone I could love and share my life with. It was quite hopeless. Nobody *in* show business was suitable, and nobody *outside* the business would be either! While I had prayed for guidance over and over again, and asked for someone I could love to come into my life, I realized I had never really given the whole situation to the Lord, without reservation. I had never totally trusted Him, for I had been busy trying to make things work my own way. Then, as the New Year approached, I finally gave up the whole situation to my Creator.

My favorite Bible verse was Proverbs Chapter 3, verses 6 and 7.

"Trust in the Lord with all thine heart;

And lean not unto your own understanding.

In all thy ways acknowledge Him, and He shall direct thy paths."

The more I thought and prayed, the more I realized that I had never sincerely acted on those words. Now I told the Lord that if His plan for my life did not include a husband, then I would accept His will graciously and be willing to go through life alone. Although I meant it, I did add a little codicil, asking that if He had anyone for me, to please bring him into my life within that year. If it didn't happen, then I would never think about marriage again. Truly meaning the prayer, and totally at peace, I fell into a deep sleep.

It was the acrid smell of smoke that woke me.

Opening my eyes, I saw over the side of my bed something very large glowing on the floor. It took a split second to realize that in my sleep, I had pushed a pillow out of the bed. It had landed on the electric fire bars, and was about to burst into flames.

The tiny room was two stories up. Next to the bed was a large chest of drawers, in front of a very old Victorian sash window. It had been my experience that such devices either only opened an inch, or not at all. Praying this one would open wide enough, I leaped out of bed in terror, reached across the big chest of drawers, and shoved up on the old window with all my strength. To my total surprise and relief, it opened all the way ! I picked up the glowing pillow and flung it out onto the snow-covered lawn below.

I have often wondered what might have happened if I had taken the sleeping pill or if the owner of the house had not kept the window in good working order. In my other lodgings, it had been *impossible* to open any of those Victorian windows without much tugging and pulling, and never wide enough to throw a pillow through!

It was some time before I worried about what the land-lady would say about her destroyed pillow sitting on her lawn. But at breakfast, when I explained what had happened, she was very gracious, and just thankful nothing worse had happened. I paid for the pillow, realizing that I might have paid with my life.

Earlier in the year, the Producer of a local drama society from home had contacted me about taking part in a benefit show for the local "Blind Children's Fund" Knowing I would be in Wallasey on those dates, I readily agreed.

It was an added delight to hear that Carol Gatley, the girl I had performed with when I was fourteen, would also be taking part. Carol had always been a wonderful stage artist, and a professional performer. So after fourteen years, we would be singing together once again at the "Floral Pavilion" the place I had first sung when I was three years of age.

Weeks later, the script arrived.

Without a doubt, it was one of the worst I had ever read in my life. One thing registered in my mind immediately. I did *not* want to be involved with that show.

It took only minutes to dream up a believable excuse to get out of my commitment. Reaching for the telephone, I began to dial the Producer's number.

But after entering the first three digits, something happened to me.

Suddenly, I had to stop dialing. I heard no voice, but my soul got the message. "You are a Christian. You gave your word to do this show. You belong to Jesus Christ. You don't make excuses and break your word."

I hung up the phone.

If that call had been completed, and I had not kept my promise to perform in that benefit show, I would never have known the incredible blessings the Lord had in store for me.

The decision to live in obedience was to take me across the world, and change my entire life.

CHAPTER 13

Hello Again

THERE WAS A darling seven year old little girl who sang with me in the benefit show. As the nights passed by, I felt a tremendous yearning to have a little girl just like her. I prayed, "Lord, I don't know exactly how you could arrange it, but I would so dearly love to have a little girl just like this precious little one. Someone I could be a mother to." Then I felt guilty. Instead of being a responsible Christian, praying a sensible prayer, here I was asking for something totally unsuitable and impossible! And anyway, the Lord was far too busy to bother with the foolish yearnings of a silly woman bent on spending her life tearing around the country entertaining people.

Once again Carol Gatley and I shared the same dressing room at the Floral Pavilion Theatre, just as we had fourteen years before, when we sang together in the children's Chrysanthemums Pantomime Society. Now grown women and experienced professional stage artists, it was a delight to be entertaining in our home town.

During the intermission the Stage Manager knocked on our dressing room door. "Angela, there is a Vera Bomford in the audience who would like to see you after the show" he called.

As a child, Vera had been in the same dancing school as my sister Olive. Our mothers waited together while their small girls were in class. Vera had grown up to be a superb dancer and choreographer, appearing in productions all over Europe including Paris and London. I had not seen her since she had been the Choreographer for the summer season "Melody Inn" shows for several years in this same theatre. Now it seemed, we had reversed roles, as she was in the audience, and I on the stage.

"Tell her I will go out front after the finale" I shouted to the Stage Manager.

At the end of the show, I changed out of my costume and made my way to the front of the auditorium. By now the public had left the theatre, but two people stood near the main exit. Vera greeted me with a big smile and embrace. There was a tall, extremely good looking man standing near her, and the thought struck me that she had obviously married a very good looking husband. Then Vera was saying, "You remember my brother Douglas don't you?"

A pair of twinkling blue eyes smiled into mine as I held out my hand to a tall, fair haired man. His glorious smile rested on me, as he grasped my hand.

We were standing in the very same spot in the Floral Pavilion theatre, where I had shyly asked him for his autograph when I was fourteen years old, half my lifetime ago. He had taken my album in his hand and written in it, "To Angela. My charming leading lady. With love from Doug Bomford."

I had read the words again only months before, when at my mother's urging, I had finally gone through a lot of old books and papers, before throwing them out. Unfortunately, that autograph album had been one of the discards.

"We'll wait for you and drive you home if you like." Douglas offered. "That would be lovely. I'll just get my coat", I replied heading towards the backstage area.

Vera followed me, no doubt remembering the hundreds of times she had danced on that stage with the "Melody Inn" shows.

Years earlier, my mother's letters had included news she had heard from Vera's mother when they ran into each other shopping. Now I remembered something important. "I heard that Douglas was married and had a family now," I said. "Oh, I am afraid there was a divorce five years ago." Vera explained.

The thought of a marriage ending has always made me feel sad. However, this time it was different. It still makes me blush when I remember how my heart rose, even as I heard myself saying, "Ooh noooo! What a shame!"

As I retrieved my belongings from the dressing room Vera told me that she had gone overseas to live with her brother to help him, as he had full custody of his two small children. Their mother was not in the picture, as she lived a thousand miles away from them, in Chile. Doug's job entailed a lot of travelling, and his sister helped to provide a stable family life. But for now the whole family was back in Wallasey on vacation.

On the drive home, we two gals hardly stopped for breath. Douglas couldn't get a word in edgewise. We had still not caught up with our exchange of news, so Vera called me the next day and we arranged to go out together that evening. "Oh, and Douglas will be our chauffeur" she added. "Oh good" I thought.

CHAPTER 14

A Time To Laugh

ENGLAND WAS EXPERIENCING the coldest winter in eighty years, and the snow was turning to slush as Vera, Douglas and I hurried from the car park into the welcoming warmth of the Grand Hotel in New Brighton, the seaside resort area of Wallasey.

It would be another ten years before the majority of houses in England had central heating. However, larger hotels did, and it was a relief to feel the warmth surround us as we entered the lounge.

Douglas helped us out of our coats, and ordered drinks. I sipped on some non-alcoholic concoction, while Vera and I once again gave our tongues a good workout.

I was aware of our handsome companion, but he didn't talk a lot. I remembered Douglas as a quiet sort of person. Even when he had directed me in the show as a child, he had not been anything like many directors who were so often overbearing egotists.

After an hour or so, Vera addressed a remark to me that was more a statement, than a question. "So you are twenty-eight years old, and you have never married?" I answered her honestly. "To me," I declared "Getting married would be the same as jumping into a grave and having soil shoveled in on top of me."

Just then, the quiet voice of her brother Douglas was heard. "Who do you think you are kidding.?" He teased.

"Cheeky chap," I thought, "He doesn't even know me!"

Later as Vera and I repaired our make up in the hotel ladies room, she complained to me that although Douglas still had six weeks left of vacation time in England, because it was so horribly cold, he wanted to go back to South America as soon as possible. "We are booked to sail on the Reina del Mar on March the twentieth. It is like a cruise ship, with music and dancing and a swimming pool," she enthused. "But now," she continued disappointment reaching her voice, " Douglas says it is too cold here, and wants to go back earlier. That would mean three weeks on a 12 passenger *cargo* boat."

It was clear that Vera did *not* like her brother's new plans. "Well we'll just have to think of something that will keep him here longer," I said brightly, as applying fresh lipstick in the mirror. "What do you think would make him forget his new plan, and just stay in England till you can go on the big ship?"

Vera's voice was very clear. "You" she said.

How I kept the lipstick from sliding up my nose, I shall never know. I was in total shock as I turned to Vera and almost shouted "ME?"

"Yes," she said, "You could keep him here."

Douglas and I had hardly exchanged a word to each other. I thought she was grasping at straws in the hope she would get her trip on the beautiful company flagship. I thought what a truly silly thing Vera had said.

However, a bubble of laughter began somewhere deep inside me, and in spite of my non-alcoholic drink, I felt slightly light-headed, as Vera perambulated me back downstairs to my childhood crush.

As the evening ended, Douglas dropped Vera off first then continued to drive me to my home. Alone in the car, the conversation turned to our mutual enjoyment of music and ballroom dancing. Douglas walked me to my parent's door, and bade me goodnight. I was fumbling for my key, when he turned at the gate, and asked, "How would you like to go dancing Saturday night?"

I had been writing to a very nice chap who was teaching engineering on a Naval ship. I had only dated Jim very briefly, but he was a good dancer, and would be returning in mid -March. Meanwhile, I had nobody to go out with. It struck me that the timing would be perfect. "That would be great," I said.

I would be leaving Wallasey to join a new show in a couple of months anyway. All this was just a nice way to pass the time. I wasn't being flighty, just practical!

In 1962, dinner-dances were a very popular form of entertainment.

During the meal, Douglas showed me photographs of his two lovely children in their school uniforms. They stood hand in hand, the perfect "Jack and Jill." Michael was almost ten, and Suzanne was seven.

Douglas was talking about his life in Lima. Unfortunately, I had forgotten my geography and was thrashing around in my head trying to remember if Lima was the capital of Chile or Peru! I recalled my geography teacher, Miss Blackman scolding me for placing Santiago and Lima in the wrong country. I had always managed to get them the wrong way around. Now twenty-eight years of age, I was ashamed to realize that I *still* couldn't remember which was the capital of Chile, and which the capital of Peru! South America was a very long way from England, and it wasn't a subject that usually came up in conversation. But at that moment, I dearly wished I had listened more in school, for I dreaded appearing to be an ignorant moron to this lovely man.! "Oh! Miss Blacklock! Which one is it?" I thought in desperation. Thankfully, Douglas eventually mentioned Peru and I was off the hook.

By the time dessert arrived, I was thoroughly enjoying myself. Doug obviously had a superb sense of humor, and we laughed a lot. My whole spirit felt happier and happier.

Suddenly my handsome companion stood up, reached out his hand to me, and said, "Would you care to dance?"

I remember distinctly sending up a fast but very important prayer. "Please Lord, make him a good ballroom dancer. You know I can't marry anyone who isn't a good dancer."

Douglas swept me onto the dance floor and into his arms.

Suddenly my heart took wings. I had never felt like this before. It was as if everything in my life had been leading me up to this moment.

And it didn't hurt that Douglas danced as well as Fred Astaire!

The next morning in Church, I prayed the Lord would take away the overwhelming attraction I had already developed for Douglas. "Please," I begged, "Don't ask me to go and live in Peru! I just don't want to."

Even if the T.V. announcing job didn't pan out, my agent had some good work lined up for me for the rest of the year. "My life is just great as it is Lord," I assured the Almighty.

Some time during that first date Douglas had asked me which Church I went to. Now exiting the portals of the Claremount Road Methodist Church, I spotted a familiar car slowly driving past.

Doug has never told me exactly how many times he had cruised past the Church before I finally emerged with the rest of the congregation, but suddenly my handsome escort from the previous evening was waving and offering me a ride home. "By the way, this is Michael," he said, indicating an adorable little boy sitting in the back seat. He had dark, wavy hair atop plump, rosy cheeks. Like his father this handsome child had a lovely smile, and very good manners.

Monday night we took in a movie, and Tuesday we spent with Valerie Evans. Val and I had been in the same class from the age of twelve to graduation, had played piano duets, and had always been great competitors for "top of the class" in English Composition. Valerie had followed a career in journalism, and wrote for the "Wallasey News". As a moneymaking sideline, she sang with her guitar, and I had promised to see her perform when she appeared at an entertainment center.

I invited Douglas to come with me. Val sat with us until her "show time", and again for the rest of the evening, when Douglas offered her a ride home. He went to get the car, while Valerie and I stood together in the doorway, with our coat collars up and teeth chattering. I assured my friend once again how good her act had been.

Suddenly she said, "So now I suppose I'll have to send the Wallasey News to you in Peru."

I looked at her as if she was quite mad. She knew I had only been seeing Douglas for three days and evenings. What was the matter with her? I took it as a funny joke. But it worried me. There was no way I would be stupid enough to get caught up with a man I had gone out with a couple of times, who had two children, and lived on the other side of the world! He was going back to his job and home in Peru, and I was going on with my career, which after ten hard years of work, was finally taking off. Val *had* to be joking!

Douglas had promised to take the two children to the Circus near Manchester, and asked if I would like to go along with them. He picked me up the following afternoon, this time with *two* adorable children in the back seat. Now I was introduced for the first time to his precious seven year old little girl, Suzanne.

Her demure little face was framed by light brown hair. She was dressed in a camel colored winter coat with dark trim. It was a bit short for her as winters in Lima were too mild to warrant heavy clothing, so both children had borrowed warmer garments from their English cousins.

Like the rest of her family, Suzanne had beautiful manners. She chose a quieter venue than her brother during the sixty minute car ride. Soon I felt a gentle touch on the collar of my nylon fur coat. It was the dainty little hand of Suzanne. I turned my head to look at her. "It's nice," she smiled, still stroking the fur. She gave me a beautiful smile. Suzie had no clue exactly where this strange woman with the furry coat had popped up from, but she didn't seem to mind. At the circus Douglas and I sat together with the children on his left. The clowns were funny and the acts were great.

However, by the time the alligator wrestler was demonstrating the art of putting the six foot reptile to sleep by stroking his tummy, Suzanne was complaining that her brother was pushing her, while he in turn, complained that she started it by kicking him. I hid a smile as I recognized the normal behavior of siblings only a couple of years apart from each other. Norman and Olive and I had never experienced sibling rivalry, perhaps because with seven years between each of us, there was no sense of "competition".

No doubt wishing he could copy the alligator man and put the pair of them to sleep by rubbing their tummies, Douglas decided to separate them. So Doug and I spent the rest of the performance holding hands across the back of Suzanne's seat.

The memory of my feelings over fifty years later, are still vivid. It all felt so very natural. I was in a state of total euphoria, and could not get a permanent grin off my face.

It was pouring with rain when we stopped en route home for a meal. We were all very hungry, and soon Douglas, Suzanne and I were demolishing large helpings of British "fish and chips with mushy peas".

Michael had pie and chips. I remember it very well, because there suddenly appeared a deep frown on his father's face when Michael, using all the enthusiasm only a ten year old boy could muster, began with the aid of a large piece of bread to mop up the gravy on his plate. Suddenly he caught sight of his father's expression. Douglas with wide disapproving eyes, was telegraphing to his son that such an action was *not* on the list of good manners expected when trying to impress a new friend! The speed which Michael's bread was tearing round the plate gradually decreased until it ended with its' owner surreptitiously sliding the tasty gravy-laden bread into his mouth, his head almost under the table. I gave the performance of my life, with my eyes glued elsewhere, apparently not noticing the little comedy being played out across the table, while my tummy ached with suppressed laughter. Michael was a totally natural little boy, suddenly remembering he was supposed to be on his best behavior!

CHAPTER 15

A Time To Build Up

I PRAYED TO THE Lord constantly for wisdom and guidance as my attraction to Douglas grew stronger every hour.

Day- time was spent with the children. Bundled up against the cold, we haunted the local parks, playing ball with them, sometimes Douglas throwing the thing as far as possible so the kids would take off running to retrieve it, giving us a chance to giggle and snuggle closer for a precious moment or two. This little family enthralled me. The daddy with his two children were totally natural, relaxed and obviously happy together.

One day, we headed for the beach dressed in coats, scarves and gloves in an attempt to block the bitterly cold British wind. We were clambering across the sand-hills that overlooked the River Mersey, when we were suddenly stopped by seven year old Suzanne shouting, "Oh daddy, look! A poor dead bird!"

We grouped round the beautiful grey-feathered body of a seagull. It was a sad moment as the four of us looked down on what had been a happy creature just a short time before, winging its' way over the water. "Why don't we bury him here, facing the sea he always loved," suggested Douglas. The children agreed, and helped their father to dig a deep hole. Douglas ceremoniously lowered the beautiful little body into the grave. There followed a few moments of quietness, ended abruptly by Michael declaring he was getting hungry, and we took off at a canter to the warmth of the car.

Many of his sex would have shrugged the death of the bird off as "Just one of those things that kids have to get used to". But this was a man who cared deeply about the feelings of his children. He was a wonderful father. He was a wonderful man.

We had spent three days with Michael and Suzanne, and five evenings alone on dates, when suddenly, my mother asked me the question, "What is Douglas *really* like?" Without having to think for one moment, I replied, probably in a truly soppy voice, "Oh he's just lovely!" If my mother had suspected I was getting involved with this man, I am certain that the idiotic look on my face confirmed it.

My father, however, was taking a very dim view indeed of my association with Douglas. Both sets of parents had worked together on committees for the Chrysanthemum Pantomime Society for years, including the production when Douglas had been the Director. His sister Vera had danced in shows with Olive when they were young, and our mothers had been acquainted for years. Our families knew each other. We were not total strangers. However, the threat of a man suddenly appearing and carrying his only remaining daughter off overseas, did not sit well with my dad. As far as he was concerned, I had two things to accomplish in my life, the first being to get over this acting nonsense, (it annoyed him that I was still in show business) then work in his shop. Also, being the only daughter since Olive's death nine years before, I was supposed to keep myself available to take care of him in his old age. Douglas was a threat to his security.

To my great embarrassment, my father refused to allow Douglas in the house.

My suitor was thirty-seven years of age, but had to knock at the door, then go and wait for me in the car like a naughty teen-ager! The fourth night Douglas had come to pick me up on a date, I had begged my father to please just let him in the house and meet him for the first time in fourteen years. Without taking his eyes off the television, my father said "He doesn't exist. Kill it now."

I tried to understand his fear for me. I was consorting with a divorced man, who had the responsibility of two children. But the real threat to him, was that Douglas lived on the other side of the world. It was all foolishness anyway, as in just a few short weeks Doug would be returning with his family to his job, and his home in Peru

At twenty-eight years of age, I was truly in love for the first time in my life. But this was playing out like a soap opera! However, whenever I was with Douglas, the world was perfect, and nothing else mattered.

It was Friday night. We had been going out together day and evening, for almost a week. Douglas parked the car on the promenade, close to the Floral Pavilion.

The lights of the City of Liverpool twinkled across the River Mersey. Suddenly to my utter amazement, Douglas asked me to be his wife. My reaction was immediate. It needed no thinking out. I said, "Oh yes please, when?" It was the most natural thing to say. I guess I just didn't believe in playing hard to get!

We drove to the nearest public phone box, and I called my Pastor asking for an appointment to see him the next morning to arrange a wedding date. As I hung up the phone, the thought struck me that I had just agreed to leave everything and everybody I had ever known, along with all that had meant anything to me in my life; my career, my family, my dear friends, and my country, to live in a foreign land, and be a wife and mother to people I had only spent time with for less than a week! I had always declared that people who married anyone they had not known for at less two years were crazy. "So why," I asked myself, "don't I feel scared?" It made no sense. But I knew without a shadow of a doubt, that this was the plan the Lord had for me, and I had never been happier in my life.

We decided it would be wise to keep the good news from my parents until the wedding date was firmly set at the Church.

We knew that one person in particular would be delighted with our news - Vera, for her plan had worked! Instead of travelling home on a small cargo boat, she would now be able to enjoy all the amenities of a cruise ship for the three week voyage from Liverpool to Peru, while accompanying her brother and his children, on his honeymoon! While she had enjoyed her five years with the family, she would finally be free of responsibility, and be able to lead her own life, with the option of possibly marrying if she so desired; something she could not have done before I appeared on the scene.

The wedding would have to be on a Saturday to accommodate our working friends, and the one just before the "Reina del Mar" was to sail. The would be Saturday March 17th, and both my Pastor and I agreed that would be perfect.

However, as he was about to write in his big Church calendar, Douglas cleared his throat and suggested I may not want to choose that for our wedding day. "Why not?" I asked in surprise. Very sheepishly, he replied, "Well, March 17th was the day I was married the first time." Out of 365 days in the year, it had to be the same one! "Great," I declared, "You will never forget our Anniversary." And he never has.

We left the Church with the date and time of our wedding all set, and drove home to break the news to my parents.

This would be a challenge. Douglas and I had been dating for a week. I was about to live on the other side of the world, and only get back to England and see my folks once every three years.

I realized that this was going to be a shock to them.

Only two years before, the very thought of leaving Wallasey to live less than two hundred miles away in Scotland, had frightened me. Now I found myself asking the Lord why I didn't feel panicky now, about living *six thousand* miles away.

I can only remember that I felt a warmth and total assurance that all would be well.

We arrived at my home to find that mom was alone in the house, as my father was at work in the shop. She invited us in and said she would do what all Britishers do when faced with visitors, illness, death, or a possible dilemma. She would "Put the kettle on and make a cup of tea".

I remember saying, "No mother. I think you should sit down, and soon *I* will make *you* a cup of tea."

Then I dropped the bombshell.

"Douglas and I are getting married at my Church at four o'clock on March the seventeenth." It was now mid- February.

My mother turned her head first to Douglas, then back to me. She did this a few times, and said. "Oh, really?"

Perhaps the reality of the situation did not hit home, but three cups of tea later, she was smiling, and talking about where to have the reception. In England we call this "Being a real brick about the whole thing."

But the biggest hurdle was still ahead of me. Telling my father our news!

CHAPTER 16

A Time To Love

MRS. EATON HAD been a lifelong friend of my parents, and the mother of my closest friend, Jill Eaton. How a meeting was ever arranged between Jill's mom and my dad, and exactly what was said, I never discovered. I strongly suspect that Mrs.Eaton told my father to wake up and realize that at twenty-eight years of age, I must know my own mind, and he should get out of the way. I only know for certain that suddenly my father became a pussycat, and agreed to a meeting with Douglas. Both of my parents fell under the spell of my wonderful bridegroom, and from that day onwards, Douglas could do no wrong in my parent's sight.

It was with a sense of shame that I remembered the problem I thought even the Lord could not solve; that of my being unable to marry anyone *outside* the entertainment industry as they could not possibly understand my love of the theatre, while I did not want to marry anyone *inside* theatrical circles either, as it makes for a negative family life.

As usual, the Lord's plan was infinitely better than mine!

Doug's sister Vera, was a spectacular dancer and choreographer, as well as a splendid actress. With this experience in his family, Douglas had no problem whatsoever understanding "theatricals". He became my greatest audience and encourager, and proved to be more than a competent entertainer himself!

We drove through the Mersey Tunnel to Liverpool to make an all important purchase. An Engagement ring. Then we headed to my future in-laws house, a ruby encircled by dainty diamonds flashing on my left hand.

Apparently Douglas had been hinting to his parents about his plans during the previous day or two, but now we had to break the news to them officially. We walked into the living room. Doug's father was sitting in his usual chair, reading his newspaper. "Go ahead. Show dad the ring," Douglas said.

I stretched out my left hand. Mr. Bomford inspected it with a quizzed look on his face. Then he looked up at us obviously thinking it was a joke. Surely his son had more sense than to marry a woman he had been dating only a week! And an actress at that! No. It had to be a joke. But I guess we looked too happy for that dear man to make any negative comment, as he dropped his beloved Liverpool Echo in shock, looked up and said "You're really serious about this aren't you?"

My future mother-in-law had been married before. Her husband had been killed in France during the First World War, leaving her alone to raise a small son and daughter. Later, she had married Mr. Bomford, and they had Vera and Douglas.

While serving as a Nurse in England during the Second World War, Doug's mother received news that her first son, serving in the British Merchant Navy, was missing. Harry was never found. It was concluded that his ship had been torpedoed off the coast of Africa. Now he too, left grieving parents, siblings, a young widow, and a baby boy named Keith, a dear nephew we telephone frequently in England.

In common with so many women of her generation, Mrs. Bomford had lived through the big Depression, as well as loosing a husband and a son in two different wars. It would take a lot to upset that strong, courageous woman. Her reaction to our whirlwind courtship and impending marriage was to serve us an enormous meal, replete with both chocolate and cream cakes. Nothing would ever beat my mother-in-laws cooking.

Douglas chose a typically nonchalant way of breaking the news to the children. The four of us were driving along in the car, when Douglas casually pointed out of the window, saying "That's the Church where Angela and I are getting married." There was stony silence in the back seat, while I prayed hard that the children would accept me. Apparently ten year old Michael stammered whenever he was excited. "You mean she-she- she's going to come and live with us in Peru?" He asked, his voice rising. "Yes", was his father's brief but truthful reply.

There followed the longest three seconds of my life, while I prayed "Please Lord let them be happy."

Suddenly I heard clapping. Turning in my seat, I saw Michael's hands were over his head as he shouted "Ay-ay-ay!" That precious ten year old boy had executed a perfectly wonderful, Latino -style shout of approval. Moments later, a small hand gave me a very lady-like touch on the shoulder, and I heard a whisper from little Suzanne. She apparently had only one concern. "Can I be your bridesmaid?" "Of *course* you can", I replied. Little Suzie was all smiles, and our joy was complete.

Now I had six weeks to arrange a wedding, buy a trousseau, get my passport updated, get the mandatory vaccinations, choose what to take, pack , and get married, before the long voyage to my new life as a wife and mother, on the other side of the world.

A smile played around my mouth, as I dialed my agent's phone number in London. Over ten years had passed since I had been told by his receptionist that they only wanted "Mature, experienced actors, not tennis girls". My smile became a grin, as I happily requested that agent to cancel all my future engagements, as I was getting married and going to live in Peru. He was happy for me, but probably sorry for his pocket!

South America has reverse seasons to Europe, so we were heading for a Peruvian winter, which both Vera and Douglas assured me were always very mild. No bitter, biting winds or snow. In fact Douglas told me he was taking me to a place where it never even rained, as Lima only experiences a fine "Scotch mist". A far cry from the constant downpours of jolly old England! I had warned Douglas that the only climate I could never live in would be the tropics, as I had experienced sun stroke one hot summer day on the New Brighton beach. It had been an experience I would never forget.

It had been my own silly fault. I had reached the age of great wisdom--- fourteen, and had refused the offer of sun tan lotion. "Don't need it. I feel fine," I had insisted whenever a concerned adult offered it to me.

Hours later, on reaching home, I became extremely ill. My skin was so badly burnt that it was impossible to lie down without incredible pain on my back and arms, even the touch of a sheet driving me mad. For three days I found it impossible to walk without the help of sticks, as the skin of my arms, legs and shoulders were so badly burnt. After that, the idea of hot weather had never appealed to me. However, Douglas assured me that the Pacific Steam Navigation Company only had one tropical post. That was Panama, and he would never be sent back there to work, as he had already done two stints there totaling five years.

I had spent one busy morning alone in Liverpool buying new clothes I would need for the ship and my future life. At Vera's suggestion, I had armed myself with light wool dresses, plus a few formal gowns for the voyage. Choosing my wedding gown was easy. I was so thoroughly happy, I could not find a fault with anything, so decided to buy the first one I tried on. Also my arm was in a sling from a bad reaction to the previous days vaccination, so the idea of scrunching my bad arm through numerous armholes was not appealing. The shop assistant asked me if it was raining outside, and I looked at her with a smile as I couldn't remember! "Oh, you brides are all the same," she said, laughing.

Suddenly it was two days before the wedding. The invitations had been sent out, the replies received, my Passport arranged, and the wedding ring purchased , along with a large steamer trunk. Now I had just completed one last minute shopping spree in Liverpool, and the bus was taking me towards the Pier Head where I would catch the Wallasey Ferry home.

It dawned on me that this would be one of my last trips in familiar surroundings for a very long time. Suddenly, through the window of the bus, I recognized Doug's car parked outside the building which housed the Liverpool head office of the Pacific Steam Navigation Company.

Gathering my packages, I hurried to get off the bus. Deeming it wiser to phone and let Douglas know I was coming into the office, than just to appear for the first time in front of his colleagues unannounced, I entered the red public telephone kiosk near the entrance to the imposing building.

In those days one put in a few coins, and dialed the number needed. If the person spoke at the other end, one pressed "Button A" so that the conversation could take place. "Button B" was pressed if there was no reply, and the coins would drop back down into a metal cup.

During our brief courtship, I had never actually used Doug's last name. So when the company receptionist answered the phone, my mind had gone blank. Suddenly I had no clue who to ask for! The name I was to take as my own forty-eight hours later had deserted me! I hastily pressed "Button B", and heard the coins clang down the metal shoot. Only then did the name "Bomford" finally enter my overloaded memory. The term "Senior Moment" had not yet been coined, but I had one when I was only twenty-eight years young!

After being put on hold for the briefest of moments, I was asked to please come on up to the office. I was shown into a room where Douglas was seated, listening to a Senior Company Director telling him that instead of returning to Lima, he was needed immediately in the Republic of Panama, to train a new Manager for the office in Panama City. We were assured it would only be for a few months.

I had no way of knowing that the clothes I had just bought for a Peruvian winter would never be worn, as we would live in the tropics for many long, hot years!

CHAPTER 17

A Time To Embrace

Finally, it was March 17th, 1962. Our wedding day!

In the morning I had gone to the Church to arrange the flowers. The excitement had grown steadily, culminating in the arrival of my two bridesmaids. I had known Linda, my next door neighbor since her babyhood, and watched her grow into a beautiful young woman. She braved the cold March day in short sleeves, while Suzie looked adorable with a little white fur cape that had once belonged to my sister Olive when she was small. They went ahead with my mother in the car along with my brother Norman. Unfortunately his wife Patsy was in the maternity home preparing to give me another nephew, so she would miss the wedding.

The house fell silent.

My father was downstairs looking dapper in his "morning suit" as it is called in England, keeping a lookout for the arrival of the wedding car.

With the steamer trunk finally closed, I stood alone in the room I had once shared with my beloved sister, Olive.

Once again it seemed that I heard my mother's voice shouting at us for standing on the beds having pillow fights, and it seemed that I heard Olive telling me again about the dance she had been to on a date. I longed for her to be with me now, on my happy day. While I would never stop missing her, I knew that with Douglas beside me, I would never again feel the gnawing hunger of loneliness her death had brought.

"It's here!' my father shouted , announcing the arrival of the Bridal limo decked out in white bunting.

I stood at the top of the stairs in my wedding dress and veil. My father looked up at me. "You look beautiful", he said. That was the only time I ever remember him paying me any sort of a compliment, and was one more than my mother ever indulged in. In those days, there was a fear that a child may grow up to be big-headed, so compliments were rare. The fashion of fawning all over children to build their "self-esteem" came later. Surely there could be a happy medium?

As I sat beside my father in the limo, I remembered the recurring dream that had haunted me for years; the nightmare of being on my way to the Church in my wedding gown, shouting for the driver to stop the car, begging my father to let me go back home. Then, I had woken up in a cold sweat at the thought of being married. But now, I had the distinct suspicion that I was grinning from ear to ear in a positively unbridal-like manner, as I praised and thanked God for bringing me to this happy, happy day.

My brother Norman who had returned from the war and picked me up off my feet as a little girl, stood now at the top of the Church steps greeting me with a huge smile. He too, had many misgivings about my whirlwind romance, but had accepted the fact graciously, when he realized how happy I was.

Entering the Church where I had worshipped since I had been fourteen years old, I heard the wedding march begin. I was tremendously aware of the solemnity of the occasion. I was about to make lifelong vows before God and this congregation.

In all the weddings I had ever been to, the groom stood somewhat rigidly beside his "best man" head firmly to the front facing the alter till his bride was at his side. However, my groom was different. Looking up, through my veil, I saw Douglas, head firmly turned towards me, with an enormous grin on his face, watching my progression up the aisle to his side. I had to stifle a giggle.

I had talked with the Lord many times in that Church, through times of confusion, sometimes of anger, and many times in fear of my future. Now, I looked up at the beautiful round stained glass window which had both consoled and inspired me since I had been fourteen years old, when a friend had first invited me to worship at Claremount Road Methodist Church. It depicted "Pilgrim's Progress", the center picture showing Jesus finally placing the crown of everlasting life on his head. Now I stood beneath it, my handsome groom beside me, and my heart overflowing with thanksgiving and joy.

When the ceremony was over, the wedding party followed the Pastor into his office to sign the register and present me with a Passport with my new name on it.

A little voice said "You're my Mummy now." I looked down at Suzanne, and marveled once again at the Lord's goodness to me. Only six weeks before, I had sung with a little seven year old girl, and prayed one day the Lord would give me such a child to cherish. Now here she was.

We reached the Church steps outside, and Michael, all rosy cheeked and smiling, presented me with a silver horse-shoe, "for luck". I don't believe in luck, either good or bad, but I enjoyed carrying on a very old English tradition.

During his teen years, Douglas had belonged to a school youth group that had gone everywhere together. He went out with the same girl from that group for many years, and Pat wrote to him when he was overseas in the Royal Air Force during WW2 from the D-Day landing on June 6th 1944, on through Belgium, Holland, Germany and Denmark. Every soldier needed a girl back home to correspond with, and Pat had been that girl. She was a married lady with children now, but a friend had told her about the wedding, and there she now stood on the gravel path as we emerged from the Church. So one of the first things Douglas ever said to me as my husband was, "Oh look! There's Pat, the girl I told you about. Hello Pat!" He shouted, waving enthusiastically in her direction. One of the attributes I had looked for in any man I had dated, was a great sense of humor. While some of our acquaintances may think my husband is a "quiet sort of chap," Doug's qualifications in that area, were then, and still are, absolutely, hysterically superb!

Douglas & Angela Bomford
March 17, 1962

CHAPTER 18

A Time To Cast Away

W E HAD BEEN married three days when, on March 20th 1962 our parents along with Jill and her mother (who had convinced my father to accept Douglas) came to see us off on the beautiful "Reina del Mar" berthed at the Liverpool landing stage.

Vera and the two children were sailing with us of course, and had cabins along the corridor from our suite. Douglas and I had a sitting room and two bathrooms connected to our bedroom. It would be a perfectly romantic honeymoon, even if we did have his sister and his two children in tow!

Standing at the ship's rail, I waved goodbye to my parents, my friends, my country, and everything I had ever known in my life. White foam roared, and the deck shuddered beneath us as the ship's bow-thrusters maneuvered her further into the River Mersey, towards the Irish Sea, the Atlantic Ocean and my new life beyond.

My heart knew that the Lord God is everywhere . But I had a niggling feeling that while I was used to finding Him near me in Europe, I may have a problem feeling His closeness in Peru or Panama. While it sounds childish now, in 1962 it was a rarity for anyone other than high income folks to travel to South America, and going to Peru from the U.K. was akin to going to the other side of the moon.

My father's white handkerchief grew ever smaller as the distance between the dock and our ship, widened. I had never seen either of my parents shed a tear in my life, not even at my sister's funeral. Today, saying goodbye to their only daughter, who they did not expect to see for at least three years, was no different. The staunch British custom of keeping a "stiff upper lip" served me well, as I only had a tiny lump in my throat. A weeping mother on the landing stage however might have undone me.

Dazedly I looked at my new husband and two children, while the land of my birth shrank slowly into the distance.

Eight weeks earlier, when I had been waiting for the Wallasey Ferry boat at the landing stage, I had heard two young girls watching the passengers at the railing of a liner leaving the dockside, just as we were doing now. They had been very vocal in their envy of the waving passengers. "Oh those lucky people! I wish I could get out of this flaming country," one of them had said. As always, I defended everything British, and had told them to count their blessings, as there was no country in the world like England, and I would *never ever* live anywhere else. That was when I learnt never to say "never", as it had only been two months since I had said that!

In keeping with tradition, the ship's loud-speakers were playing "A Life on the Ocean Wave." Vera was a gem, keeping my spirits up as she grabbed Douglas and I by the arm, and the three of us performed a spirited "grapevine" step back and forth on the deck. It worked perfectly, as I found myself singing and grinning along with my new husband and sister-in-law.

Soon the Liver building which gave the name to the City, faded into the distance, and nothing could be heard but the gentle swish of the sea below.

Matthew Ch.28 v.20 "---and lo, I am with you alway, even unto the end of the world."

Suzanne spoke to a little girl who was standing at the ship's rail with her mother. The child's mother spoke, and quite suddenly

Douglas turned to her and said "You're Audrey McQueen aren't you?"

He had recognized the voice as belonging to a woman he had last seen sixteen years previously, in the uniform of the Woman's Royal Air Force with the "Chile" insignia on her shoulder.

Audrey had served during the war as a volunteer from her native country, and she and Douglas had been part of a group who were waiting for their demobilization in England in 1946. Sixteen years had passed since they had met, but he had recognized her delightfully distinctive Chilean accent.

"My daddy's going to be the new Air Attache in Lima," her little girl proudly informed us before running off with Suzanne and Michael to explore the ship.

The Captain and officers all knew Douglas and his family well, through his work and the number of times they had sailed together. I was the new kid on the block, but I was enjoying my first experience of the instant comraderie that evolves among shipmates.

The passengers were delightful. The wonderful, educated conversationalists were kind to this young bride, taking her very first voyage, and I thoroughly enjoyed it all. We played deck games and joined in the ship's quiz hour, took bracing walks round the deck, saw the movies and enjoyed the dancing. A special treat were the afternoon teas served in the lounge, accompanied by gentle music from the grand piano.

At first our coats were wrapped tightly around us, then as we drew closer to the Caribbean, white shorts and swim suits were donned and more time was spent at the ship's pool.

Dinner was always a formal affair with light music played by a five piece orchestra located on the balcony overlooking the magnificent dining room. Children had all been served earlier, as they were not allowed in the dining room after six o'clock.

Vera, Douglas and I sat with the Chief Purser Peter McSalley at his table, the sparkling glasses and silverware always set for four. Peter had known Douglas for some years and became a life-long friend, still visiting us annually at our home forty years later .

Next to each place setting, there stood a beautiful silver bowl half filled with water. I had no clue what it was for, until the Purser had finished eating his "escargot" and I saw him gently dip his fingers into the water and wiping them on his napkin. I had just met my very first finger-bowl. However, I never developed a taste for snails, believing they should remain firmly on the ground.

Until now, I had never heard a word of Spanish in my life. Douglas spoke it fluently, and addressed the stewards in their own language. In preparation for my having to deal with the language in both Panama and Peru, Douglas furnished me with a list of nouns, saying he would not pass me anything at the dinner table that I did not ask for in Spanish. Unlike our little girl Suzanne, who developed a superb aptitude for learning languages, my talent in that direction was zero. It was fortunate indeed that Douglas took pity on me and relented, or I would have been condemned to live on salt and pepper for the entire voyage!

The "Reina" was not a cruise ship, but a passenger vessel, carrying 700 passengers from England and the continent to South America and back. Jet planes were only just entering the market and sailing across the Atlantic was still the chief form of transportation.

In order to provide passage for all people, including those with smaller pockets than others, there were three different prices offered. One could choose to travel in First, Cabin or Tourist class. They each had three totally different areas where their cabins and public rooms were located.

Class envy was not yet being used widely as a self-righteous political tool, and people still had a choice. The idea that everyone should be shoved down to the lowest common denominator, and that one should feel ashamed of being successful financially, still only flourished in Communist countries.

Due to the fact that Douglas was a highly regarded overseas Assistant Manager of the shipping line, his family was given First Class accommodations on board. It was one of the few "perks" that went with his extremely demanding job which called for his working fifty hour weeks, often far from his family as he travelled all over

South America and the Caribbean for the Pacific Steam Navigation Company.

At no time was anyone travelling in one class, allowed to infringe on the areas of the other two. Everyone had an equal right to their own space. However, Doug and I found the dance music a bit old fashioned in first class, so one night, I changed my long formal gown for a short cocktail dress, and Doug and I slipped through the "Do Not Enter" sign, to join in the dancing in the Cabin Class, where the people were younger, and the music faster. However, Purser McSalley found out, and gave us a stern reprimand! He was right of course. The space of those paying less, needed to be guarded as carefully as the space of those paying more. We were infringing on their territory, and were told to go back upstairs to "First". So we continued to dance a lot of waltzes, and left the jive to the lucky folks in Cabin Class!

CHAPTER 19

Voyage To The Unknown

OUR FIRST PORTS were in France and Spain before the long voyage across the Atlantic Ocean.

The Reina del Mar appeared to be quite a large ship at 27,000 tons back in 1962. However, today's average cruise ships are more than four times her size. By today's standards, I guess the ship moved a fair amount in the March weather, but it didn't bother anybody, as we used our "sea-legs" swaying port to starboard, with a loose grip on the corridor handrails. I laugh today when a passenger on a 125,000 ton cruise ship will grumble that the ship is "rolling" if they feel any movement of any kind whatsoever.

The First class section carried only 240 people, so it never took more than a few minutes walk on deck or into a lounge to come across the same people one had chatted with before. Dates to play deck or card games abounded. The same people would be seen grouped in the deep lounge chairs at the evening dances. Many of those ship-board friendships lasted a life-time.

It was on this, my very first voyage on a ship, that I fell in love with cruising, and although it has changed in many ways, it is still a fantastic experience.

Trinidad was my first encounter with the tropics. Never before had I seen turquoise waters and felt balmy weather on my skin. Every summer of my life, when I had worn cool dresses in England, I had never been able to walk outdoors without carrying a sweater with me. While we occasionally had sweltering days, the temperature could suddenly drop like a stone. I remembered the numerous times my mother had packed up a picnic for us when the sun was shining outside, but invariably by the time the family piled into the car, it had turned cold and rainy!

La Guaira was the port of call for Caracas, Venezuela, where the ship's agent sent me beautiful flowers and perfume and took Douglas and I ashore to see the sights.

The following day, we stood on deck as the ship came alongside in Curacao. The unique Dutch architecture of buildings in yellows and pinks, pale greens and reds, enchanted me. It was so very European, and looked totally out of place in the fierce tropical heat. I dragged myself up the small hill into the town, trying to keep up with Vera and Douglas as the children ran ahead of them. I had never been so hot in my life! Entering the shops didn't help, as they only had fans which pushed the hot air around. I had been in snow in Wallasey just three weeks before and my body couldn't take the change. Making my excuses to the family, I walked back to the ship, and flaked out in the air-conditioned suite. Nobody mentioned that Panama would be just as hot, or that there would be no a/c there either!

This whole area of the Caribbean was where Douglas travelled frequently for his job, and now the agents were making him and his bride very welcome, with gifts galore greeting us at every port.

On reaching Cartagena, Columbia, a gigantic bouquet of exotic flowers along with boxes of chocolates and perfume were delivered to our suite. Later we were escorted ashore for a wonderful day out then later entertained at a Spanish cabaret. It was the first time I had seen real Flamingo dancers. I was fascinated by the brightly colored dresses on the women, layers of frills swirling, dark heads flung back, and heels clicking in rhythm to the staccato beat of their castanets.

Cristobal is the port for the Atlantic side of the Republic of Panama, and was at that time part of the American Canal Zone. As we approached the port, Douglas received news from his office. He was needed immediately for meetings in Panama City, so instead of continuing our honeymoon voyage, he was to disembark right away. After packing a small bag, he told me he would see me four days later in Peru, and kissed me goodbye.

Everyone should experience the wonder of their ship being lifted from the Atlantic Ocean up eighty feet, to sail the width of the Isthmus then lowered some eight hours later, in the Pacific Ocean. It is accomplished by use of three huge locks, the result of incredible engineering work performed almost a hundred years ago, and still in use today. The first of my many transits of the Canal had taken place however, with two children and one sister-in-law, but minus one husband!

Another "first" I was sorry to experience without Douglas, would be the Crossing of the Line ceremony, held for all first timers crossing the Equator. It was always a highlight of such a voyage on the Reina. The Purser dressed up as King Neptune, performed a comedy routine with the help of Officers dressed up as Pirates. I had been warned to wear my swim suit under my clothes. I had always been scared to death of going under water, but I had to be a good sport, or loose face horribly with Suzanne and Michael, who swam like fishes. However, it was not something I was looking forward to!

Seated in the audience beside the pool , I was suddenly snatched by two Pirates and forced to sit in a wooden "Barber's Chair" which was jutting out from the pool deck over the water. There King Neptune (alias Purser Peter McSalley) proceeded to "shave" my face with the aid of an enormous wooden cut-throat razor, Sweeney Todd style. I thought I was ready for the dunking, but King Neptune had a great line of patter, and kept me talking for a while, until suddenly, when least expected, I was catapulted backwards into the pool. As usual, I inhaled at the wrong time. Fortunately, I was pulled up from the bottom by officer Cadet "Sharks" who were in the pool ready to save rotten swimmers like me. I came up coughing and spluttering much to the delight of the all the passengers, crew and particularly my two new step-children. It was then I was glad that Douglas was *not* around to see his soaked, choking, sorry-looking bride!

It was six o'clock in the morning. I was asleep in the stateroom when I suddenly heard the most welcome sound I could have wished for. My husband's voice whispering in my ear. "Hi honey", he said. Douglas was finally back with me having flown down from Panama to Lima the day before. He had hitched a ride on the Pilot launch at dawn, and while the ship was still not alongside, I would soon be seeing the home where Douglas and his family lived in Peru.

CHAPTER 20

Lost In Lima

THE LINESMEN HAULED in the ropes and cables, securing the "Reina del Mar" to the pier at Callao, the Port for Lima.

The ship had been my home for my entire married life - all three weeks of it! I had just adapted very nicely and loved shipboard life. How nice it would be, just to stay on board and travel around in the luxury of our lovely suite, dressing up every night and being entertained!

We were very aware that Douglas had to spend the next few months in Panama training a new manager for the company office in Panama City. So while Lima was Doug's permanent home, we were faced with the realization that we would only have two weeks here, before sailing North to Panama again. We had been told that disturbing news two days before the wedding, and we had been faced with a very real dilemma. There was only one English private school for boys in Lima, and they would not guarantee there would be a place open for Michael if he was withdrawn, even for a short time.

Vera had lived with Douglas and the children in the Lima house for two years. They had a good maid, and many English friends living nearby, so it made good sense for Vera to stay in Lima with Michael for the few months we would be away in Panama. This would also save her from feeling "replaced" by me so suddenly. Suzie was only seven, and could transplant with us for those few months, and go back into her girl's school in Lima on our return. Splitting up the family was a disagreeable but necessary decision, and we all finally had to agree it was the only thing to be done.

But as all humans know, the best laid plans can go awry!

But right now, the thought of facing the totally unknown was daunting. I had spent years living in hotels, and now, after a life of luxury on the ship, suddenly my life would involve such mundane things as shopping for toilet rolls!

I walked gingerly down the gangway with my little family, and finally set foot on Peruvian soil.

The office had sent the chauffeur Raul, with the car to meet us. The children chatted endlessly throughout the half hour ride, looking forward to getting home. We finally turned down a pretty street in a suburb of Lima, then made a sharp right turn into a cul-de-sac pulling up in front of an attractive two storey Spanish style house. It had decorative curly-q iron-work across the windows. Pots of bright red geraniums stood beside the front door which was opened by a young woman in a maid's uniform. A demure smile emanated from a face with features indicative of her Inca heritage.

The children bailed out of the car as fast as they could, laughing and chattering, as a Border Collie tore out expressing his joy at having the family back, with barks, jumps and licks all over Douglas and the children. Even Raul was grinning as he helped us in with the luggage. Everyone was happy that the family was home at last.

The only stranger in the place was the new lady of the house----me!

The following days were anything but dull. The first morning Douglas left for the office and the children went next door to visit with their friends.

I realized that once the maid had finished cleaning up the kitchen, she may expect me to ask her to do something else! I felt like an idiot dodging from one room to another in an attempt to avoid the moment when I would have to really try and communicate with her. She did not understand one word of English, and I was ditto the other way around. Fortunately she seemed to follow a regular pattern of duties, and kept the floors mopped, the rugs vacuumed and the furniture beautifully polished.

I had always been a very busy person. Now with no scripts to learn, no costumes to pack and no friend to phone, I felt as useful as a chocolate fire-guard.

On the second day, Douglas had ascertained that there was an absence of prunes in the house and asked me to buy some from the local grocery store which he assured me was within easy walking distance. He told me the Spanish word for prunes was "ciruelas", and described how to get there.

Armed with the memory of the easy directions, I set off repeating "ciruelas, ciruelas, ciruelas" over and over to myself, as I walked for the very first time in this strange country.

I turned right at the end of the block as Douglas had said. Then took the second left ---or had he said the third? There was nobody on the street to ask, and as I still only knew how to ask for salt or pepper in Spanish, it would have been a futile endeavor anyway.

There were lovely houses on both sides of the wide street. I could not imagine a store of any kind being around there. But suddenly I spotted a woman carrying two string bags on her arms, coming out of a small doorway on the corner. I had found the little store! I was elated!

The tiny establishment was chockablock with a myriad of tin cans and packets. Large flour- bags overflowing with beans and rice occupied part of the small floor space. Spotting a box piled high with potatoes I smiled, remembering it was Sir Frances Drake who introduced them to my ancestors in England four hundred years before. That lesson from sixth grade rang a bell with me now. What we think of as a typical English Sunday dinner *always* has to include potatoes. But without Peru, we would probably never have tasted one!

The owners of the establishment were an elderly couple. They greeted me with a "Buenos dios" and smiled at me expectantly. I opened my mouth to speak but could not for the life of me remember the wretched word for "prunes". In the effort to find the shop, it had completely vanished from my mind! They gave me their full, undivided attention, as I attempted to describe prunes to them. I made small circles with my finger. The lady made noises that told me she knew exactly what I needed, disappeared into the small rear part of the shop, and reappeared smiling broadly, carrying two eggs .

I tried again, and a tomato appeared. Cans of various fruits were offered, but in great embarrassment, I finally gave up, and left. It would make more sense to return with one of the children to interpret for me.

Stepping out into the sunshine of the Peruvian summer, I turned for home.

But which way? I had made so many turns before I found the shop that I now had no idea which corner to turn to get back to the house. Here I was, a twenty-eight year old woman of average intelligence, with no *clue* how to find my way home! It had to be somewhere near, but in which direction? Every road looked like the next. Nice suburban Spanish style homes. Nice hedges. Nice gardens. But where was mine?

I scolded myself for not drawing a map or at least dropping bread crumbs on the way! But I had been assured by my trusted husband that it was "so easy to get there". When I finally got back to the house, I vowed never to leave it again without a map and at least one of my wonderful, totally fluent Spanish- speaking children!

Next time I visited that store, I had a longer list plus Michael and Suzanne. If one ever needs a lesson in humility, try listening to a seven and a ten year old apologizing for you in a foreign language! The look of pity on the store -owners face made me shrink like wool in boiling water.

Vera and Douglas had made many friends during their two years in Lima, and they were all very curious about this new wife Douglas had brought back from his vacation in England. Consequently, we received a number of invitations to dinner. It was a bit like taking an examination every time. Apparently I passed muster as they were all very gracious to me. Then, of course, we obviously had to return the invitations, so I held my first dinner- party.

Douglas chose a menu which included dishes he knew the maid knew how to cook. The house being spotless already, all I had to do was to get dressed and be sure everyone had finished each course, before ringing the bell for the maid to clear the table and serve the next one.

All middle-class families had a live-in maid in that part of Latin America. Not to do so would be looked upon as depriving poorer people of a home and a living. Also the Senora was expected to entertain her husband's business associates, and go out with him in the evenings. A live-in maid closely associated with the children, was the safest and best way for this to be done. Maids had a much higher standard of living this way. They had their own room and bathroom, usually little to do in the afternoons, plus they had a day off every week. It was then that they usually returned home to a very large family, to sleep on the floor of a mud hut. Some years later in Panama, I found our maid sleeping on the floor in her room instead of the mattress, as she didn't feel comfortable on a bed.

Vera disembarked from the Reina del Mar, as Douglas and I went on board to head North to the Republic of Panama again. It was heart- wrenching to leave Michael behind with Vera. But we believed the family would only be apart for a few months. We had no way of knowing as we waved goodbye to them, that it would be a whole year before we would see either Michael or Vera again.

CHAPTER 21

The Republic Of Panama

AFTER ANOTHER WEEK of heaven on board the "Reina del Mar" it was time to disembark for Panama City, where Suzanne and I would live with Douglas for a few brief months while he trained the new Manager.

The small Company apartment came with two bedrooms and one bathroom, and was to be adequate for the three of us. It was fully furnished and equipped. That meant that every cup and saucer, bowl and glass, knife and fork, had the company initials of the "Pacific Steam Navigation Company", imprinted somewhere on it. As I pointed out to Douglas, we even had his office in bed with us as "P.S.N.C." was printed on all the sheets and pillow slips!

It was temporary, and would have been fine --- except for one thing. Panama is very hot and humid all year round, and the apartment had no air conditioning.

I had been in snow in England a few weeks before, and after a couple of days Douglas came home from the office to find his bride a sweaty mess almost passing out from heat stroke.

"I just can't live here," I choked. I was promptly told by Douglas not to be so silly, as thousands of people did.

My body just could *not* acclimatize.

After a few days of this nightmare, Douglas invested in a small air-conditioner that fitted into the wall of our bedroom. That became the favorite spot in the apartment. It was the cleanest as the maid liked to work in it, Suzanne did her homework in it, I wrote letters home in it, and would have had all the meals served in it if I could have!

Our sturdy little seven year old did not notice or care about the climate. A little girl her age lived in the apartment below, and the two of them were soon running up and down stairs together.

It was 1962, and Marta had come from Cuba with her parents. Her mother told me that she and her husband had arrived in Panama with one small suitcase each. They had claimed to be coming to Panama on a "vacation" as they had become afraid for their safety when they heard Castro's soldiers walking around the outside of their house clicking their rifles. They had no way to defend themselves. So they left their loved ones, their big house, their business and everything they owned, to escape the stranglehold of Communism, and bring their little girl to live in freedom in the Republic of Panama.

Our company apartment came with a daily maid called "Oola" whose native land was Jamaica. It was a great blessing as of course as she spoke English.

For our first breakfast together in the apartment Douglas decided on a boiled egg . We had won a rather nice English style brass egg-timer while on the ship. Oola had never seen one before, and did not know what to make of the hour-glass with sand in it, so I explained it carefully, and told her that when the sand was all in the bottom part of the glass, the egg was ready to be taken out of the boiling water.

There was a sparkling white tablecloth, a china tea-pot and cups, and toast in a silver toast rack next to the marmalade which sat in a little silver dish.

We smiled at each other, and chatted, and waited, and waited. Douglas kept checking his watch. Eventually I went into the kitchen to see what the hold up was.

There in the pan sat two eggs, boiling merrily away, with the glass egg timer seated squarely between them in the bubbling water.

Apparently I was a total failure at communicating even in my own language! I left the water to cool down with the timer still in it, which saved the glass from breaking. However the brass turned black.

Over fifty years later we still get a perfectly boiled egg for breakfast using that same glass timer--- with the words "Reina del Mar. P.S.N.C." still proudly emblazoned on the top.

CHAPTER 22

A Homesick Bride

WHILE THERE WERE no regrets about marrying my wonderful Douglas, the days dragged by in that hot and humid land, where crickets made weird noises all day long. I was four thousand miles and three years away from any expectation of seeing my parental family, friends or country again.

Outside of Suzanne, Douglas and the maid, I didn't know a living soul. A hideous illness invaded my usually cheerful spirit for I was desperately homesick. We had no television, and apart from music or announcements, "The Breakfast Club" on Armed Forces Radio was the only English speaking program all day.

Our own household effects had been left in the rented house in Lima for Vera and Michael. Even our wedding presents had been left in Peru, still unpacked after the voyage from England. We had arrived in this fully furnished bachelor apartment which was to be our temporary home, with only our clothes. Douglas had a very responsible job, but keeping a sister and son in one country, and a wife and daughter in another, and both children in private English speaking schools, stretched our income to the limit. There were no credit cards then. If you couldn't afford it, you did without it. Televisions were expensive. We just had to manage without watching the English language A.F.N. programs beamed into the Canal Zone. After all, it was only going to be for a few months.

There was no question of my going out to work. It was 1962, when men provided for their families, and anyway, nobody was about to give a job to a foreign woman who couldn't speak the language and was leaving in six months. Some Canal Zone wives worked, but we did not have Zone privileges, and anyway, no English husband worth his salt would want his wife to go out to work.

I tried Spanish classes, but to no avail. It always amazed me that while I had the ability to memorize long scripts and songs in English, I could not remember one blooming noun or verb in Spanish from one lesson to the next.

Douglas needed the office car for work, and I drove on the wrong side of the street anyway! The only solution was to walk to the supermarket then get a cab home with the groceries. The first time I tried this, I clambered into the back seat of a cab along with four overflowing bags of food, and proceeded to recite the instructions home to the driver, in my carefully memorized Spanish. He stopped me in mid-phrase with the remark, "Looka leedy, we get there mush queeker if you speaka English, O.K?" Every shred of ambition to learn Spanish fled in that moment, never to return!

My homesickness grew worse.

Mornings were spent looking at the telephone, willing it to ring. But knowing it never would. Looking at the silent object one day, I suddenly noticed an army of tiny ants marching with the precision of a Marine squad, up the wall around an arch and down to the ground on the other side, then along the skirting, and out on the balcony where they trooped in a perfect line to the apartment below. Doug's reaction to this was that of any typical British male. He pointed out that ants were really quite clean creatures, had lived in Panama long before humans inhabited the place, and apart from squirting something on them now and then to keep them down, one really must simply learn to live with them. "Anyway," he added "They don't eat much."

I longed for the day when Douglas would come home and say "The new Manager is trained---now we can go back to our real home in Lima." Suzanne was a happy, independent little soul, who made friends easily and spoke perfect Spanish. Usually either in school, or dashing off with her new friend from downstairs, she didn't seem to need me.

For the first time in my life I was useless, and felt guilty being an added expense to Douglas. I hated both Panama and myself, and earnestly prayed the Lord would intervene and get us back to Vera and Michael in Peru very soon.

It was a happy diversion when the Reina del Mar was to dock again in Panama, en route from Liverpool to Chile once again. Douglas invited the Captain and Officers to a dinner party at our apartment. It was great to have something to look forward to, and I vowed to myself that I would be the very best possible hostess and make Douglas proud of me.

The big night arrived, and I looked at the table. It was set for ten, with a pure white linen cloth, laden with silver flatware and lovely china --- all emblazoned with the P.S.N.C. company initials of course. They would all feel very much at home, as the table setting was identical to the ones they sat at every evening on their ship!

Wedding cakes in England are made with lots of heavy fruit, as in a rich Christmas cake, plus a large quantity of rum that, if stored correctly, keeps for months. Thick Royal icing which goes solid and is always used for very important cakes, keeps the inside moist. The tradition a hundred years ago, was to keep the top tier for the first Christening! However I had carefully wrapped the top tier in clean cloths, put it in a sturdy tin and sealed it with three layers of Scotch tape. Our Wedding cake was the only thing we had brought with us to Panama, and Doug and I decided that, along with some delicious local ice-cream, it would be the perfect dessert.

Oola held the large tin while I cut through the Scotch tape, happily anticipating a vision of the beautifully decorated top layer of our cake that would grace our table. My mouth was watering as I carefully lifted the lid off the big tin. Instead of white icing however, the entire cake appeared to be black, and was moving. I let out a screech of horror, realizing the cake was a mass of ants. How in the world they ever got in there, I never discovered. The three layers of Scotch tape had been sealed fast to the tin.

Oola ran out of the back door to dispose of the failed dessert. I was sticking a couple of cans of fruit in the freezer when I heard Doug's voice.

"Hi honey, we're here," he called as he walked in with the Captain and the Senior Officers of his Company's flagship.

I was grateful that I was a trained actor!

CHAPTER 23

The Theatre Guild

RAIN WAS SLUICING down on the car like Niagara Falls, as a blur of shiny row houses in the capital of the Republic of Panama, slid slowly by. Learning to drive on the "wrong" side of the road had been challenging enough without this! Now having the use of Doug's car for the afternoon, my nose was pushed as close as possible to the windshield in an attempt to see what was ahead.

Stranded cars with water over the hubcaps were scattered around me, while gleeful native boys, welcoming the cool water over their young bodies, shoved on car trunks to get the vehicles moving again.

In spite of all the jokes about rain in England, six years driving experience there had done nothing to prepare me for negotiating the potholes of Panama City in a deluge of tropical rain.

A distinct sloshing sound could be heard dangerously close to the bottom of the car door. Praying I would not have to get out, as it would be impossible without flooding the whole of the interior, my only hope was to keep the engine turning over, while inching my way up and out of the deep water.

Before our marriage Douglas had told me he would take me where it never rained. "Campaign promises!" I thought out loud, gently pumping the brakes and praying the car would keep moving.

To be fair, Douglas had expected we would be living in Lima where his promise would have proved true, not in the tropics with a "Rainy Season" which would have been called "Monsoon Season" in India!

Finally the car moved forward, till it was up on higher ground. The brakes no longer worked and it was with a prayer of thanksgiving that I finally arrived back at the apartment and fell into a chair with the greatest of all British medications ----a nice cup of tea!

Soon after our arrival in Panama, we had attended a Sunday morning Service at the Canal Zone "Union Church", knowing it would be in English. However, there was no air-conditioning, and after the second hymn, the Sanctuary began to swim around me. While the eyes of the Congregation were hopefully closed in prayer, I had tugged at Doug's hand, while offering a silent prayer of my own that the Lord would get us outside and into the car before I passed out. My sweet husband assured me that my body would "get acclimatized". It never did.

We discovered the President of the local community theatre lived up the road from us. John Mayles had been born in England and had come to Panama as a teenager. He was a brilliant actor but with the good sense to have followed a career in real business, not show business. John told me that auditions were going to be held for a play called "Out of the Frying Pan" about a group of college students, and warned me there really wasn't a part in it suitable for me. However, I felt deeply that if I could get a script into my hands, the awful homesickness and depression that had enveloped me for weeks would disappear.

Driving across the railway line that divided the Republic of Panama from the American Canal Zone where the theatre was located, I mused on the fact that one would travel to a different country to rehearse!

I parked and walked into "The Ancon Theatre Guild" for the first time. It had seating for a hundred and fifty, and was blessedly air-conditioned.

The director gave an outline of the characters. There were parts for six college age actors, an older man, and a New York landlady. At twenty-eight, I was immediately labeled too old to play a student, so I auditioned for the part of the land-lady.

Although I felt my accent was pretty good, I discovered later that it had been deemed more appropriate to use a real native of the area who was available. At the end of the evening, the names of the cast were read out, and mine wasn't one of them.

Whatever depression I had felt before the audition was peanuts in comparison to what I felt now. Here I was, a trained professional actor who had earned my living performing on stage for several years, totally incapable of getting myself into the cast of an amateur play to work for nothing!

The fact that there might be other opportunities in other plays later was no comfort to me, for as soon as Douglas had trained the new Manager, we would be sailing back to Peru.

For the first time in my life, I felt that I was an abject failure.

Why would the Lord put me in this humid, foreign land where I was just a drag and an added expense to my wonderful husband? None of it made any sense.

Sitting around waiting for Suzanne and Douglas to come home was not enough. I needed to be involved in something productive I could enjoy now! If *only* I could have been in the play, I thought.

Two weeks later the phone rang. It was John Mayles. The lady who had been cast in the comedy role of the New York landlady had been transferred back to the States. Could I possibly take over her part?

Could I just!

Performing in front of a mainly authentic American audience, a large number of whom had been born and raised in New York, was going to be a real challenge. Remembering that I had perfected at least five British dialects to performance level only months before, there was no reason why I couldn't do it again-- with a New York dialect. I had once earned my living as an impersonator. So I told myself to get impersonating!

There was only one person I was acquainted with from New York with that distinctive accent. It was the lady in charge of props. She, plus my memory of Danny Kaye when he put his Bronx accent on in movies, was all I had to work with. I had three weeks to learn the lines, the dialect, hone my character, and hopefully, make the audience laugh- for the right reasons!

The day after the play opened, the review in the English version of the "Panama Star and Herald" read: -

" *As Mrs. Garnet, the pixellated landlady, she is a sheer delight, her marvelously mobile hands, limp as wet gloves, dangling from the wrists in the Zasu Pitts manner, all form part of what must surely be one of the finest comic portrayals to have appeared on the Guild stage'.*

Suddenly the phone started to ring. The newspaper called. Could they send a reporter over to interview me? This resulted in a full page article with a large photograph and details of my career in England.

Invitations to parties in the Canal Zone started to arrive. We had been in Panama six months. There was still no sign of us returning to Lima, but life in Panama was suddenly not so bad after all.

In the "Theatre Guild" fall production, I was cast in the leading female role.

Three of the main characters were played by military personnel from the Canal Zone bases. They were good actors and rehearsals were in full swing in October 1962.

It was all great fun, except for one thing. A friend showed me a magazine, with aerial photographs of Russian ships carrying what looked like missiles to Cuba

Suddenly, everything changed.

John Mayles phoned me. All rehearsals for the play were cancelled. The Panama Canal Zone was on full alert. A major confrontation between Russia and the United States seemed imminent. The first strike could be on the Panama Canal. The "Missile Crisis" had begun--- and we were living right on its doorstep.

CHAPTER 24

Reunion

THE WORLD HELD its breath, as it teetered on the edge of nuclear war.

My mind filled with childhood memories of England in 1940 when Olive and I had listened to the whistling of the bombs and the booming of the anti-aircraft guns, while huddled in a cupboard under the stairs.

I recalled one night walking outside with my mother after the all-clear had sounded, and seeing the sky lit up, bright red from the fires of homes and hospitals, schools and businesses across Liverpool, as Hitler fought to bring the British people to their knees. He had sought to demoralize the civilian population, and the human cost had been terrible.

But now it was unwise to dwell for even a moment, on the thought of what a nuclear attack would do.

We kept the usual routine of life. I hugged Douglas a little longer each morning as he set off to the office. The maid Oola came to work each day and mopped the tiled floors. Suzanne went to school, and I tried to concentrate on learning my lines for the play, and failed miserably. Nothing could push the fear from our minds. I suspect that even avowed atheists turned to fervent prayer that this cup would pass from us all.

It is described in history as a time when the Premier of Russia, Nikita Khrushchev and the young President of the United States, John F. Kennedy went eye-ball to eye-ball, and Khrushchev blinked first. For finally, on the eleventh day of excruciating fear, the news we had prayed for came through. The ships heading for Cuba bearing more nuclear war-heads, had turned around heading back to Russia, and an agreement had been reached that the missiles already in Cuba would be dismantled.

It is a miracle that the combined sigh of relief from the inhabitants of the free world did not blow the globe off its' axis.

Douglas had warned his company that the man they had sent to him to train to manage the Panama office, was totally unsuited for the position. However, the decision makers five thousand miles away thought they knew better, and months passed by as Douglas attempted to prepare someone with neither the ability nor the personality for the job.

This meant that sadly, our family was still split up. Michael and Vera were still in Peru, while Douglas, Suzanne and I spent our first Christmas together and welcomed in 1963.

My permit to be in Panama was only valid for six months, by which time we had expected to be out of the country. Now in order to stay legal, I would have to leave the country, and come back in again. So in early January, when Douglas had a business meeting scheduled in Costa Rica, the company agreed that I should accompany him. Susie was excited about staying with Marta and her parents in the apartment below while we were in San Jose for three days, and I was thrilled at the idea of getting out of the humidity of Panama while seeing yet another country.

At the airport check- in counter I was asked to step aside while Douglas went through the line to the other side of the barrier with the rest of the passengers. Soon everyone had walked across the tarmac and up the steps into the small plane while I was still waiting for permission to pass through.

Douglas was waiting for me on the other side of the barrier while the inspector kept insisting that I did not have permission to be in Panama, but nor did I have permission to leave it. Officially I couldn't stay and I couldn't go!

Finally, as we heard the plane's engines turning over, the official thrust my Passport back at me, telling me in rapid Spanish to get my permission to leave *and* to stay when I came back.

And I thought the Irish could be confusing!

We ran across the tarmac and leapt up the metal steps a moment before they were pulled away, and the plane door slammed behind us.

Costa Rica was beautiful. It was green and cool, and the wives of the officials Douglas had business with were extremely hospitable. They did not speak English, but took me in a chauffeur driven car all over the city of San Jose, while the men were working. Both daughters were engaged to be married to Costa Rican men, but apparently in keeping with the local custom, neither of them had ever been alone with their future husbands. A chaperone had been with them at all times, on every date. It was 1963 and I had believed such customs had been abandoned in the previous century! On meeting the young men, they complained to me in perfect English, that the old chaperone custom was a "real pain in the neck", as they had been to college in the U.S. and were used to dating without a mother or an aunt having to be included in the invitation, as well as the bill!

Doug's job entailed a lot of travelling in the Caribbean and South America, and he was away when we should have been celebrating our first anniversary. It was a shame that we could not have been together, as I had a life-changing piece of news to relate to him.

We were going to have a baby.

Douglas was still trying to train the new man, who was bereft of the decision making skills required for the position with Pacific Steam Navigation Company. Part of the job entailed occasionally going out in a launch to board a ship via a rope ladder which was slung down the side of the vessel. Both ship and launch were still moving when one had to step over the side with no life-jacket, and a canvas bag of documents slung over a shoulder. The last straw came when the trainee took one look at the high waves, and simply refused to leave the launch.

Almost a year after Douglas had warned his company that their candidate was not capable of doing the job, they finally agreed. Realizing that Douglas himself was the only person available with the experience to run that extremely busy office, they asked him to stay permanently in Panama. This was something we definitely did *not* want to do. However, Doug's career was with P.S.N.C. We really had no choice but to agree.

Now we had to find a larger apartment, sail down to Peru, pack everything up, take Michael out of his wonderful school, and bring him with Vera and the dog, back to what would now be our permanent home in the heat of the Republic of Panama.

Apparently my body had not been apprised of the fact that "morning sickness" was supposed to be just that, for I was plagued with nausea from the moment I woke up throughout every waking moment. Walking to the Doctor's office in the humidity for shots to stop the continuous sickness, made matter worse. I discovered that even my beloved tea had a smell and I couldn't bear the thought of drinking it. Proof indeed, that I was a very sick lady! Three days in hospital cured it for forty-eight hours, then it was back again. Such a condition had never been heard of among my friends who thought

I was making a huge fuss about nothing. Half a century would pass before a member of the British Royal family would have the same problem, and the world discovered it had a fancy name, hyperemesis gravidarum. It had *not* been my imagination after all!

My wonderful husband came home from a business trip to Miami, laden with a superb maternity wardrobe for me. It cheered me up quite beautifully. On asking Douglas how he had managed to get such a perfect fit for me, he said that he had asked a passing lady on the street where the best store would be to buy such apparel, then picked out a shop assistant who looked about my size. Indeed, I had *the* most perfect, clever and thoughtful of husbands!

Douglas was due to go overseas again on a business trip, and it became my mission to find us a new home which would be large enough to entertain but within our limited budget. Finally, I found a very nice brand new apartment only ten dollars a month beyond the limit we had set. Three stories up, it had a huge oblong living room with sliding glass doors at either end, opening onto two large covered balconies. I found myself imagining rows of chairs with parents sitting facing the "stage" as they watched their children present their elocution and drama pieces, then exit "back-stage" to the maid's quarters. It would be an ideal place for me to run an Elocution and Drama School for children! I talked the owner into keeping it for me till Douglas returned to Panama. Three days later we signed the lease.

Once again we sailed south to Peru in the dear "Reina del Mar" to pack up the house there, and bring Michael and Vera back to Panama with us. We had not seen them for over a year.

Vera stayed on the ship for a holiday round trip South again. Thus it became my responsibility to pack up a house I had never lived in. There is something distinctly weird about opening cupboards and drawers full of stuff one has never seen, and having to decide what to throw out and what to claim for one's own. I felt like a burglar!

The present manager of the Lima office had a pilot's license, and use of a company four seater Cessna aircraft. He was flying down to Mollendo, a small seaside town at the southern tip of Peru, where the company maintained a small office and house on the beach.

Terry, a skilled pilot, invited Douglas to accompany him on the short trip down to pick up another company employee and his wife, and bring them back to Lima. Knowing that flying on a small aircraft was infinitely more dangerous than on a scheduled airline, the thought of biting my fingernails off for six hours waiting to hear that Douglas was back safely, scared me to death. I had always enjoyed flying, and since my miserable pregnancy symptoms had passed, I persuaded Douglas that I *loved* flying so much, I wanted to go in his place.

Flying West out of Lima, we then turned South, following a straight ribbon of road, the only thing remotely associated with civilization to be seen. It ran beside the Pacific Ocean down the entire length of Peru. Everything to the East of it was desert, and to its West was the Pacific Ocean.

Leaning forward to look down through the big windscreen I felt like a bird. I told Terry that next to being in the theatre, I would love to have been a pilot, so Terry being an easy-going sort of chap, asked me if I would like to fly the plane. "Me ? Really ?" I squeaked.

He explained some of the instruments to me. One showed a horizontal line, with a matching line which showed us how we were travelling. The two lines had to match at all times, until coming in for a landing. After a brief demonstration of what would happen if the steering wheel went too far left or right, I got the picture. I told Terry I was busy remembering to be sure to walk West towards that ribbon of road if we came down, as there was nothing East of us but desert! He told me not to be a pessimist, and after a few more instructions, gave the flight over to me. I honestly thought he still had control of the plane, until the line started going a bit slanted before me, and we started into a slow decent. I gently brought the two lines back level to each other. It was a thrill I will never forget! It would not have been surprising if our baby had become a pilot after that experience at five months in the making, but he chose a more dangerous career, in demolitions in the United States Marine Corps, and later with a career as a Firefighter!

Although it was only a little four seater aircraft, on the return flight after picking up our passengers, it carried six souls, as the employees wife was five months pregnant also!

As soon as Michael and Suzanne were together again, they took up where they had left off. It was good to hear them running round the house, and squabbling over a game of cards. It had been a terrible thing to have the family separated for so long. We would not have allowed it to happen. However, the threat from Michael's Lima school that they would not have him back if he was absent for a few months, would have put Mike's education in serious jeopardy. Douglas had no alternative. The added months of separation were entirely due to the head office refusing to listen to Doug's advice regarding the replacement Manager, and nothing ever made up to us for the sad loss of a year of Michael's childhood.

CHAPTER 25

A Family Affair

ERA SHARED AN apartment with her beloved dog Brett, just five minutes away from us in Panama City.

We finally had our television and opened the wedding gifts not seen since our marriage fifteen months before. We engaged a young live-in maid named Petita, who actually understood my "kitchen" Spanish. At last an air of permanence was setting in, albeit in a country whose climate I would never enjoy.

When one of the girls in Douglas's office was getting married, we were invited to attend.

Arriving a few minutes before the appointed time, we were surprised to see the bride in a full white veil and a long train worthy of a Royal Princess, already entering the enormous Catholic Church. We parked and following the bride into the Church, we slipped into a pew at the rear. Although cool to begin with, the air grew hotter as time went by. Being eight months pregnant, I was very uncomfortable as there was a great deal of kneeling and standing then kneeling again involved. The service went on interminably in Latin and Spanish, and was followed by Holy Communion .

Thankfully, at last the bride and groom, now man and wife, turned to walk down the aisle towards us.

Douglas took a deep breath, and whispered in my ear, "I hate to tell you this. But it's the wrong bride!" His employee was just arriving for her nuptials more than an hour after the invitation had stated, so we had to go through the whole thing all over again! We should have remembered that unless the invitation says "Hora Inglesa" meaning "English Time", it behooved one to arrive an hour later, as being punctual for a Panamanian or Peruvian dinner invitation would very likely result in the embarrassment of catching the hostess in the shower!

That summer a very talented young man named Bruce Quinn, was to produce the musical, "South Pacific" at the Theatre Guild. This would have been " Right up my street" as the Brits say. "Oh great!" I moaned to myself. "A musical show, just when I look like a beached whale!" I realized that the only bright lights I would be appearing under, would be the lights of a delivery- room !

The idea of producing a large cast show in the little Theatre Guild looked impossible. But Bruce Quinn was about to make artistic history.

Doug and I took Vera along to the first auditions, knowing that a really good choreographer would be needed. My sister-in-law's entire career had been as a professional dancer and choreographer in England and in Paris. I remember distinctly walking through the empty auditorium seats, and introducing Vera to the young producer. We had no way of knowing that this would be the beginning of an artistic partnership which would result in top -of -the -line musical productions over the next thirty years, raising thousands of dollars for the "United Fund". Nobody would ever top the ingenuity of the productions of Bruce Quinn, and the incredible choreography of Vera Bomford.

Bruce reconstructed the stage, with space on either side to house different scenes, plus a place for the small "orchestra". It was amazing what he did with such a small area.

The production date drew closer. Douglas and Vera had rehearsals every night as Doug was playing a part in the men's chorus. It was obvious they were both enjoying themselves immensely. The urge to be part of this, the first musical that had been produced in that theatre, was intense. The call of the boards to be under my feet and the longing to be a part of all the excitement, was overwhelming. So one night I went along with them.

"Rotten timing" I thought, plonking my eight month pregnant body down in a tip up seat. "Why now Lord?" I questioned. It was a wretched feeling.

I didn't *mean* to resent the large lump that was keeping me from all the fun. I just did. After earning my living singing in these things, why did I have to be left out right now? It just wasn't fair. The guilt I felt about my feelings was awful.

However, I should have known that the Lord's timing is infinitely better than mine, as fourteen years later, I was paid to play the leading role of "Nellie" in "South Pacific" in a two thousand seat theatre on Miami Beach. There I faced the challenge of two obstacles - my age and my accent! Good lighting and make –up took care of the former, and the latter was overcome after many hours of study! Apparently it worked, as the show at what would soon be known as "The Jackie Gleason Theatre" was a hit.

But for now, I was sitting nursing my resentment, when suddenly, a miracle happened.

One of the young women of the chorus had arrived late for rehearsal. She thrust a tiny baby into my arms. "Hold him for me," she said as she rushed down the aisle. "How old is he?" I shouted after her "Two weeks", she cried over the music as she shot onto the stage to join the back-up for Nellie as she "Washed That Man Right out of her Hair."

A moment later, that diminutive scrap of humanity moved gently against me. Looking down into a tiny face, I saw trusting eyes gaze up into mine. In an instant, I knew there was nothing in the whole world I would rather be doing, than holding a little baby in my arms.

How gracious the Lord was to me! The excitement of the music and the whole production which had enveloped me only moments before, receded, and I longed only for the arrival of my own little child.

Most of our friends had "Canal Zone Privileges" which meant they could use their American hospitals and schools. Many also had "Commissary Privileges" where they paid half the price people living in the Republic of Panama who had no such privileges. This was all very fair if one knew the history of the canal. Construction had taken place in the early part of the 20th century when the area was very primitive and extremely uncomfortable. In order to attract engineers and workers needed to work on the Isthmus, the United States had built their own houses, schools, medical facilities and shops. Only those working on the canal had use of them. Now, fifty years later, the same rules applied regarding those who worked for the Canal Zone in some way.

Some Canal employees chose to live in the Republic of Panama, and go to work each day across the border. We lived in the Republic, but as Douglas did *not* work for the Canal Zone, we did not have commissary privileges. Hence our next-door neighbor who worked in the Zone paid half as much as we did for everything from ketchup to shoes.

The time came for me to go to the hospital to have my baby. But of course I was not allowed to use the American hospital, and had to go to the Clinica San Fernando which was fine, if one was totally fluent in Spanish.

However, lying in the delivery room in a stupor of pain, trying desperately to think of the future tense in Spanish for, "I am going to throw up", was not my idea of fun.

Various figures in white had been coming and going from the room for a number of hours. They all just chatted on in very loud Spanish, apparently quite unconcerned about the enormous squirming lump lying on the gurney. Two other babies were safely born in the next cubicle, while I remained a writhing lump.

I remember that Douglas was allowed in the room for a brief moment. The hands of the clock above my head were on twelve, so I asked him why he wasn't at the office. I had been raised at a time when *nothing,* but *nothing* was allowed to interrupt a man at his work. My mother had never phoned my father at the shop even though he owned it! Doubtless, it was a hangover from the terrible days of the big "depression" of the thirties, when people were starving. A man and his job were the number one priority in all households, and I had been raised to respect that idea. So I had never phoned Douglas at his office unless it was urgent, and now it worried me that he was away from his job. However, Douglas smilingly explained that it was twelve o'clock midnight, so my guilt was assuaged.

The days of inviting the father, plus in-laws, siblings and half the neighborhood to view the delivery of one's baby, had thankfully not yet arrived. It was a distinctly private matter between the mother and her doctor, with the father being kept firmly out of the way till it was all over.

At noon the next day, our baby son was born. And what a wonderful production he proved to be!

CHAPTER 26

New Arrival, Sad Departure

WE NAMED OUR baby, Malcolm. I had been told that babies slept a lot. They lied! In fact his vocal energy could be heard throughout our home day and night. I dragged my exhausted body to the pediatrician, who examined the baby and suggested he may be hungry. "You could perhaps increase the baby's bottle from four to six ounces of milk at feeding time," the good Doctor suggested. I didn't know how to tell him the kid was already consuming over eight ounces every three hours day and night. The tiny boy was a noisy vacuum cleaner, while I was a walking zombie!

One night, in desperation, we moved the howling child into the bathroom, sticking his carry-cot between the loo and the bath, and managed to get a couple of hours sleep. However, I soon noticed the maid was now getting bags under *her* eyes. It was then that it dawned on me that our bathroom backed onto Petita's bedroom, and now *she* was getting the benefit of the baby's all night crying concerts!

We put the child into a big crib in his own room. Malcolm was four months old when, one night, I woke up automatically at three o'clock in the morning. The silence worried me.

Leaping out of bed I shot into his room, terrified that something was wrong with him, only to find Suzanne and Michael standing over the crib. They too, were worried because the baby wasn't crying! A moment later, Douglas joined us and we all looked down at the miracle before us – a plump, apparently contented sleeping child, whose silence had still managed to wake up the entire family.

And Baby Makes Five

Parenting is not easy. It is similar to being a tightrope walker. Lean too much one way, and the child will become an obnoxious, selfish lay-about, but lean a fraction too far the other way, and today's child specialists would have us believe the kid will be a resentful misfit. My parent's generation had no such problems. You behaved yourself or it would hurt!

However, being a step-parent is twice as difficult as anyone who has been one, knows. Any form of discipline tends to earn one the title of wicked step-mother or step-father. However, responsibility of keeping *someone else's* child safe from harm is infinitely more formidable than caring for one's own flesh and blood.

Returning from the supermarket one day, I walked through the front door, glancing briefly at the balcony on my far right. There was a parapet which was an extension of the tiled balcony floor. It was three feet wide, to allow for any heavy rain run-off, but was used by workmen and burglars alike. Right now, however eleven year old Michael had climbed over the railing, and was walking nonchalantly along it. We were three stories up. A slip and he would plunge to the cement beneath. Terrified of frightening the boy and possibly making him slip and fall, I pretended not to have seen him, and walked to the bedroom in a cold sweat.

Shaking from head to foot, I imagined what the consequences could have been. It was obvious that Petita must have urged Michael not to do such a dangerous thing, and it was equally obvious that he had taken no notice of her. I said nothing to Michael, but reported the incident to his father when he came home. To my horror, Doug's reaction was to ignore the whole thing, saying any eleven year old boy with any guts would try walking along the outside of the railing, as it was a challenge, and one would have to be pretty silly to fall off! Admittedly the ledge was almost three feet wide, but chills still run through me when I think of what could have happened. After Michael and Suzanne were parents themselves, they told me they both used to walk out there. However, if one of them had fallen, I have no doubt whatsoever that the "neglectful step-mother" would have been blamed.

Nobody old enough to remember November 22, 1963 will forget where they were, or what they were doing when they heard the tragic news that shocked the world. I was standing in the hall of our apartment in Panama City, when Douglas phoned from his office to say the handsome, beloved young president of the United States, John F. Kennedy, had been shot in Dallas.

It was the end of an era.

British parents working overseas always sent their children back to the U.K. to be educated. Sometimes girls escaped the tradition, but it was always taken for granted that sons would go to boarding school, usually by eleven years of age. Arrangements for Michael's British education had been made before I had appeared on the scene, and while I thought it a barbaric idea, Vera and Douglas had already trained Michael to see the prospect as one to be looked forward to. In fact, one of the worst threats to the child was that if he didn't behave, he may not be *allowed* to go away to boarding school, which incidentally, would not accept a boy over the age of twelve. So the little chap really was looking forward to what he saw as a privilege. He would soon be above the accepted age, and he had to leave.

The idea of not seeing this wonderful little boy until the summer vacations five months hence, distressed me. I just had not had him long enough! But I could hardly go against the arrangements that had already been put into motion long before I had come on the family scene. The school was close to Doug's parents, where he would stay for the short vacations times, and he would come back to us every summer.

The morning of his departure, I heard Michael singing in the shower, so in spite of my heavy heart, I knew at least *he* was happy about it!

I remembered the longing I had to go to boarding school when I had been twelve, after reading stories about midnight feasts, and all sorts of fun and adventures that the characters in books about boarding school seemed to have. Once I had begged my mother to let me go to one. Her answer had been brief and to the point. "Don't be so stupid." So that was the end of that idea. I still think I would have had a whale of a time!

Michael was to fly to Trinidad, where he would be met in by the Ship's Agent, and taken to the "Reina del Mar" for the Trans-Atlantic crossing to Liverpool, something he had done so often during his short life that the Captain and Officers all knew him well. Now at the airport with his big new suitcase, a camera over his shoulder, and a huge smile on his face, after more reminders to "Change into your warm clothes when you see the Officers change from their White to Navy blue uniforms" we said our goodbyes. I cried for three hours, and dragged around for days, missing his high spirits, and cheeky grin. But I felt cheated. I had not had long enough with that precious young boy.

Only days after Michael's departure, events in Panama took a very frightening and unexpected turn.

CHAPTER 27

Canal Zone

I N 1903, PANAMA was only a department of the country of
Columbia, and while the former had welcomed the idea of
a canal being built through their area, Columbia did not.
Local Government officials in the Panama region understood the
tremendous advantages there would be for them locally, so with
the help of the United States and without a shot being fired, on
November 3rd 1903, they declared their Independence, and a new
country, the "Republic of Panama" was born. A treaty was signed
ceding control of a strip of land to the United States in perpetuity.
This strip running either side of the canal from the Pacific Ocean
to the Caribbean, became a U.S. Territory, and would be known as
the "American Canal Zone".

In order to attract Americans to work under hardship conditions
in the humid foreign country, American schools, hospitals and
special shopping areas were built. The Zone had its' own Police,
Post Offices, Courts, and eventually, its' own Television and
Radio stations. The Zone provided a lot of employment for local
Panamanians, who crossed each day into the Zone from the
Republic. Both American and Panamanian employees were entitled
to use all the facilities including the Commissary, where food and
clothing were much cheaper than in Panama.

Employees of the Panama Canal Company carried a special pass.
But as Douglas was employed by a British shipping agency in the

Republic, we did not qualify for one. Suzanne and Michael had friends who were going to the Circus at the Canal Zone theatre a couple of miles from our home. I believed that if I took my children along with them, Suzie and Mike may get in also. However, we were turned away at the Box Office which was really only to be expected, as I didn't have a Canal Zone pass. I felt awful, walking back to the car with my children, while their friends were allowed to go in. However, we attended Church in the Canal Zone, and enjoyed volunteering in the theatrical productions there, raising funds for the United Way.

Our neighbors in the next door apartment in Panama paid much less for clothing and groceries than we did, as the husband worked for the Canal Company. They were wonderful Christian friends to us. However visiting for a meal one day, I could not help but notice the sticker price on their ketchup was one third of what I had to pay in the local Panamanian grocery store. We understood it, and accepted it, but we were only foreigners. It was inevitable that such an arrangement would rile a great number of the local Panamanian population. It was too easy to feel that those with the privileges, were the "have's" while the rest of us were the "have not's". The resentment of these arrangements came to a head, and boiled over on January 9th 1964, with tragic consequences.

In order to appease this growing resentment of the Panamanians towards the United States, President Kennedy had agreed to fly the Panama flag alongside the U.S. flag at all non- military sites in the Zone. He was assassinated before his orders could be carried out, and a month later, Governor Fleming issued a decree that *no* flags would be flown, except on military bases. This angered the Zonians who were used to seeing the U.S. flag flying outside their American schools, Post Offices, and their own Police Department.

On January 9th, 1964 Balboa High School students raised the U.S. flag. This outraged the Panamanians, and then *their* High School students marched over from Panama to the Canal Zone High School with the Panamanian flag, intent on raising it beside the United States flag. Reports much later showed that adults on both sides of the border, egged the teenagers on.

Unfortunately, as so often happens in these instances, in spite of a strong Canal Zone Police presence, scuffling took place, during which the Panamanian flag was unfortunately torn. As nightfall came, the Canal Zone police force of eighty officers were facing a hostile crowd of five thousand. Underestimating the gravity of the situation earlier in the day, Governor Fleming had left for a meeting in Washington. When the Lieutenant Governor arrived to survey the scene, a Panamanian mob stoned his car.

News came that Panama had severed relations with the United States.

The next three days saw rioting, cars turned over, and buildings set on fire. As happens all over the world during times of unrest, hooligans took advantage of the situation and roamed the streets of Panama, intent on revenge against Americans.

There had not been enough housing in the Zone for all the military families, so some were billeted in apartments in Panama City. We could see some of them from our rear balcony. As the day wore on, it became obvious that Americans were at risk in the Republic, and the Guardia National (Panamanian Police) were deployed to evacuate all military dependants.

I will never forget seeing Christmas wreaths still on one door, as a woman with her baby in her arms, and another by the hand, hurried out, pushing a stroller with all it could carry.

We stayed indoors.

Then the phone rang. It was Vera who had been rehearsing for a show the night before at the Theatre Guild, and was now virtually trapped in the Canal Zone. She was alright, and would be staying in the Zone at a friend's house, but asked us to evacuate the dog Brett from her apartment.

The television showed rioting and looked as if the whole of Panama City was on fire. It wasn't of course, but the Television Producers as usual, salivating at "newsworthy" stuff, looped the

167

same scenes of rioting and destruction over and over again. We realized that seen in England, our family and Doug's home office in Liverpool, could think we were in a desperate plight. Our Turkish landlady had the sign "Americana Building" taken down and our Panamanian neighbor from the floor below kindly knocked on our door, and offered us a gun for protection. Later the Guardia National offered us safe conduct out, but having nowhere to go, we draped a very large Union Jack over the balcony, and stayed put. We remembered the motto of the British during the war. "Stay calm and carry on." So we did.

The situation worsened. Douglas drove to his office to send a telex to Liverpool, letting them know we were O.K. and asking them to notify our families in Wallasey. Meanwhile, I had been delegated to walk up the road to Vera's apartment and bring her dog home to stay with us. Dear Brett would be our refugee.

The usually busy thoroughfare to Vera's apartment was deserted. I remember very well praying for safety as I walked along the normally busy street, hearing the click- clicking of my heels on the pavement in the uncanny silence. Taking the precaution of covering my head with a scarf, I kept my eyes down in an attempt to negate my American appearance.

Not a living soul was on the street. Not one vehicle was on the road. The lace curtain of an apartment moved as I passed by and I picked up my pace. I had never walked faster in my life.

The return trip was better with the dog on a lease beside me, for while Brett wouldn't stop a bullet being fired, he would no doubt take a bite out of an attacker! It was a relief to finally reach my own front door.

Later, I learned that my Panamanian supermarket down the road had been machine-gunned, which made no sense. As happens so often during hostilities, the ordinary decent working people of Panama were suffering from the destruction and looting carried out by their own people. Rioting went on for four days.

American owned businesses in Panama were set on fire. The Pan- Am building, which housed American businesses, but was Panamanian owned, was gutted. The next day the bodies of six young Panamanians were found in the wreckage.

By the end of the rioting, twenty-five people had been killed, including four United States soldiers. Dozens more were badly injured by gunfire.

I eyed the remaining spoonful of baby food at the bottom of the can with concern. All the stores had been closed for two days now, and we had no way of knowing when they would open again. Malcolm was still three months old. I tried putting milky tea in his bottle. Being of sound British stock, he of course loved it.

As soon as the first reports of trouble had reached us, we had given Petita the option of going home to her parents, but she had chosen to keep off the roads and stay with us. Meanwhile, Douglas still had to go to his office. The ships were still transiting the Canal, and needed his attention.

On the third morning, while hostilities were still in progress, the telephone rang. It was the First Secretary of the British Embassy asking for Douglas.

We knew Alan quite well. We had been to many social events at the Embassy, and he had been a guest in our home a number of times. Nevertheless, I found myself gripping the phone tightly, nerves taut with apprehension, convinced we were getting orders to leave all we owned, and evacuate.

I explained that Douglas was at the office, but offered to take a message. It was very reassuring to hear the familiar British voice. "The Embassy is making up a cricket team, and just wondered if Doug could join us" the voice said. I almost dropped the phone in relief.

When Douglas came home, I told him the Embassy had called. "What do they want us to do?" He asked.

"Play cricket of course" I replied.

Eighteen months later, the brilliant young Producer Bruce Quinn, who had presented "South Pacific" put together a wonderful production of Rogers and Hammerstein's " The King and I " in the Canal Zone. The scenery and costumes were first class.

I was honored to play the part of Anna, with the fantastic Panamanian actor Adolfo Arias, as the King.

Since the riots, there had been virtually no social intercourse between the population of the Canal Zone, and Panama. Now, thanks to this production, parents from the Republic were bringing their little boys and girls cast as the King's children, across the border to rehearsals. Dancers from both societies worked together. Only yards from the Balboa High School flagpole, where the terrible hostilities had begun, we rehearsed "The King and I" together.

Tickets for the show were in demand on both sides of the border, as now folks from both populations came together for this beautiful musical. Friends of the American and Panamanian cast arrived every evening at the "sold out" performances. Thanks to Bruce and his fantastic army of helpers, the sets and costumes were superb. Smiling Panamanians and Americans loved the show, which became the main topic of conversation throughout the area. The production proved to be an enormous instrument of healing between the two nationalities.

One day, I received an invitation to meet Governor Fleming of the Canal Zone. It was a wonderful surprise when, on August 17th 1965, along with Producer Bruce Quinn, Director Fred Berest, and my "King", Adolfo Arias, the Governor presented each of us with a Key to the Locks of the Panama Canal. Keys have been presented to cast members since then. Indeed, my sister-in-law Vera Bomford was the recipient of a Key years later, but this was the very first time people participating in a theatrical production had been so honored. It had been deemed appropriate, as the production had brought great healing between the people living on both sides of the border.

Angela with Adolfo Arias in "The King and I"

Some months later, a group of us attended a performance at the Community Theatre in Colon, fifty miles away on the other side of the Isthmus.

Just before curtain time, Adolfo Arias and I, along with our spouses, entered the auditorium to take our seats. As we walked down the aisle, a ripple of applause began. The curtain was not yet up on the stage and as the applause grew louder we wondered what it was all about. Noting a sea of upturned, smiling faces pointed in our direction, Adolfo and I suddenly realized it was for us. It was hard to realize so many remembered our performances from months before! It was a very nice feeling.

**Gov. Fleming presents Angela with the Certificate
and Key to the Locks of the Panama Canal.**

Forty-five years later, taking a cruise which included a stop at
Panama City, Douglas and I visited my "King" at his beautiful home
on the Panama Bay. Adolfo Arias, still a handsome, straight- backed
gentleman now ninety years young, greeted me with outstretched
arms, and the greeting "Mrs. Anna". What a joy it was!

The character of Anna had a song about her certainty that no
matter what happened, she would never forget the King's children.
Indeed, I never have forgotten them, and often wonder how all those
lovely little boys and girls grew up, what professions they followed,
and where they all live now. I wonder if they ever told their own
children, of that beautiful time when, strident music playing, dressed
in the finery of nineteenth century Siam, they marched onstage, and
bowed to "The King and I".

CHAPTER 28

First Leave

VERA AND I appeared in several plays and shows, including "The Boy Friend", a delightful British musical set in the twenties. The morning after the opening night, the Social Section of the "Panama Star and Herald" headline was, "Those Bomford Girls Make Boyfriend Big Success." We were always thought of as sisters, but were in fact only sisters–in law, but it was all great fun.

Douglas was now officially the Manager of the Panama office, and being a tropical post, we would be entitled to home leave every two years, instead of the usual three, The months passed and my excitement grew. Finally, passage was booked for us back to England on a company ship. This time however, instead of the Flag Ship of the fleet carrying seven hundred passengers, we would be sailing on a cargo vessel, the "Salaverry" with only twelve.

In the early sixties, it was still popular among the well heeled Brits to get out of the cold English winters by taking a long cruise. This was before the cruise industry as we know it today, was in existence. The Pacific Steam Navigation Company had ten cargo vessels that could accommodate up to twelve people on the round trip from Liverpool to South America. They sailed full every winter.

Douglas reminded me there would be absolutely no entertainment of any kind on board, and that playing bridge would be the only social activity available after dinner.

I had been warned by Purser McSalley of the "Reina del Mar" two years before, when I had first left England and was still on my honeymoon, that I would become "a useless wife, who did nothing but play bridge." Determined to prove him wrong, I had purposely avoided any chance of learning the game. However, the specter of my being the only one sitting with a book in the corner of a small lounge, while the rest played cards for fourteen straight nights, appalled me. I begged Douglas to teach me the wretched game.

After learning the ropes, we talked a couple of friends into a trial game or two with us. I began to look forward to these "bridge nights", and when the time came to start packing, I was utterly and totally hooked on it. I could hardly wait to get on board to start the first game! Douglas was an excellent player, able to remember exactly who had played what card, and when.

As soon as we had sailed from Balboa, I sought out the other eight passengers. I smilingly asked each one if they played bridge. One by one they answered, "no". Not one of them played the wretched game I had spent months learning! Douglas told me that in his fourteen years of travelling on board his company's cargo boats, this had never happened before. Fortunately, one lady knew how to play an English card game called "whist", so the Captain made up a foursome with us every night after dinner. We kept the same game going all the way across the Atlantic Ocean. I never played bridge again. .

Soon after dawn, I stood on the deck of the ship. Seagulls made their noisy flight overhead as I watched the skyline of Liverpool emerge on the horizon. The cranes beside the docks, the sight of the Liver building, everything screamed "you are home" to me, and I thanked God for keeping us all safe for this moment. Soon we would be seeing our parents, relatives and friends! I had dreamed of this day so often during those long lonely first months in Panama. The bouts of homesickness had never really subsided.

It was wonderful to be with our relatives and friends again, particularly Michael. We had not seen him for five months. He had taken to Boarding School life like a duck to water. Over those school years, he developed into a first rate sportsman, in rugby and soccer and eventually became the top wicket taker for his school cricket team, resulting in beating another "unbeatable school" for the first time in ten years. Then he looked very smart in his blazer with his Pocket Crest of Gold, the full colors for sports.

Everyone came to the Church we had been married in, this time to witness the Baptism of our baby son. During those weeks in England however, something strange happened. I found myself saying "back home" referring to Panama.

While my body would never adapt to the heat and humidity of my new country, and I still prayed the Lord would move us somewhere else, slowly I realized that "home" was wherever my beloved Douglas was. And for now that was Panama.

CHAPTER 29

A Royal Visit

SOON AFTER OUR return to Panama, we received a large, embossed envelope from the British Embassy.

It was an invitation to meet the Duke of Edinburgh, Prince Philip of England. Only one person from each British business operating in Panama was invited. Douglas was chosen to represent British shipping, and I was included.

The husband of Britain's Queen Elizabeth was to arrive in Panama on the Royal yacht "Britannia". The instructions were that ladies must wear cocktail dresses, plus hats and long gloves were mandatory. In Panama, we had little use for either, and I combed the shops for suitable headgear that would go with my red cocktail dress. I was not about to waste money on something I would only use once in my life, even for Royalty!

Having a lovely apartment and a live-in maid sounds today, as if this was part of "Life-styles of the Rich and Famous". However Douglas and I were obliged to entertain on behalf of his company sometimes with dinner parties for as many as forty people. Also the entire apartment needed the tiled floors mopped every day, so both space and physical help were required. Foreigners were expected to give employment to the local people, and we were providing a good home and an income to Petita, which helped to support her numerous younger siblings. I looked for bargains in the supermarket, aware of a budget which had to also cover expensive school bills for our two older children. So I gave up on the search for a hat, and made a confection of white tulle, which I secured atop a small headpiece. The hat turned out just fine, but I hated having to waste money on long white gloves!

Finally the big night arrived and we headed out of the door.

Unfortunately, Malcolm was at the time of his life when seeing mom and dad exiting together did not sit well with him. He was two years old now, and I will never forget the awful feeling of guilt, as howls of "maameee" and gut wrenching sobs followed me over the balcony to our car below. I looked up and saw Petita hanging onto the squirming child who was determined to convince the entire neighborhood that he was being murdered!

On our arrival at the Embassy door, we joined a reception line.

A staff member appeared and proceeded to instruct us in the protocol for the occasion.

Contrary to the usual custom in Western society, the gentlemen were to be introduced to His Royal Highness first, and the ladies second. The latter, (we were instructed) upon presenting their gloved right hand to the Prince, would give a very slight curtsy, and move on.

Finally, the reception room doors opened, and we began to file in, two by two.

Suddenly I heard Douglas being introduced, and saw him shake hands with Prince Philip. Then it was my turn. Smiling up into the Royal eyes, I did my "bob curtsy" and extended my only- to –be-used once gloved hand to his Royal Highness, then moved on.

I remembered the number of times when fourteen years before, I had been introduced to the Prince at the ball on stages across England when I played the role of "Cinderella", loosing my glass slipper as I ran out of the Palace. Little did I think then, that I would one day meet a *real live* Prince of the realm!

There were only fifty guests present.

The Prince had chosen to wear a grey suit very similar (in all but the price I am sure) to that which Douglas had on. The two men were of similar height.

Douglas and I had always made a habit of splitting up at parties to speak to different people. He had told me how glad he was that I wasn't a "clinging vine" as he called wives who just could not function socially without dripping from their husbands arm all evening. I spotted Douglas talking with a small group of people. He had his back to me, and I was just about to put my arm around his waist, when he turned around. It was then I found myself looking into the smiling face of Prince Philip. Their stature at that time was identical.

With a fixed smile of shock on my face, I stood next to the Prince listening as he spoke of his visit to the Galapagos Islands that he had just visited on the Royal Yacht. A few minutes later, Prince Philip moved on to another group of people, and I let out a sigh of relief that I had not inadvertently squeezed the Royal waist!

I grew hotter and hotter as the evening wore on.

We had visited the Embassy in the past when the balcony doors were closed, and the room had been air conditioned. But that was when a very small group had visited the Ambassador and his family. Now the big shutters leading to the large balcony had been thrown open to the tropical air, and the humidity was getting to me.

We mingled as one does at such events, all nursing glasses and chatting amicably.

I was just about to make my way to the ladies powder room to rescue my dripping make-up, when I saw that the His Royal Highness was about to honor us once again by joining our small group. I knew that one definitely must *not* move away from a Royal personage no matter *what* the emergency! One stays until *they* move away from *you*.

Now the Prince stood next to me and spoke his mind at some length about the architecture of Mexico City, while I became acutely aware of a large rivulet of make-up running down my cheek. Remembering the old adage that "the show must go on" I gave the Prince my best smile, while the wretched stuff shivered down my neck.

As we say in England, I felt "a right Royal mess". But I did get home before midnight, and with my footwear intact!

A surprise bonus for us was a further Embassy invitation this time to tour the "Royal Yacht Britannia".

We were met at the top of the gangway by the boatswain who piped us aboard, then were greeted by the Officer of the deck.

The yacht carried twenty-one officers and two hundred and twenty-nine crew members.

After a short reception in the ward room, we were shown over the beautifully appointed vessel. I was struck by the lounge area and imagined Princess Margaret, the Queen's sister, playing the grand piano during the family trips of bygone years.

Seventeen years later, Princess Diana and Prince Charles would spend time here on their honeymoon.

The star attraction however, was the incredible engine room. It resembled a jewelry store! Every railing, every nut and bolt, and every piece of machinery was shining so much, one almost needed sunglasses to look at it! There was not one drop or smudge of oil to be seen anywhere. It was explained to us that the crew wore dusters on their hands like gloves, thus ensuring that every time they touched anything in the engine room, it was being polished!

The ship had carried Britain's Royal family on goodwill tours and vacations around the world for forty-four years, when in 1997 I watched on television, as that lovely vessel was decommissioned.

The plaque from "The Royal Yacht Britannia" still hangs in our house today.

CHAPTER 30

Contrasts

IT HAS ALWAYS amazed me how the Lord has brought people into my life at just the right moment, and how friendships have followed me across the years and miles.

Gladys and Elmer Anderson had been missionaries in Columbia and Venezuela before coming to Panama with their five children. Gladys brought her precious little four year old daughter with her to the weekly Bible study she led, placing a small rug on the floor with a few toys on it for the child. I was in awe of the fact that at no time did that sweet little girl ever interrupt our lessons! Ten years later, and a thousand miles away, that little one became our son's baby-sitter.

After I opened my elocution school Gladys sent her older girls to my classes. Two of them joined my "Charm Course" for Senior High girls, tailored to improve deportment and Public Speaking skills as they prepared for College. Twenty years later at an Anderson family reunion in Florida, a handsome young man approached me and said, "My wife was in your classes when she was in Panama. I would like to thank you for making her so charming." Only a teacher can feel that thrill of satisfaction, when hearing their work made a positive impact on a young life.

Determined to thank my own past mentors, I tracked down my wonderful High School music teacher. We had been blessed to have the brilliant pianist and organist from the Liverpool Philharmonic Hall, so now I wrote to thank Dr. Jarvis and addressed it to the Hall. I thanked him for teaching me a love of good music. By then in his late eighties, he replied saying that until he got my letter, he had often wondered if he had wasted the years he had spent teaching at Oldershaw High School. I never found any of my other wonderful teachers, and too late, I learned just how important a prompt and sincere thank you letter is.

Another example of the Lord's great timing and grace came soon after the Anderson family left Panama, when a fellow Brit, Beryl Adams, who also taught Bible study came to live down the road from us. Our children were soon running around together, and both Beryl and I wrote and presented a weekly fifteen minute spot on the Christian Radio station H.O.X.O. It aired in Panama and the Canal Zone during the morning commute time. I always started with a light comedic introduction, which led into a Bible based theme. Beryl alternated with me, writing and reading her own program. It sounded as if the Christian air-waves were suddenly inundated with British accents!

Forty years later, with all our children now parents themselves, Beryl and I still have long phone conversations, laughing together in the good times, and drawing strength from each other in the bad.

The women's British Panamanian club brought me face to face with desperate poverty. I was on the committee which purchased basic non-perishable food items and necessities and took them in boxes to the now very elderly Jamaican residents who had helped to build the Panama Canal.

As young people, they had left their homeland to seek a better life. They could earn good money during the construction days of this modern wonder of the world, and they had raised families in Panama. Now over eighty years of age, their working days were over. Jamaica gained independence from Britain in 1962, so the British government no longer had any legal responsibility for them, and Panama had more than enough desperately poor people of their own to take care of. So these very old and poor people had fallen through the cracks, and the British Panamanian Club had been formed specifically to raise money to help them survive.

We purchased rice, beans, canned milk, coffee and other non-perishable items, including soap and soap powder, then working in twos, we delivered the grocery boxes every month.

The sickening odor of decaying garbage and stewed coffee assailed our nostrils as we climbed the rickety, wooden stairs to locate the correct doors. Some on our list were now in their nineties, and lived alone. Although their faces were lined, we invariably encountered large smiles or laughter as we carried the boxes in to their one roomed homes. Sometimes there was a thin curtain hanging on a string; in a desperate attempt to keep a tin bowl and stove separate from the bed-sitting area. Our box of non-perishable items would help to tide them over, till we returned the next month.

I always left with a feeling of hopelessness, and bombarded the Lord with the everlasting question of why some are born to such a hard life, while others flourish in comfort. After a long hot shower, I would once again ask the Lord to forgive me for thinking I should have all the answers, and for feeling I could run the world better than the Creator.

John Ch.3 v 16 "For God so loved the world , that he gave his only begotten Son, that whosoever believeth in Him, should not perish, but have everlasting life."

The summer weather in England on our next "home leave" was not good. Most mornings we heard the question all parents dread on a rainy vacation day. "What are we going to do now daaaadeee?"

It had been wonderful spending time with Michael, now a very healthy, confident teenager, standing proudly in his school cricket blazer. He excelled at sports and was a very sociable person, liked by all. However, school vacations in England were much shorter than elsewhere, and he was already back in boarding school when we were to sail back from England, this time on the original "Queen Mary."

Built in 1934 in Clydebank, Glasgow, she had been famous for carrying movie stars and millionaires across the Atlantic Ocean. After the outbreak of WW2 however, she was outfitted as a troop ship and played a vital role, sometimes carrying as many as 15,000 troops at one time to their destinations.

Douglas was agent for a number of shipping lines, including Cunard . Thus it was, that for our return back to Panama from our second leave in England, we had the privilege of sailing on board the first Queen Mary. She had been restored once again to her former glory.

Opening the tall built-in wardrobe in our first class suite, I hung up my long evening gowns, the memory of my beloved big sister Olive filling my mind. I remembered the day we sat together in our local movie house when I was five years old. The newsreel had shown every female's heart-throb of the 1930s, Clarke Gable on board this very ship. As I closed the wardrobe door, I whispered to my late sister in my mind, "Who would have thought it Olive? Fred Astaire, Judy Garland, Winston Churchill, and now me!" I could almost hear Olive giggling.

The suite consisted of two adjoining bedrooms with separate bathrooms. Suzanne was almost twelve now, and shared a room with Malcolm who was nearly four. Just as on the "Reina del Mar", children under fifteen years of age were not allowed to sit with the adults for dinner, so I had to dress them up and take them at five o'clock sharp, for their evening meal. The custom had been put in place when first class families would have a nanny taking care of their children. But on this voyage, there were no other children travelling in first class.

The dining room was three decks high, and the full width of the ship. I still remember the loud "click -click" of our heels on the hardwood floor, as we walked to a table set up with snow-white linen. Two waiters and a bus boy fussed and cared for them each evening, helping them to choose from their special menus.

On our first evening home in Panama, at dessert time, Malcolm announced in his high pitched three year old voice," I think I will take a little chocolate pudding ." "You'll have your jello and like it young man!" I retorted as I unceremoniously parked it in front of him on a plastic table-cloth.

By now, people were flying Trans-Atlantic as Douglas had on his first trip to the United States a few years earlier. But for Suzanne, Malcolm and I, this would be our first view of "The New World".

Suzanne had not appreciated being woken up before dawn to be hurried out on deck, but I didn't want her to miss an event of a lifetime. I believed she would remember, and one day appreciate that her first view of the United States was the classical one, right out of a book.

Dawn was just breaking, and a crowd had already gathered along the entire starboard side of the deck. They were all pressing against the ship's railing, as we sailed up the Hudson River.

All eyes were straining in the same direction.

I felt, more than heard, the hushed murmur around me, as I deftly wriggled Suzie closer to the front of the crowd.

Suddenly, voices grew louder in excitement, as out of the mist, the beautiful and world famous Statue of Liberty, came into view. She held her lamp aloft as our ship passed in front of her, and the crowd became strangely silent.

Probably we were all thinking of the thousands of immigrants who years before, had seen Lady Liberty just as we saw her now. Most had brought nothing more than a willingness to work hard, while seeking a better life. It would be the work of those people and their descendants, who built the wonderful free land that lay before us, "The United States of America." Strangely, the land seemed to say "Welcome home" to me. It made no sense, for my little family and I were only passing through---- weren't we?

CHAPTER 31

A Taste Of America

THE SAILING DATE of the Queen Mary from Southampton had left us ten days on Doug's vacation time. We decided to use it in New York and Miami.

Walking down the gangway of the famous ship sent a shiver of excitement down my spine, as for the first time in my life I stepped onto United States soil.

Humming the "Lullaby of Broadway'" we walked along that illustrious street, then just like thousands of others who have visited the top of the Empire State Building, we relived the scene from my favorite movie, "An Affair to Remember", when Cary Grant was looking at his watch, waiting for Deborah Kerr to arrive.

Walking around any big city is tiring, especially for a small child, so on the morning of the second day in New York as soon as we left the hotel, obviously realizing he was in for another "walking day", Malcolm complained that his feet hurt. "They can't possibly be hurting. You just got out of bed!" Douglas reminded him. The answer came back "Yes, but my shirt hurts." His resourcefulness won him a ride on his father's back then, and a lifetime of achievements since!

A few days later, we were in a cab, being driven from the airport to Miami Beach along a wide five mile long causeway. Incredible blue waters flowed on either side of us, while ahead, dozens of tall, pristine- white buildings stood proudly in the sunshine, like sentinels guarding the Atlantic Ocean beyond.

It was a joy to watch our children playing together on the beach. Suzanne was a wonderful big sister to Malcolm, building sand pies and castles and running with her little brother in and out of the ocean.

A few days later we rented a car and toured south Florida, stopping at a brand new development in West Palm Beach. The four of us stood, fascinated to see beautiful forty foot long royal palm trees, being transported on enormous trucks for planting. There was no way that our three year old little boy could know that one day he would be a Battalion Chief in that City's Fire Department.

Disneyworld had not yet been built, but we were charmed with the swimming fetes of the cast at Wiki-Watchee and the water skiing show at Cypress Gardens.

Olive and I had seen Olympic swimmer and actress Esther Williams perform in some of our favorite movies at the Wallasey cinema when we were children. Now I could not believe that I was actually standing on the side of that pool where she had water danced with all those lovely, swimming chorus girls.

We spent our last two days in Florida in a pretty motel on the beach front of Fort Lauderdale, a resort the whole family fell in love with. It was there that I entered the first shopping mall I had ever seen. Both Douglas and I were mesmerized with the scope of items available all in one place.

The beach was beautiful, the promenade wide and clean, and everyone was super courteous. We had found excellent service even at the most modest lunch counter. People went out of their way to make us feel welcome, and were particularly kind to Suzie and Malcolm. Entertainment available in the promenade area of Fort Lauderdale included a fantastic Ice Show and Ballroom Dancing with a terrific band. Our time there had been unforgettable.

Our wonderful vacation time over, we turned the rented car in at Miami airport, and boarded the plane back to Panama. After seeing the children into their seats, I crossed the aisle, sat next to Douglas, and buckled up my safety belt. The plane started taxiing out on the tarmac.

I have never forgotten what happened next.

Turning to Douglas I asked him a hypothetical question. "Just for fun, if money was no problem and we had the choice of living anywhere in the world we wanted, where would it be?" Douglas turned to me and smiled. In the same instant, we both said, "Fort Lauderdale."

We knew how futile such a dream was. Douglas had worked over twenty years for the British shipping company which had nothing whatsoever to do with North America. It serviced *South* America. There was no possibility *whatsoever* of us ever living in the United States----- let alone Fort Lauderdale! As the wheels of the plane left the ground, I knew the Lord had far more important things to consider, than the supplications of a woman already blessed with so much. So my prayer to live one day in Fort Lauderdale was just a whispered one.

CHAPTER 32

Chile

DOUGLAS WAS NOW Assistant General Manager for the Pacific Steam Navigation Company in South America. He had a manager's meeting in Chile, and I was invited to accompany him.

The first two days were spent in Santiago at the home of the General Manager of the company, a title which Douglas was to inherit when our host retired. His wife Nancy was a perfect hostess, making us extremely welcome and comfortable.

It was spring in Chile, and the view of the snow covered mountains all around the city was a delight. The change of climate and scenery after the humidity of low lying Panama City, I found invigorating.

Two days later, we were driven to Vina del Mar, a delightful old colonial coastal town about two hours from Santiago .

Three other managers and their wives from Chile and Peru arrived later to stay with us in the lovely company house overlooking the Pacific Ocean. A man-servant and his wife would take care of us during our stay, so there was no question of having to help out in the kitchen.

Huge windows gave a panoramic view of the Pacific Ocean, the white foam of its enormous waves crashing onto the rocks below.

While the men talked shipping during the day, the wives were chauffeured around the area. Each lady was just that - a perfect lady, with delightful manners and kindly ways. I found myself praying that when Douglas became General Manager, and we were transferred to Santiago, that I too, would be as gracious a hostess as Nancy.

Petita our Panamanian maid had been in our employ since before Malcolm had been born, and we had not hesitated to leave the children in her care for the four days we were gone. One of the great benefits of our living in Latin America was that one's children became totally bi-lingual. Indeed, although Malcolm had only been on the planet four years, his Spanish was infinitely better than mine!

The flight back from Santiago to Panama was a long one. It was three o'clock in the morning when, on reaching home we checked on the children. Apparently they were peacefully asleep, so we clambered into our night clothes and fell into bed.

I woke up to the voice of twelve year old Suzanne. "We had an addition to the family while you were gone," she announced. Crawling my way out of the depths of a sleep experienced only by the totally exhausted, I opened my eyes. Thanks to the moonlight filtering through the drapes, I could see the two children next to our bed.

They must have been standing there for a minute or so, for as I asked what she meant, I felt a strange movement under the sheet near my arm. "The school asked who would like to have a white mouse, so I brought him home with me" Suzanne explained. "He's nice Mommy," Malcolm assured me, pointing down under the bed-sheet. It was at that moment that I felt a scampering movement across my stomach. Apparently a small boy's idea of a welcome home present was to pop his pet mouse into bed with his sleeping parents.

Suffice it to say that at no time in my life either before or since, have I ever leapt as high, or as fast out of bed!

Mouseytung became a permanent part of the Bomford household.

Then one day, the mouse was missing.

He was not in his cage. I searched the apartment for him, but to no avail. The children came home from school, but apparently neither could shed any light on the mystery. My mother's instinct however, made me feel that Malcolm knew more than he was admitting.

It was then that I remembered the English " Mother Goose," nursery rhyme I had shared with Malcolm in his early years.

"One, two , three, mother caught a flea,

Put it in the tea-pot and made a cup of tea."

We had a small Chilean silver tea-pot displayed on the credenza. Suddenly I knew *exactly* where the mouse was.

I shot over and lifted the lid. There, sitting up on his haunches like a little dog, was Mousetung. His tiny pink eyes looked up at me trustingly. Obviously he had not doubted for a moment, that someone would eventually get him out of his cramped, metal prison!

Our dog Pancho apparently enjoyed having Mousey running down his back and along his tail, as he never attempted to hurt the little animal.

At Malcolm's fifth birthday party the children were gathered on the balcony for the ritual opening of the "Pinata". It was then that the birthday boy decided to give his young guests a demonstration of the unusual phenomenon of a mouse running down his dog's back. I had my eight millimeter camera ready to film the children hitting the papier mache figure, which would eventually spill out toys to them.

But before the first child could take aim Malcolm placed the mouse on the dog's tail. Unfortunately Pancho decided that was the moment he should flick his tail very hard, and we have a movie showing the mouse flying through the air, and over the balcony. Mortified, I leaned over expecting to see a flattened and very dead mouse on the pavement four stories below. Amazingly however, the little chap was hanging onto the balcony with his forelegs, looking up at me with beady, pleading eyes, just like a Disney cartoon. Much to everybodys relief, I reached down and brought him safely back into the apartment. The mouse seemed alright. However a few days later, we found Mouseytung lying on the floor of his cage, apparently having passed from this world due to "delayed shock".

Although Doug's company provided our transportation round trip to England for our home leave, I realized that too much of our savings were winding up in British movie houses and restaurants. Even in 1966 gas in the U.K was close to four dollars a gallon. Renting a car to drive round visiting friends and relatives plus keeping three children occupied in inclement weather, with no friends in the area, was an expensive business.

When I first went to "view" our apartment, I had visualized rows of chairs with proud parents watching their daughters presenting their poems and acting in the comedy dramas I had taught them. Douglas earned the bread and butter for the family, but I decided I would earn the "jam".

Starting with one class a week for two different age groups, soon dedicated parents were dropping off little girls to our home three days a week . Now there were two Bomford schools! Vera's for Dancing and mine for Elocution.

I loved teaching. It was a joy to see a shy young girl blossom out in confidence, as she became accustomed to standing alone in front of a group, reciting her special piece. Girls who had moved awkwardly became poised, standing tall and proud, and speaking up with expression and clarity. Word soon spread, and I had students from Panama City and the Canal Zone, including daughters of Ambassadors.

The sixties had unfortunately ushered in an era when young women, in an effort to win equality with men in areas like wages, had unfortunately abandoned much of the ladylike behavior prevalent in previous years. It was becoming the in-thing to be as rude as possible, while throwing oneself around in a gross and unseemly manner. No matter how good the home training has been, as all parents know, once in their teens many youngsters tend to replace home training with the fashionable form of behavior. So it was at the suggestion of Elmer and Gladys Anderson, my stalwart friends, that I added a charm course for High School girls. The Andersons were the first to enroll their daughters in the classes. Their girls were already beautifully trained as respectful, lovely girls. But learning how to get in and out of a car in a ladylike manner, how to introduce a speaker and learning how to pitch one's voice correctly, were all part of the course.

While a mother may know all this, learning from a stranger is often easier for a teenager. My own mother used the term "she is lovely till she opens her mouth." That was why she had sacrificed money from the housekeeping allowance, and sent Olive and I to elocution classes. It saddens me today that so many lovely young women have voices that resemble a scratchy imitation of Minnie Mouse.

The time was approaching for our annual presentation to display their new skills to their parents and friends. But there were more students now, and the girls had progressed to the point where they needed to perform on a real stage.

I approached the Rabbi of the Ancon Synagogue in the Canal Zone. He was extremely kind, and was more than willing to allow our little show to be presented on the stage of his lovely hall.

With the girls rehearsed, and the costumes ready, I suddenly realized the one thing we needed was a spotlight!

"The Theatre in the Round" was another theatre where both Vera and I had performed many times. I knew the Director Lucy Tonsfelt very well, and called on her one day, asking if she knew where I might borrow a spotlight. After a quick phone call, she filled out a form and handed it to me along with directions to a warehouse on a military base. The officer in charge would be expecting me. "Tom will take care of it for you," she said waving me off along the narrow causeway.

The interior of the warehouse looked very strange. The entire area was "behind bars" which were guarding enormous amounts of equipment. Seated at a desk on the inside, looking for all the world like a prisoner, was a young officer

He stood up. I was looking at an incredibly tall, blonde, handsome man. He had blue eyes, and a smile that would have melted Mount Everest. "Can I help you ma'am?" he asked. In England that term is used only to Her Majesty the Queen, or to an elderly lady. Still in my early thirties, I felt like his grand-mother!

After inspecting the request form, he disappeared for a few minutes, returning with a large, heavy spotlight. The young officer opened his "cage", and carried it to my car.

Some time later, this handsome man proved to have a wonderful baritone voice, and I had the pleasure of appearing in a show with him.

That was in 1968.

However, the young officer who had put the spotlight in my car would become a television star; a favorite cast member for sixteen years with "The Lawrence Welk Show".

His name was Tom Netherton.

CHAPTER 33

Tough Times

MY PARENTS CAME out to Panama for Christmas. We had a party for them, and many of our friends reciprocated. We had a wonderful time, and all seemed well when we finally saw them off at the airport.

On our next leave in England however, my mother adopted a very strange attitude. Nothing the children or I did was pleasing to her, and my father was even more critical than usual. It took a while to realize that my parents resented the blessings of my lifestyle. The real thorn in my mother's side seemed to be that I had a maid. Until then, I had no idea that parents could actually become jealous of their own children. Hurt and confused, I was glad when the day finally arrived for us to leave England, and go home.

Our six month stay in Panama had now turned into six years, and we were still paying "dead rent" on an apartment. Whenever we found a house we would like to buy, Doug's company would advise us against it, warning us that we could be transferred at any moment. Our circumstances were very unsettling.

All the assurances that I would "get used to the heat" had proved groundless Electricity was cheap in the Canal Zone, but expensive in Panama where buildings had decorative "holes" built in to the walls in the shape of flowers. It made any attempt to air-condition the living room of our apartment, impossible.

One day I was shocked to find myself unable to stand up without feeling deathly ill. Every few hours I would have to go and lie down.

The weakness was frightening as it felt horribly like "fading away" as in dying. The doctor said I was suffering from a sudden drop in blood pressure. Then sore throats dogged me for weeks at a time, until eventually I had a permanent case of laryngitis.

Over a number of months, I consulted three different throat specialists. Each prescribed different antibiotics. They all, without exception, made me feel very ill and did nothing for the painful throat. Eventually I could not speak without considerable pain. I could no longer sing or act in shows, and not being able to teach, had to close my school. All the activities I enjoyed, slowly and insidiously began to disappear.

At first, determined not to stay at home feeling sorry for myself, I had accompanied Douglas when we had a party invitation. However, within minutes of arriving, the same boring routine would begin. Every man in the room felt obliged to tell Douglas how lucky he was to have a wife who couldn't talk, "ha ha ha". I resented these thoughtless people who always believed they were the first to think of that "funny joke."

It was frightening, hurtful and humiliating to be unable to join in conversations: a fact that has since made me very aware of the plight of the deaf. People would look through me or walk past me. I had always been a good communicator. But that was no longer the case. The telephone would ring, but I could not answer it. I didn't need a voice to speak to the Lord, but as weeks turned into months and my prayers were not answered the way I wanted them to be, I became disgruntled.

Somebody told me I should count my blessings. I tried. I counted my patient husband, precious Suzanne and my lovely little son. With a maid to clean my spacious apartment, and no shortage of good food on our table, I still could feel neither thankfulness nor joy. That was when I learned a valuable lesson. Never tell a person to count their blessings when they are living in a ghetto of despair!

I found it difficult to read my Bible, and eventually, impossible to pray. My usual cheerful spirit was under attack and my faith was at zero.

Describing how I felt one day, I told Douglas that it was as if I had been thrown out of a space capsule, and was totally lost, cut off from the world. I felt totally alone in the vast eternity of space. I had no idea what was happening to me.

Walking along the aisle of the supermarket one day, I saw an acquaintance who came over and started talking to me. I felt buoyed up for a moment. Then she remembered my throat condition, and said with a scowl, "Oh, I forgot it is no use talking to you, you can't say anything." She flounced off apparently annoyed that she had wasted her time on me. I stood holding the shopping cart, tears running down my face. Until that moment, I had no idea that if I couldn't talk and entertain people, I was worthless.

It was a shock to discover that apart from Douglas who patiently read my scribbles on a note pad, most people have little patience with someone who is unable to answer them immediately. Suggesting to Suzanne that she should face me while I mouthed words to her didn't work, as with the natural impatience of a thirteen year old, she said it took too long, and walked away. At the realization that I could no longer communicate even with the children, my heart broke.

One day I saw five year old Malcolm, determined to get a better view of something three stories below, standing up on a chair he had pulled to the edge of the balcony. I tried to shout to him to get his attention, but nothing came out. Terrified, I ran and pulled him down as he was about to lean over the railing.

My throat was permanently inflamed, and one night the pain was so bad, and the frustration so overwhelming, I started to bang my head against the bed's head-rest. The doctor's said they knew of no reason why I had such a bright red throat. Worse than the pain, was the realization that absolutely *nobody* seemed to understand how frustrated I was.

One day when Douglas was at work and the children were making no effort whatsoever to understand me, I hurled a plate against the wall. This behavior was totally foreign to me, and I knew I needed help. Picking up the phone, I dialed my doctor. Apparently the very act of throwing the plate across the room had done something to relieve my wretched condition, as to my great surprise, I was able to just squeak out enough words to ask him to get me an appointment with an English speaking psychiatrist.

It took many long months of therapy before my voice came back. However, it was not until we finally left Panama, that I was totally cured.

From my ordeal I learned a number of things that I could not have discovered any other way. First, that mental pain is something that is indescribably difficult to bear, and secondly, that intercessory prayer can work miracles. It was many months after my recovery that I discovered just how many friends had been constantly praying for me, when I could not pray for myself.

There had been just one oasis during those tough months. A copy of Bob Hope's autobiography had come my way. His writing was as comical as his performances, and during the moments when I was reading his book, the depression lifted, and I felt almost normal, even laughing at times. More irrefutable evidence that as usual, the Bible is correct, as in Proverbs Chapter 17 verse 22 it is written that,

"A merry heart doeth good like a medicine: but a broken spirit drieth up the bones."

The power of prayer and the power of healthy laughter are a winning combination. Perhaps that is why I so enjoy making people laugh.

Years later, I came across the piece called "Footprints" about a man who had always seen two sets of foot-prints on the sand, his and those of the Lord. Then suddenly, when the man was in deep despair, he saw only one set of foot-prints. "You promised you would walk beside me always," the man cried to Jesus. "Why, when I needed you the most, did you desert me?" "My child," the Lord said "I would never desert you. In your greatest hour of need, I carried you."

Fourteen years after this experience, I was fortunate enough to sing with the "Festival of Praise" team, travelling with them for a brief time across the Western States. It was then that I learnt how to use sign language, and still use it sometimes to sign the words of the choir anthem at Church. It is one of the greatest joys of my life, for it is then, sometimes even when I am just rehearsing, that I feel the Holy Spirit most near.

CHAPTER 34

Home And Away

MICHAEL HAD FINISHED school in England, and was finally home with us in Panama City. He spoke perfect Spanish, and with winning personality, a lovely British accent along with his Michael Landon good looks, he was obviously destined for a career dealing with the public, and secured a job as a trainee under the careful watch of the Swiss Manager at the Panama airport hotel.

The family was together again, and we sighed with relief as although we still had two children in private school in Panama, there would be no more huge Boarding School fees. Then quite suddenly Suzanne, now a very lovely fifteen-year old, made her announcement. "You said you couldn't afford two in boarding school, but now Michael is home, I want to go," she declared.

British fathers were always gung ho at sending *sons* home to the old country, but the idea of their little *girls* leaving, was a different story. Like daddies all over the world who feel their little girls should stay just that, and never grow up, Douglas was more reluctant to address Suzanne's request. The thought of loosing her to Boarding School when we had just got the family together again, was awful. In my heart I knew it would be grossly unfair to penalize Suzanne, denying her the chance to broaden her horizons just because she wasn't a boy. I remembered how much I had wanted to go to boarding school when I was her age, and how quickly my mother had dismissed my suggestion! Now, after a lot of prayer, I began the research to see if Suzanne's wishes could be fulfilled.

Calling in at the British Embassy, I approached the Consul, who was a good friend of ours. She kindly allowed me to take the big book of "British Boarding Schools" home with me, and while Douglas was at work, I poured over the pages. It was soon very obvious that there was only one school we could possibly afford, which was geographically close enough to Doug's other sister who lived in England. Bunt had a daughter the same age as Suzanne, and after a phone call, she agreed to have Suzie for the short vacations.

The normal age to enter boarding school was twelve, and at first the school of our choice balked at taking Suzanne, for at fifteen she was deemed "too old". Suzanne was an excellent student however, so I wrote again, this time enclosing the glowing reports from her current school. A few weeks later we stood at the airport, again saying goodbye to one of our children. Suzanne had been a little girl of seven when I had married her father and I hated to see her go.

Parents have to make decisions that have far -reaching consequences in the lives of their children. It is a huge responsibility. But now when we see the lovely, responsible woman she is now, her career as a nurse, her excellent choice of husband, and having raised three fine sons of her own, we know we did the right thing.

My singing voice was finally back, and I was cast in the leading female role of Magnolia in the musical, "Show Boat".

Tom Netherton, the young officer who had loaded the spotlight into my car the year before, was asked to play the leading man's role with me. But he turned the part down as the rehearsal and performance schedule would have interfered with his promise to teach a Bible study to the San Blas Indians. While I was disappointed not to play opposite such a superb singer and actor, I was pleased and impressed that Tom was doing the right thing. A fine Christian gentleman, Tom richly deserved the stardom he attained later with Lawrence Welk .

Written in 1927 with music by Jerome Kern and the book and lyrics written by Oscar Hammerstein ll, "Show Boat" was the first ever musical which combined spectacle with a serious theme. Almost every song became a hit of the time. "Can't Help Loving That Man of Mine", "Only Make Believe I Love You" "Why do I Love You," and "Old Man River" had been constantly played on radios on both sides of the Atlantic . I had grown up on that music.

Just as the writing of Charles Dickens in England had put the spotlight on the cruelty of sending little boys up chimneys, and the terrible conditions in orphanages of the previous century, so now "Show Boat", based on a novel by Edna Ferber, made ordinary people stop and think about injustice. The show paved the way to a much needed change in American anti-mixed-race laws, the last of which amazingly had only been repealed in Virginia in 1967, just two years before our performance.

The story spanned almost fifty years, so as I was supposed to be seventeen in the first scene, and sixty-seven in the last, I would be my own real age just before the intermission! Good wigs were not yet available, and while a grey one would suffice for the very short final scene, looking younger in the first half of the show presented a challenge. Being convinced that a blonde Magnolia would look younger than a mousey brown one, with the Director's blessing, I made an appointment with the hair-dresser at the Tivoli Hotel. Douglas would meet me there for lunch after the transformation had taken place. My heart was in my mouth as I wondered if he would like my new look. In actual fact, he liked it so much that I never went back to being a mousey brown-head again. Vera later told us that someone had "dutifully" reported to her that Douglas had been seen having lunch in the Tivoli Hotel with a blonde!

We had a performance on July 21st 1969, the day scheduled for the first human being to walk on the moon.

As usual, Bruce Quinn organized everything perfectly, arranging that when the moon walk was imminent, the show would be stopped, and television sets put both on stage and back-stage, so nobody would miss this incredible, historical event.

We knew it was coming, but suddenly being transported from the 1880s, of "Show Boat" to a man walking on the moon was a weird experience.

After seeing the miracle of Neil Armstrong walking on the lunar surface, the cast had to line up on-stage. As the leading lady I had to stand in the center of the front line as the magnificent Air Force band that played for the show, struck up "The Star Spangled Banner".

As the American Canal Zone audience came to their feet, a terrible thought hit me. Being born and raised in England, I suddenly realized that my education had been sadly neglected. For while the tune was familiar to me, I had no clue what words came after "The twilight's last gleaming"!

Fixing my eyes firmly on the lips of the Musical Director, I prayed that he would sing as well as conduct. Fortunately he did, and I was able to lip read and sing the words only the tiniest fraction behind everyone else.

CHAPTER 35

Adventuring

ARLY ONE SUNDAY morning I was woken up by a shout from Douglas. He jumped out of bed and ran to the bedroom door. "Someone just left the room!" He said. "I saw his back as he left." My brain was not in gear yet but I knew that only Malcolm, Douglas and I should be in the house. It was impossible for any other adult to be on the premises. Something was very wrong.

A quick glance on the floor beside me confirmed my fear. My purse always left there at night, was gone. I thanked God that I had not woken up a few moments before, or I would have seen a thief with his face only inches from mine.

The chain on both front and back doors were still in place, indicating that the thief was still in the apartment. Fear clutched at my throat.

Malcolm's bedroom door was closed, and I was terrified at the thought that the perpetrator might be in there with our sleeping child. I breathed a prayer of thanksgiving when Douglas opened the bedroom door, searched the closets, and saw that our son was still sleeping peacefully in his bed.

In the panic of the moment, I had tried to arm myself with some kind of weapon. Nothing had come to hand. I had just grabbed what I could. What idiotic things one does in a panic, for later I realized I was creeping around the place, throwing open closet doors, while holding a shoe- tree. I guess I could have stroked the thief on the cheek with it! The intruder had got in and out *somehow* climbing up the flat side of the five storey wall, then over our balcony to open the sliding glass door. The only damage done was to our nerves, but my handbag was gone for good.

Our brave dog Panchito Lopez Fabriga Bomford, was sound asleep on the mat in our bathroom until the police arrived at the front door, at which time he gallantly barked and leapt for the detective's throat. From then on, he was known as just plain Pancho!

There had been one other incident of an intruder in our home.

It had been the day before we moved from our previous apartment. As soon as Douglas had left for work, and Suzanne was on the school bus, I began tackling the last of the packing boxes. I had dressed in a hurry in old shorts and top and left the curlers in my hair, planning to shower and dress properly later.

Needing the maid to help me with something, I had shouted her name. There was no reply, so I walked into the hallway.

Apparently Petita was bent on cleaning off the kitchen "pass through" counter. My vision was blocked for the most part, and all I could see was her hand on my purse as she lifted it up to wipe the surface beneath. "Surely she could lift up my bag and wipe under it faster than that," I thought. Then the bag started to move away from the counter, out of my line of vision.

I bent down, and stuck my head through the "pass through" opening.

I was face to face with a strange man.

I screamed.

He ran.

Perhaps we all react automatically under these circumstances, as without stopping to think for even a second, I did something really stupid (surprise?) I ran through the living room, out of the front door to cut him off, intent on getting my handbag back! Anger makes us do the truly idiotic things I guess, and while today we are trained better to face such circumstances, at that time, I didn't "act", I just "re-acted".

Apparently the modus operandi of petty thieves was to watch until all the maids were chatting together after taking the garbage out in the morning, then nip up the staircases and try all the back doors of the apartments, which of course the maids had left unlocked. A thief could be in and out in a minute, while the maids chatted on.

This is exactly what had happened. A startled Petita and her fellow maids watched in horror, as they saw the lady of the house tear round the corner screaming "Ladron" which is Spanish for thief, as she tore in the direction that passers by pointed to.

Suddenly a large black Mercedes drew level with me, and the smartly dressed driver shouted, "Jump in – we will follow him." Then again, reacting automatically, I jumped in beside him and we shot off together, looking for any sign of the perpetrator.

It was two minutes later that I began to feel very awkward, and extremely foolish. I was in a car with a total stranger who was dressed in a perfectly tailored business suit and tie. However, as common sense began to dawn, I realized I could truly be "Out of the frying pan into the fire". Moments later, realizing what a foolish thing I had done, and also what a total fright I looked, I thanked the gentleman, and requested that we disband our chase of the miscreant who had disappeared from view. The gentleman gave me a charming smile, leaned over and opened the door for me.

My shouts had brought neighbors onto their balconies. Now they witnessed a very embarrassed and disheveled Senora, slinking along the pavement home.

It would be a week before I discovered that I had been in the car with the President of the Xerox company, dressed in my "grungys" and sporting rollers in my hair.

Our next home leave was due and we looked forward to seeing Suzanne who was about to finish her first year in boarding school. However, jet travel was now a reality and instead of a sea voyage the company offered us first class flights to England.

My research showed we could take the two boys to see something of the United States for ten days. Then while Michael flew back to his job at the Panama Airport Hotel, the three of us could fly economy class to England. The total cost for all this, would be very little more than three first class airline seats paid for by the company.

Mike was promised his ten days off, and I set about planning our "trip of a lifetime". I did not know it at the time, but this would be my first of many experiences in planning trips, usually for other people!

My childhood had been filled with songs from America. Every kid my age in England knew the words to "Swanee" and "California Here I Come". Olive and I had sat together in the movie house, watching Judy Garland singing "The Atchison Topeka and the Santa Fe". We had felt it would be very glamorous to ride on such a big train! Now, after spending our first night in Albuquerque, the four of us stood on the railway station platform, waiting for that very train to take us West.

A thrill went through me as, with bells clanging and horn blowing, the steel V shaped wedge of her cattle catcher leading the way, the mighty El Capitan of the Aichison Topeka and the Santa Fe railway came into view.

I could hardly believe my eyes! I knew the train would be a lot bigger than those I had travelled on during my show business days in England, but the sight and sound of this enormous locomotive, her double deck carriages snaking behind, put goose bumps all over my skin. "Oh Olive! " I breathed in my heart, "Just look at this!"

Through the picture window beside our seats, and later upstairs in the big dome lounge, we watched the changing scenery as we crossed from New Mexico into Arizona.

We passed what looked like a movie set from the beloved cowboy movies of my childhood. Enormous boulders slashed up from the desert floor towards a deep blue, cloudless sky. Surely at any moment John Wayne would gallop out from behind one of them, chasing the bad guys!

I remembered that as a child, someone had given my mother a small cactus plant in a pot. I thought it very exotic. Now my eyes bulged, seeing huge cacti of all shapes and sizes. Some grew round, wide and low to the parched earth, but some were as big as trees.

We alighted in Flagstaff that evening, a little sad to see the great train disappear on the horizon. But what a start it had been to our travel adventures!

The next morning we picked up our rental car, and drove up the mountain to the Flagstaff ski resort. Although it was summer and there was no skiing, the lift was open, and we rode to the top. Malcolm, seeing snow for the first time in his seven years of life, took a running jump into the white stuff expecting it to be soft like cotton. He got a shock and a sore backside!

The next day we arrived at the breath- taking "Grand Canyon National Park" and stood in awe at the sight before us. We were looking at one of the seven natural wonders of the world.

The sheer size of the Canyon is overwhelming. We looked along the different layers of colored rock, then down the one mile to the Colorado River. Once again I was reminded that no matter how clever man becomes, he will never be able to create anything with the beauty and majesty of God's handiwork. The words of the Hymn "How Great Thou Art" went through my mind. Years later, travelling with the "Festival of Praise Singers," I had the opportunity to stand near the Cross which overlooks the Canyon, and join in singing that beloved hymn with them.

The next day we boarded a very small aircraft and literally flew through the Grand Canyon, watching a half dozen sight-seeing helicopters in the sky around us on our trip to Las Vegas, the city in the middle of a desert.

As we entered the terminal, we saw rows of slot machines, aptly called "one armed bandits" inasmuch as they steal both money and in many cases, a person's dignity from them. Anyone who has counseled with the poor souls who are addicted to them, will attest to the negative and sometimes very dangerous impact they can have on people's lives.

Fruit machines were everywhere one looked in that town, flashing and whirring their enticing promise of easy money. We even saw them just inside the entrance to supermarkets, and later heard of families who had suffered because mom or dad were hooked on the seemingly innocent habit and had put their cash into the machine instead of into food.

After a tour of the incredible Hoover Dam we set off to pick up our rented camper.

After much research back home in Panama, instead of using one of the big rental companies I had chosen to book with a one man business, called "Joe's Car Lot". My parents had provided for their family by opening a small furniture store, and I like to support private enterprise. It worked out beautifully. Joe proved to be close to senior citizen status, and was all smiles as he led us to a beautiful brand new three quarter ton cab-over vehicle. The interior was so new it still had the cellophane on the sofas. There were twin beds which turned into a dining room by day, plus an adequate kitchen and bathroom, with the one thing I had stipulated as being essential - a flushing toilet! The queen sized bed was situated over the driver's cab area, and the two boys would sleep in the living area which at night, turned into twin beds. Everything promised was there. Joe's wife insisted on filling up the salt and pepper shakers then invited us to stay for lunch in their home before we hit the road. My faith in small businesses was once again vindicated!

Within hours, we were in a different world.

Death Valley is the hottest and driest place in the United States. With temperatures in summer around a hundred and twenty, and less than an in inch and a half of rain a year, it truly is a desert. We filled up at the "Last Chance" gas station, named as a warning that no more petrol would be available till we got out of the arid valley, then drove for three hours without seeing another vehicle. The tourist season was over, and we were most definitely alone.

As I looked at the ribbon of empty road ahead, the parched earth around us and the mountains in the distance on both sides, I prayed that Bert Cram's vehicle would keep up the steady, comforting rhythm of its motor, for this was *not* the place to break down!

My eight millimeter movie camera was never far from my grasp, and I urged Douglas to let me out so I could take a movie of the camper moving off showing the arid, lonely area all around it. Perhaps I should have had more sense than to trust three members of the male species, for as soon as I shouted "Action" the camper started moving away from me, and kept on going. They could not have heard me shouting "cut" and "hey stop!" but I shouted anyway. I am sure my beloved husband and sons would have given a lot to have been holding the camera to film mama as she started to walk faster, then eventually start running after them. The camper finally came to a halt, and I clambered aboard, sweaty hands clasping my camera, and totally out of breath. Of course it was some time before the male laughter died down!

When we pulled over to spend the night in that vast wasteland, we still had not seen another vehicle. It was June Fifth, but it was not till later that we learned that nobody in their right mind went through Death Valley after June First. Today it would be safer, but then it would be three more years before the cell phone was invented. We had no form of communication whatsoever.

Our next overnight was in the incredible "Yosemite National Park" where we were happy to see miles of green grass underfoot, while almost vertical cliffs soared up to three thousand feet around us. We explored on rented bikes, and saw the tallest waterfall in the United States cascade over twenty-four hundred feet.

We camped the next night in the Sequoia National Park, home of the giant Sequoia trees, believed to be the largest living things on earth. We saw the two hundred and sixty seven foot General Sherman tree, which the guide book assured us was over two thousand three hundred years old. It was incredible to realize that tree was already old when Jesus was born.

Driving away from these natural wonders, we headed to a completely different environment --- the old boom town of Virginia City.

We walked into a former silver mine, and strolled the boardwalk viewing the shops and businesses, all restored to their mid-nineteenth century glory. The Comstock Lode was discovered in 1859. As prospectors crowded the streets bent on getting a share of the 400 billion in silver, the population grew to 10,000. The vein ran out forty years later, so now the population of Virginia City was just over 600.

In 1862 one of the many young men arriving with dreams of making his fortune from silver and helping his extremely poor mother, was Samuel Clemens. Along with many other hopefuls however, for him, it literally didn't "pan out". In desperate need of a job, he applied at the newspaper office of the Territorial Enterprise which still stands on the main street. It was there that he took the pen name which would become so famous - Mark Twain.

The television series "Bonanza" had been a favorite of my mothers. Whenever I had been home from my show business commitments, we had sat together and enjoyed the wholesome but fascinating stories of the Cartwright family.

Virginia City had been referred to in the script as the nearest town to The Ponderosa. Discovering that it was really so, we were soon clambering out of the camper at the ranch which had been used to film all the outdoor shots for the series

Years later I was to become close friends with Victoria Jolson, whose husband, David Levy, Executive Director of Programming at N.B.C. had pushed to get "Bonanza" on the air. He had met with strong opposition some citing it was "just another Western." David Levy pointed out that it was a story about a family that happened to live in the West. Eventually, he won the day, and "Bonanza" became one of the longest running shows on television, bringing family-friendly delight to millions around the globe.

I found it a marvel to be standing there looking at the same views I had seen from my father's armchair in Wallasey years before.

The last night of our camper trip was spent in the Mojave Desert, where we slept outdoors beneath the stars, and listened to the howls of the coyotes in the mountains. Probably ignorance was bliss, as we fortunately did not think of the tarantulas or rattlesnakes which could have disturbed our slumber!

Somewhere in that itinerary, we visited Los Angeles Natural History Museum, where, as we were examining one of the exhibits, our seven year old decided to find out where a small door led to. He covered the few yards back to us in rather a hurry, as the air around us was suddenly filled with loud sirens and bells. Malcolm had opened an Emergency door. The Bomfords made a hasty exit!

We visited "Disneyland", saw the stars in the pavement in Hollywood, and took the tour of the movie star's mansions in Beverley Hills. Michael had no way of knowing how useful this trip would be to him when some eight years later, he would be a Tour Director showing British guests across much of the area he was now enjoying.

After dropping off the camper in Las Vegas, we saw Michael off on his flight back to our home and his job in Panama City. He was an adult now with responsibilities, and anyway he had recently spent six long years in England.

After waving Mike farewell, we took our flight to San Francisco where we would spend three nights in the home of the British Consul. Elsie Squires had been our good friend when she was with the British Embassy in Panama. She had been transferred to San Francisco, and now we looked forward to seeing her again.

We were to be with Elsie over the birthday of Her Majesty Queen Elizabeth, which was celebrated by all the British Embassies and Consulates round the world. Elsie had told us to bring evening dress for the occasion which was to be held at the famous Top of the Mark hotel.

That party was to add something very special to our lives.

All the guests were in their finest array.

The ghastly fashion of black for women's evening wear had not yet arrived, and instead of being dressed in the color used at funerals, ladies danced by in gowns of emerald green, sky blue, silver, gold and every shade in between. Luxurious satins and beaded chiffons rustled by in soft elegance. I was happy in my powder pink floor length gown of satin, with an overlay applique of tiny white leaves.

Entertainment was to consist of a typical dance from both countries. The closest thing Britain could come up with was a Scottish Sword Dance executed quite perfectly by members of the San Francisco Scottish Dancers.

However, the United States presentation blew us away.

Eight couples appeared on the floor, and formed two squares. They were beautifully dressed in matching outfits, with the ladies sporting enormous circular underskirts. The music began, the Caller shouted "Honor your partners, and honor your corners," and the show began.

To get the best view, Douglas and I had decided to stand up with our backs to the wall. The music and movement of the swirling skirts was a delight. Following the instructions of the caller, the dancers made intricate patterns, always quite miraculously winding up in exactly the right spot with their own partner again. The skill of caller and dancers, and the excitement of the music were awarded by thunderous applause from the audience.

I was shocked however, as Douglas murmured in my ear, "When we get back to Panama, we are going to do that."

I made no response. But I thought to myself, "Not on your life! I don't want anybody telling me what steps to do next. And anyway, I couldn't *possibly* learn all that stuff. I would turn the wrong way, and bump into people." Never before had I known my sensible husband to have such a crazy idea! It would be weeks before we got home to Panama after our leave in England, so I decided I would think no more about it, and hoped Douglas would do the same.

However, within a week of returning to Panama, Douglas had us signed up for Square Dance classes in the Canal Zone.

There was no air-conditioning in the High School Gym where we danced, and I dreaded Tuesday nights. Half the time I felt as if I was going to faint. But this was clearly something Douglas wanted to do. He needed a partner and I was it.

Douglas and Angela

Thanks to the experienced dancers who came every week to help us (they are called "Angels" in Square Dancing) we finally graduated, becoming members of the Star in a Circle Square Dance Club of Balboa, and we have square danced almost every week since. Those who think they can't have a good time without booze being served, will never be Square Dancers as no alcohol is ever allowed where the dancing is taking place. This is a world -wide rule which in forty-three years, I have never seen broken. It was probably wisely introduced when the West was still being won, and cowboys had to check their guns at the door.

Square Dancing flourishes wherever Americans have had an influence. The language barrier disappears as the caller always uses English. The wife of our first teacher was Japanese, and was one of our "Angels". Incredibly, we have danced with Germans who hardly spoke a word of conversational English, but proved to be fantastic Square Dancers.

Through this wonderful hobby, we have made life-long friends, danced to delightful music every week, and kept physically very fit.

All thanks to a Square Dance demonstration at the Queen's Birthday party, a persistent husband, and some "Angels".

CHAPTER 36

Changes

THE SIX MONTHS we had originally expected to live in Panama had now turned into nine years. Whenever we saw a house we liked, and told the company our plans to buy instead of paying dead rent year after year, they warned us we could be transferred "any time soon". So the years dragged by.

Then we received the telephone call which was to change our lives.

Douglas had been on many business trips to Miami and had got on extremely well with the owner of his company's shipping agent there. The phone call was from this gentleman, who told Douglas he was expanding his business, and wanted him as his Vice-President. He invited us to visit for a few days to see how we would like the idea of living in Miami.

Because of our friends and our contact with the Canal Zone, we had both grown to love everything American. Douglas particularly enjoyed the Square Dancing and Country and Western music, so it took him about three seconds to decide he wanted to live in Miami.

I, on the other hand, was not so sure. According to what we read in the Miami newspaper the Hippie movement the Flower people and the drug scene were in full swing across the United States, and the idea of raising a child there did not thrill me.

During all my years in show business, I had never heard anyone even *talk* about marijuana or drugs or any kind, let alone use them! There was a vague memory of an article I once read about girls in

London having something slipped into a drink, but as I had never frequented bars, it didn't concern me. While some of the cast had a habit of "going for a drink" after the show to be sociable, I had never accompanied them. Sometimes dubbed "a pain in the neck" for not doing so, it never bothered me. I had once heard a sermon based on Genesis Chapter 4, verse 9 *"Am I my brother's keeper?"* high lighting the responsibility we have for helping others. The Sermon included details of the difficulties those fighting a drinking problem can have in a social setting where liquor is offered. He explained that those he had counseled found it easier if someone *else* ordered a soft drink. I decided that this was one thing I could certainly do in my life. There is no way of knowing if my refusal to drink alcohol has ever made any difference to anyone else, as few of us ever know the problems others face. However my early life had followed a pattern of mixing with a myriad of worldly show biz people, and I know of careers and family lives ruined by alcohol. So the decision made in my mid-teens probably saved me from a whole heap of trouble.

But now Douglas and I were at a cross-roads in our lives.

The decision regarding a move to Miami had to be made not just for *our* future, but for our nine year old son's future also. While reason told me that probably the bad publicity was exaggerated as newspaper thrive on negative stories, still the ogre of fear haunted me.

I argued with myself incessantly.

England was still our "home base." Two of our three children were already building careers in London. Suzanne was training to be a nurse and Michael was working for a hotel chain there. Our parents, my brother and family and my lifelong friends lived there. England was home, and the place where we would retire. Wasn't it?

Perhaps it was the fear and the worry about such a decision that caused it, I don't know, but I became too ill to accompany Douglas to Miami on his "look see" visit.

Life changing decisions are never easy, and this one was a doozey. Douglas said he would not accept the job if I was not happy about the move to Florida. However, big changes were happening in the British shipping industry in South America, and my husband feared his company might not have a future as great as its past had been. However, the final decision it seemed, rested on my shoulders.

While Douglas was perusing Miami, I was suffering from sudden bouts of low blood pressure which made me weak and depressed.

I was constantly asking the Lord for guidance.

We could not mention to anyone that there was even the remotest possibility of Douglas leaving his present job. He had worked for the Pacific Steam Navigation Company for almost twenty-five years, and anyway, I just could not see us giving up Great Britain to live in the United States.

A lady in my Bible class had recently got out of Cuba having been a Missionary there for a number of years, and was staying with her daughter in Miami for a while. I knew I could trust her as my confidante, and sought her counsel.

"Miami is booming, and has wonderful Churches and great Christian people there. My daughter and her family love it. By the way, she teaches third grade at Miami Christian School," she added. That would be the grade Malcolm would be going into! She promised to phone her daughter in Miami, and ask about the possibilities of Malcolm getting into her class if we lived there. She was as good as her word, phoning me the very next day. "If you live in Miami, and Malcolm passes the entrance exam, my daughter will be sure he gets into her class," she said.

Once again, the Lord had "planned ahead" for me, putting me in a Bible class with just the right person, long before I ever knew what a pivotal role she and her daughter would play in our lives.

Doug's favorite song at that time was "Snowbird" sung by Ann Murray. The day he was due back from Miami, I heard it on the radio. It was then that I decided I could not refuse to live in the United States, when it was obvious that Douglas wanted it so much. Americans were warm, welcoming, loving people. As the last strains of Anne Murray's song faded in the background, a warm glow of His blessed assurance filled my heart. The direction was clear. Suddenly, I wanted to live in the United States of America more than anything else in the world!

We could not share our plans with anyone until the courts had reviewed our application for a Work Permit, and that could take weeks, as the job Douglas was needed for, had to first be advertised in the trade papers in the States, to see if a U.S. citizen was qualified to fill the position. This excellent law was to prevent foreigners from taking jobs from United States citizens, and in 1970 was strictly enforced.

As the days passed, I found myself thrilled at the thought of moving to Florida.

Then the unbelievable happened. Douglas came home with the news we had been waiting nine long years for. P.S.N.C. was finally transferring us.

We had three weeks to pack, and board their ship. The company needed Douglas back in Peru.

"What now Lord?" I cried in frustration. "Everything was going just right! I don't understand!"

Now we told our friends we were leaving for Peru, but had to keep the idea of the job in Miami a total secret. Attending "despedidas" the lovely farewell parties friends gave us, made me feel like a phony, as they talked with me about Peru while in my heart I was hoping we were going to *North* America, not South! The only person who knew of our dilemma was Doug's sister, Vera.

Things which we knew would be very expensive to buy in Peru, like the refrigerator and dryer, would go on the ship with us. Some furniture we had sold and would be picked up, while stuff we wanted to keep, would go in storage till we knew what country we were going to live in!

The U.S. Courts had still not approved our Work Permit when the day arrived for us to move out of our apartment. We would have two nights in a hotel before we sailed on a cargo boat to Peru. That day proved to be a nightmare.

I explained to the three tall, burly removal men, that green labels meant "Leave it Here" blue labels meant "To go in Storage" while yellow labels meant "Ship to Peru.". I followed them around to be sure we didn't wind up in Peru with something somone had bought from us already! Our books, kitchen utensils toys and all the other myriad of items that go to make a home were in labeled boxes piled around the rooms.

A lady arrived with more movers to fetch the dining room set she had bought from us. Other people were coming and going with lamps and side tables, while someone else came to haul off the beds. Meanwhile our own movers were working on our stuff.

In the midst of all this confusion, the telephone rang. It was my gynecologist's secretary. She told me it was very urgent that I come in and see the doctor right away.

I tried to explain that I was moving out of my home that day, and sailing to Peru two days later. "You can't do that" she exclaimed, insisting how urgent it was that I see the Doctor right away.

On the brink of tears of fear and frustration, I phoned Beryl Adams who had alternated her Christian Radio Program with me years before. She was still my Bible study teacher and best friend.

After explaining that I had not heard from the Doctor since my annual exam eight weeks before, quietly and confidently Beryl said, "There has been a mistake. Phone Douglas and tell him to get to the doctor's office right away and sort it out."

She was right. They had called the wrong Bomford. My sister-in-law had recently had her check-up, and it was she, Vera Bomford who needed immediate surgery.

Doug's company was relying on him to take over in Lima right away. So with assurances from the Doctors and Vera herself that she would be fine, and knowing she would have the help of her many wonderful friends, we boarded the ship, and headed for Peru.

Vera made an excellent recovery, and lived to teach and choreograph many more musical shows in Panama for another three decades. It was she who had introduced Tap Dancing to Panama. It had never been taught in that country before Vera Bomford arrived, and Panama was to be her home for the rest of her life.

CHAPTER 37

Welcome To Peru - Again!

THE THREE OF us watched from a forward deck, as a large crate hung precariously from the jaws of a crane over a large hole in the deck below. "That's our stuff," Douglas said, recognizing the markings on the container.

It looked as if our washer and dryer together with all the belongings we were taking to Peru were in imminent danger of falling out and smashing to pieces all over the deck! I held my breath until it all finally disappeared into the bowels of the ship.

I reminded Douglas of our honeymoon trip from England to Peru nine years earlier when he had disembarked half way through the voyage to attend business meetings, leaving me on board with his sister and children. "I trust you won't leave me half way through *this* voyage," I teased, laughing up at him.

While sorry to leave good friends I had prayed for nine years that the Lord would move us away from the heat and humidity of the tropics which my body just could not deal with. Now I breathed a prayer of thanks, as Panama slowly disappeared on the horizon.

Thirty-six hours later while alongside at a port in Columbia, Douglas received a message from his office. He must disembark immediately and fly to Chile for meetings. He would get to Lima as soon as he could. A hastily packed bag, a quick kiss, and he was gone.

This time I was left on board a cargo boat to spend a week with one child, a container of appliances, a fishing line, and a dog. What *was* it with this guy that he was never able to stay on a boat till we got to where we were going!

One of the duties I now had to perform which Douglas had done on board was to walk the dog. On a ship this obviously entailed some delicate organization and careful timing on the part of the dog's caregiver. The trick was to watch very carefully indeed, and just time it right to slide one's glove- and- newspaper- covered hand beneath the animal's derriere. This became a great source of embarrassment to me, as I was painfully aware of the smirks and giggles of the young Officers on the bridge. Let us just say that it gave a whole new meaning to the Nautical term, "Poop Deck".

It was six o'clock in the morning as the ship approached Callao, the port for Lima. After checking that everything was packed in our cabin, I took Malcolm to the dining room and ordered us a hearty breakfast.

We were still steaming into the harbor of Callao when the steward placed a large helping of eggs and bacon, sausage and tomato along with milk and a pot of tea on our table. At that moment, an Officer came to inform me that the Immigration officials had just boarded the ship, and Malcolm and I were to go immediately to the lounge with our documentation. There was no way any official of any country was going to make me give up my first cup of tea of the day, and my child needed his food. So some ten minutes later we appeared before three disgruntled Peruvians Immigration Officers.

First I was asked for the address we would be staying at in Lima. I didn't have one. Doug had told me we were to be met in by someone from the office and taken to the home of the Assistant Manager who was on leave with his family in England. We were to "house sit" while they were gone, by which time P.S.N.C. believed we would rent a house of our choice.

"You don't know where you are going to live?" I was asked. I had to admit that I had absolutely no clue regarding the address.

The next question was, "How much money are you bringing into Peru?"

Douglas had left the ship in a hurry. He knew the office would provide me with Peruvian money till he arrived. The search through my purse produced only eight U.S. dollars, which I gingerly placed on the table before the disbelieving Immigration officials. They were having a hard time wrapping their minds around the fact that this odd English woman was arriving with a kid and a dog with no home to go to and no means of support! They went into a huddle, fast Spanish being exchanged between them. I feared they were discussing the wisdom of allowing this cookie blonde into their country. She had kept them waiting ten whole minutes too!

I spent some time wondering what I would do if they wouldn't let me off the boat. It was with the greatest relief that Malcolm and I finally walked down the gangway onto Peruvian soil.

I recognized John and Daphne Dunn from our previous two visits to Lima. They drove us to what would be our home for three months, till the residents returned from their vacation in England. John handed me Peruvian currency, the keys to an office car which was on loan to me, then left.

Pancho and Malcolm were soon very much at home in the large four bed-roomed four bathroom house, complete with two maids.

Foreign residents liked to have their homes occupied for the months they were away on vacation in their homelands. It was much safer to have the premises occupied, thus deterring vandals and robbers, and the servants would be fed and kept busy in their absence. Good maids were a treasure, and the custom was that while the owners continued to pay their wages, the temporary occupants would feed them.

But once again I was a stranger in a strange place, not knowing when Douglas would be able to join us.

I prayed long and hard for my husband's safety and for guidance in this strange land.

Our first Sunday in Lima, Malcolm and I attended an English speaking Church and after the Service went for coffee in the hall.

Not knowing a soul there, I asked the Lord to just put me in conversation with the people He wanted me to meet. The prayer had hardly left my heart, when I saw a lady walking straight towards me from the far end of the hall. She stopped in front of me and said with a slightly exasperated and very British accent, "I don't suppose you happen to sing do you?"

The next day, I was a member of "The Lima Ladies Chorale".

Armed with a road map and the borrowed office car, I was en route to rehearsal, when I noticed all the traffic coming to a halt. I couldn't understand why and continued to drive round a large circle of flowers, steering in and out of the stationary vehicles. My car engine was making strange knocking sounds, but I was afraid to stop till I got to my destination in case I couldn't start it again.

Pulling up in front of the rehearsal hall, the lady who had hooked me into the chorale came running out. She looked extremely worried.

"Are you alright?" She asked in an anxious tone.

"Of course," I said smiling as I alighted from the car. "Why wouldn't I be?" "Because we just had an earthquake," she replied. I finally figured out why all the cars had stopped, and why my car engine had been knocking so much. While the center of the quake had been miles away we had apparently caught the edge of it. And I thought all those nice Peruvian drivers had stopped to let a strange foreign lady get past them!

We had no idea how long we would be in Lima. However, believing that life should never be put on hold, I called the British Embassy, and discovered there was an English speaking drama group. "Gigi" was to be their next production. I got the script, and auditioned for the part of Gigi's elderly grandmother. I wasn't too sure whether to be pleased or insulted when I got the part!

Douglas arrived ten days after us, by which time my gown for the chorale was being made, and I had the two rehearsal schedules to show him - one for the concerts and one for the play.

"Sorry you've been bored without me," he laughed, hugging me close.

The Southern hemisphere has seasons opposite to the North, and the schools were closed for the summer. This meant I had to Home School Malcolm, so he would not fall behind. The lady of the house was a school teacher with four children of her own, and I was able to use a fantastic collection of history, geography, math and story books for Malcolm. Once again, the Lord had taken care of even this detail for us.

The weeks flew by, and soon the Assistant Manager and his family were due back from their leave in England. There was still no sign of a United States work permit, so we had to find somewhere else to live.

Wives of the men working for Douglas would phone me, assuring me they had seen an ideal house for us to rent. We couldn't tell them that we didn't want to lease a house long term, as we hoped Douglas would soon be resigning and we would all be moving to the States!

Once again, we were living week by week in a sea of uncertainty.

On Christmas day, Douglas was doubled up with pain. Doctors found a stone hooked into a kidney, and he went for surgery. In between visits to the hospital, I found another family who were delighted to have a British couple to live in their house while they left for eight weeks. Douglas returned from hospital to a different home than the one he had lived in a week before!

Don Quinn phoned us from Miami to say the U.S. Courts had turned down our application for an American work permit. However, Don said he definitely wanted Douglas in his company, and was going to apply to the Courts again.

Eight weeks went by, and once again, we had to search for yet another house. This would be our third move in eight months.

Driving back from Church one Sunday, Malcolm noticed brightly dressed people knocking on house doors. He asked who they were. "They are Gypsies" Douglas explained. "What are Gypsies?" The child asked. His father gave what he felt was an appropriate reply. "People who have no permanent home and keep moving from one place to another," he answered.

A few seconds later, a small voice from the back of the car whispered, "Daddy, are we Gypsies?"

Still in my thirties playing the part of a very elderly grandmother in "Gigi" had been a challenge I loved. Skillful makeup, a grey wig and one blacked-out tooth helped.

Each night, in order to get home as fast as possible after the performance, I took off the wig, changed into my own clothes, but left the time-consuming of job of creaming and washing off the make-up till I got home.

One night, my car was idling, waiting for the red traffic light to change, when I heard shouts of "Oye! Oye! Chica!" as a couple of young men in an open sports car drew level with me. Obviously they had seen my blonde hair from the back, and noted I was alone.

I turned to them with a huge smile showing off my "wrinkles" and blacked out tooth. Not waiting for the light to turn green, they shot off at record speed!

Months later, we were still living in Peru, when the "Lima Theatre Workshop" held an awards ceremony.

The theatre was full. On stage was a table with a number of beautifully fashioned brass Inca statues resembling "Oscars". The brass plate at their base was covered up, thus keeping the inscribed winners names a secret until the time came for them to be read out.

There was some entertainment then awards for best Set Designer and best Director. Then the names of all the female performers who had acted in productions for the year were read out. The President of the company opened an envelope, looked at it, and said, "And the winner for Best Actress of the Year is----" and I heard my name.

A sort of glow seemed to grow in my heart, as I walked up onto the stage to accept the heavy brass statuette. I felt extremely honored as there were many talented actors in the group. I had only been in Lima a few months, and had not for one moment expected to be selected. My brass "Peruvian Oscar" is still a treasure in our home.

Playing the part of a woman in her seventies, when I was only in my thirties had apparently worked. However, I cannot help but think what an achievement it would be today, if I could win an award for playing a part the other way around!

A Church friend told me about a Swiss couple who were going on three months leave to Europe. They had been frantically looking for a suitable family to occupy their home as they were leaving the next day. The house came with a live-in maid, a cook, a house -boy, a gardener, a laundress, and a large St. Bernard dog.

As was the custom, the owners would continue to pay the staff, but we would pay for their food. It sounded like a wonderful deal. Again, Douglas was away on business, and the decision and the actual move would be my responsibility. But by now I was getting used to the drill!

A few hours later I had the keys to the door of a magnificent four bedroom, three bathroom, one storey house. Its roof was covered in cascading pink bougainvillea, and was built on three sides of a large terraced garden descending in three layers of manicured lawns.

The first morning I woke to the sound of doves cooing, and the gentle sound of water trickling from the ornamental fountain outside the large glass door.

Douglas telephoned to told me he would be back a few days later, which would be the evening of our tenth wedding anniversary. He reminded me to be sure that the office chauffeur, who would meet him at the airport, had the new address.

The office had put a chauffeur at Doug's disposal, and Raul had driven Douglas to work and back each day. If Douglas was not going to need him, Raul could be sent back to the house to pick me up and take me shopping. Parking in Lima even then was difficult, and it was a wonderful luxury to be dropped off at a store. I never did fathom out how Raul knew when I was finished my shopping at that particular store, but invariably when I walked outside, there was Raul with the car at the department store entrance.

Peru was becoming understandably more Nationalistic, and foreign business was growing more difficult to conduct every day. So in spite of our apparently luxurious life-style, Douglas was anxious to work in the States.

While it was fun to have the house beautifully taken care of, it was becoming very expensive to feed the staff, who apparently thought it quite in order to invite half their family over to our kitchen for meals as well!

At one time the Government rationed red meat, only allowing it to be sold the first two weeks of each month. We had no problem with this, as tuna and chicken were in good supply. However, the servants and their families refused to eat anything but red meat and considered sweet potatoes as only dog food. It was odd to go into the kitchen and see them sitting down to roast beef at a plastic table top, while we sat at the beautiful oak dining table covered in pure white linen, eating tuna!

This time, while Douglas was away, another challenge presented itself. The school year was about to begin, and it was the last possible day to enroll Malcolm in the only English speaking boy's school in Lima. This entailed paying a very expensive, non-refundable

"Matriculada" registration fee. Michael had attended "Markham Boy's School" years before, and we knew how limited the number of student places there were. If we were to reside in Lima, I had to enroll Malcolm immediately. There was still no word on the work permit for America, and now the last possible day to pay the expensive non-refundable registration fee for the school year, had arrived.

Sitting in a room just outside the enrollment office of the school, I prayed earnestly for the Lord's guidance in this very awkward situation. Malcolm could miss the chance to get in to the school, which would be a disaster to his future if we had to continue to live in Lima. However, while our standard of living appeared high, we certainly could not afford to loose all the money I was about to hand over to the school, if we were *not* staying in Lima.

The uncertainty about our situation was nerve wracking. Sometimes, when under stress, the simple answers just do not dawn on us. I prayed, sitting on the bench in that hallway. "Dear Lord, there is only an hour left. Please show me what to do."

Immediately, my mind cleared, and the simple solution popped into my mind. Speak to the Headmaster. I did so, explaining the situation to him in strictest confidence, and he kindly told me to register Malcolm, and if we were to leave Lima due to business decisions before the first few weeks of the semester were over, he would have the registration fee returned to us. I thanked the Lord for waking me up to that simple solution, then breathed a lot easier.

The house was perfect for entertaining, and I decided to surprise Douglas with a party for our tenth anniversary, which would be the day he was to arrive back from his business trip to our new "home".

It was a beautiful starlit evening. Twenty guests were on the patio enjoying ceviche and hors deuvres, when the doorbell rang. It was Douglas.

After a long kiss, he expressed his delight at our newest house, and to his surprise, was soon surrounded by our guests. I hugged the fact to myself that I had the best possible anniversary surprise for him, as an hour before the first guest arrived, I had received a phone call from Don Quinn in Miami. Douglas had been granted the permission to work in the U.S. We would both receive a coveted Green Card. We were going to live in the United States of America!

Finally we would be looking for a permanent home, but this time in Florida!

CHAPTER 38

A Time To Keep

OUG'S RESIGNATION FROM the Pacific Steam Navigation Company after a twenty-five year career with them, and so close to a promotion to the top executive position in South America, came as a shock to friends and colleagues alike. Even his parents thought that Douglas had taken leave of his senses!

However, within two years of Douglas leaving, the company was taken over by a foreign entity and sold off piece by piece, until the one hundred and thirty year old Pacific Steamship Navigation Company, no longer existed.

The job offer from Miami proved to be the greatest blessing our family could have had.

But at this time, the old company was obliged to repatriate us home to the U.K.so while Malcolm and I took advantage of the free flight to England and visited the grandparents, Douglas flew to Miami to commence a new career, this time in American shipping.

Panama was en route to Miami, so Douglas stopped over a couple of nights to visit his sister Vera. He had our beloved family pet Pancho with him. Born in Panama, and having lived in Peru, the dog was now en route to a new life with us in the United States.

The day of Doug's flight from Panama to Miami, the airport personnel put our black Labrador into a crate, and as was usual with larger animals loaded it into the cargo hold.

It was fortunate that in those days the Panama airport had no comfortable departure lounges, for as Douglas was about to walk across the tarmac for his flight, out of the corner of his eye he saw a dark shadow running from the back of the plane. He gave his usual whistle, and our faithful dog came panting up to him. In spite of two Veterinarian prescribed tranquilizers, Pancho had bitten his way through his wooden kennel in the cargo hold, and escaped out of the back of the plane! The family had come horribly close to loosing our wonderful dog.

On his arrival at Miami Airport, as Douglas walked through the Customs and Immigration lounge, he saw an official already standing on the other side of the barrier with the dog on a lead. Thus our beloved pet officially named Panchito Lopez Fabriga Bomford was the first member of the family to arrive as a legal, permanent resident of the United States of America.

However, Malcolm and I were still in England, visiting family. By now Michael was working as an Assistant Manager with a Hotel chain, while Suzanne now twenty-one, was a trained nurse. It was so good for Malcolm and I to see them both, and spend time with family and friends again. But I missed Douglas horribly. Life was never just quite right without him near me.

At last the great day came when, with our X-rays under our arms to prove we were not bringing any lung diseases into the country, and having been finger-printed and our back-grounds checked innumerable times, nine year old Malcolm and I came out of the Customs and Luggage claim area at Miami International airport and finally breathed the air of our new country – America!

Douglas had rented a house for a few months, giving us time to explore the area before we bought a place of our own. The first thing I noticed was a lovely bouquet on the dining room table. I read the romantic note of welcome attached.

Then I saw something I could not believe.

We stood in a large Florida Room surrounded on three sides by jalousie windows that had no bars on them! Something I had not seen *anywhere* before. Nobody in Panama or Peru would have lived in a building with bar-less jalousies! Such a lack of security struck me as being extremely dangerous.

"It is a good job I won't have to sleep here alone!" I exclaimed. "Anyone could get in here in minutes just slipping those windows out." Douglas went very quiet for the next few minutes, as I walked through the other rooms, repeating under my breath "No bars on the windows! Crazy!"

Douglas started clearing his throat, always a sure sign that something was bothering him. Then he dropped the bombshell. He was leaving the next morning on a three week business trip to Europe.

The flowers seemed to droop!

The next morning Douglas walked out of the strange door down the strange pathway, into a cab and off on his trip.

Once again, I was a stranger in a strange country. I was the only adult in the house, but at least this time I could speak the language -----well, more or less anyway!

Disappointment enveloped me. I moaned to the Lord for a while about the bad timing, then ashamed of my self-pity, I apologized and asked to be led to good friends.

Within the hour, there was a knock on the door. When I opened it I could hardly believe my eyes. For there stood Gladys Anderson, who had been my Bible study teacher and friend eight years before in Panama. She had a smile on her face and a home-made cake in her hands.

I never felt lonely in the United States again.

Back in Peru I had mentioned to Douglas that the Andersons might be living in the Miami area. During the weeks he had been there on his own, he had located their family, and told them where we would staying when I arrived.

The Lord answered my prayer regarding Malcolm's education. He passed the entrance examination for "Miami Christian School," and his first teacher was indeed the daughter of my missionary friend in Panama, who had encouraged me to choose to live in America.

Douglas had never known when P.S.N.C. would transfer him to another country, so renting a home had been the most sensible arrangement. The result was that now, already in our middle-age, we had no lump of cash to put down from a previous property sale. With limited resources, we plumped for a small two-bedroom, one bath house, where we found ourselves living in total contentment, among welcoming, caring and generous people - Americans.

I remembered the young soldiers I had met as a child during the war, when they taught me "Mares Eat Oats and Does Eat Oats" and recalled the G.I .who had given me pennies to put in the game at the amusement park when I was evacuated from the bombing. Now I was surrounded by the same kindness and incredible zest for life they had shown me then.

My brother Norman had always described Americans as being a people who had a passion for working hard, and playing hard. Now I discovered how right he was. While we would forever treasure the old country, with family and the dearest of loving friends, we would feel blessed beyond measure to be privileged to live the rest of our lives among the wonderful people of "The New World". We vowed we would become one of them as soon as the law would allow it.

Indeed, five years later, after being proved to have been "good residents" and passing the oral examination, the great day would arrive when we would be sworn in as citizens of the United States. That night our friends at the Square Dance club would present us with a special cake. On it would be written, "King George looses two more".

Putting down roots among these friendly people was easy. We found a good Church home. Then, blessing Douglas for insisting we take lessons in Panama, we went Square Dancing.

Douglas enjoyed his work, Malcolm was happy in Miami Christian School, and I trained with the Chamber of Commerce to become a "Miami Tour Guide".

One never-to-be-forgotten time, I had a bus load of Japanese business men. They were all most courteous and respectful, as I pointed out the highlights of the area. After a drive along famous Collins Avenue on Miami Beach, the driver made his usual stop to give the passengers a chance to shop awhile.

They were a cheery group, full of smiles and laughter as they re-boarded the bus. A gentleman sitting near me had purchased a souvenir ash-tray, with a very attractive colored picture of Miami Beach on it. He turned it over and started to laugh. Of course it said Made in Japan on the bottom. The classic joke, but it really did happen!

My training in the theatre was not being used at all. I missed it badly, and after the bus Tour Company closed down, an office job I held was boring and unfulfilling. I prayed to be led to employment where I could use my talents to earn something more towards the family budget.

Spending a small fortune on my photo "head shots" required by all aspiring actors, I joined the "Screen Actor's Guild" and registered with their Talent Agencies. Once again I was haunting offices in the hope of work, just as I had done in London over twenty years before.

Movies were being shot in the area, but although everyone liked my accent, there just weren't any parts for middle-aged English ladies, and obviously nobody needed someone with a fake American accent in a place that abounded with the real thing!

All my efforts resulted in a bit of photographic and modeling work, and a couple of commercials. It was fortunate that the family was not relying on my income for the food and mortgage, or we would have been hungry and homeless!

Then I heard of auditions for two vastly different professional Theatrical Productions.

The first was the part of Eleanor of Aquitaine in "A Lion in Winter," and the other was the leading role that I had wanted to play nine years before in Panama, when I was pregnant --- Nellie, in "South Pacific."

I auditioned for them both, and to my utter amazement, I got both.

Although the production dates were not exactly the same as each other, they were very close. Rehearsals for "Lion" would be during the day, and "Pacific" would be evening hours.

"Oh noooo! After all this time with no work, which one will I turn down?" I wailed to Douglas. "Do them both", he answered.

I was shocked.

Switching from the character of Eleanor to Nellie, the gal from Little Rock Arkansas, which involved my adopting a very different accent, didn't worry me. But I knew that learning all the lines would be a nightmare. Queen Eleanor, the estranged wife of England's Henry the Second, had been one of the richest and most powerful women during the Middle Ages, while Nellie was a young American nurse in love with a French man on a South Pacific island during the second World War. The characters could *not* have been more different.

With Doug's encouragement and assurance that I was capable of doing it, I gave up my day job and accepted both roles.

There were times, at three o'clock in the morning in particular, when I was up learning lines, that I feared Doug's faith in me as an actress was ill- founded. I berated myself for being so stupid as to take on such a work load.

Queen Eleanor was rarely off the stage in "Lion", which meant endless lines to learn in two weeks. I would have four to learn all the songs, script, dialect and routines for "South Pacific".

The tours of South Florida were from Friday through Sunday, so I was home during the rest of the week. The two shows hop-scotched each other over a period of some months, and it all fitted in. Show biz is always either feast or famine!

It was a busy few months, working both productions, but I loved every minute of it. Malcolm was doing well at Miami Christian School and loved being able to have his father to himself sometimes.

It was nerve wracking to perform at the Jackie Gleason Theatre on Miami Beach. I knew it was a very sophisticated all American audience, but they seemed to receive my newly acquired Arkansas accent very well indeed!

Then one day my agent sent me on an audition for a part in a movie.

There were just two people in the room: a lady who handed me the script, and a jolly, plump gentleman, who read some lines with me a couple of times. Then, the audition obviously over, he extended his hand to me.

As I had not quite got the name he had said when I came in, I asked him if he would repeat it for me.

I wondered why his assistant kind of rolled her eyes. It sounded like a very unusual name, so I wrote it down. "No, it's M not N," plump gentleman remarked, looking over my shoulder. Then he patiently wrote his name out for me.

D-o-m D-e-l -u-i-s-e.

Still having no clue that I had just been reading lines with one of America's most famous and best loved comedians, I shook his hand and went home. The next day my agent phoned. I had got the part. For the first time in my life, I would be on the Big Screen!

CHAPTER 39

The Big Screen

EVERYONE IN THE industry knows that a large part of making films consists of hanging around waiting for something to happen, while the lighting and camera crew get things arranged as the director wants. This gave me a chance to talk at length with some of the wonderful actors on the set like Ossie Davis, who was having fun playing the role of an undercover - cop who was pretending to be a "Godfather" figure.

While the extras were given boxed meals in a tent outside, those of us who were lucky enough to be designated as "Principles" in the cast sat together near the set to eat our full meals from the portable kitchen.

It was kind of nice having lunch and dinner with Jerry Reed and Suzanne Pleshette, folks whose faces I had only seen on the big screen or television.

All stars have their own 'trailers' on location shoots, and one day I was walking past Suzanne Pleshettes, when she invited me in. She was a brilliant artist, and was working on designs which if I remember correctly, later appeared on her own brand of linens. During our short chat together, she was kind enough to make some very encouraging remarks about my comedy "timing" in the scene she had seen me rehearse with Dom. I am so glad I had the chance to tell her how unforgettable her performance was in "Fate Is The Hunter" with Glenn Ford in the early 60's. While she will always be remembered for her work in comedy, Suzanne Pleshette was an incredibly skilled dramatic actor. Douglas was one of her greatest admirers, and never missed the "Bob Newhart Show". One night I asked him why he didn't just pick up the television set and put it on his knee! She was a very beautiful lady.

With my main scene completed, I left for the day, knowing I would be called back some time the next week for the party scene.

I expected a phone call from my agent with details about my call date and time. So when the phone rang one evening, I was shocked to hear the voice of Dom Deluise himself. It is unheard of for a Director let alone a big star, to call a cast member about organizational details! But that was very typical of the beloved comedian.

Finally my last day on the set arrived. I finished up the paper work, and signed out. Dom saw me as I was leaving, and he gave me a big hug. I asked if I might bring my husband by to meet Ms. Pleshette "Of course," he said, "I would like to meet him too."

The next day, Douglas parked the car near the movie lot, and we were walking towards the set, when the door of Ms. Pleshette's trailer opened and she came down the steps. I introduced her to Douglas. She took his hand and greeted him with her usual gorgeously husky voice. They chatted together as the three of us walked to the set, and I smiled to myself, pleased that I had managed to get Douglas much closer to his favorite movie star than just putting the television set on his lap!

As well as directing the production, Dom Deluise played the leading male role. He was supposed to be an undercover cop, working a "sting" operation by taking over a small shop suspected of dealing in stolen items. Behind a two way mirror, was another Police Officer taping the transactions between the supposed owner of the store, (Police Officer Dom) and the people who brought in the stolen or otherwise illegal items. I played the part of an upper class English lady with her husband both bent on selling "pot".

Angela working with Dom Deluise

Fortunately by the end of the movie, all of the criminals including my character were arrested along with all the members of "The Mob," and the Police and good guys came out on top.

Being a committed Christian can be hazardous in any work place, but for actors it can be fraught with distress. One has to follow the Director's orders. But even back in the eighties it could be tricky after signing a contract, to find something in the script one didn't like.

I feel saddened for today's actors who are too often expected to use foul language, and participate in scenes that would never have been written years ago. As Maurice Chevalier once sang , "I'm glad I'm not young any more"!

Being a local production, the World Premiere of the movie was held in Miami with a red carpet and all due fanfare.

As Douglas and I sat in the audience along with Suzanne Pleshette and a packed house, I recalled the dreams my sister and I had discussed when we were children – dreams that helped to block out the sound of exploding bombs, and the thumping of our hearts. "Oh Olive!" I whispered as I saw my large pink hat arrive on the enormous screen and heard my voice speaking my lines, "It happened! I am in America, and I am seeing myself on a huge screen, in a movie!"

Once the film was released locally, it provided me with some very interesting experiences.

The car industry had not yet come up with the brilliant idea of attaching gas tank tops to the car by a little wire, and once again I had driven off after filling up, forgetting to screw the cap back on, and loosing the wretched thing. Arriving at the local 'car parts' shop, I asked the young assistant if he had a tank cap for my make of car.

He looked at me with a stunned expression on his face. Then his eyes grew wider, and I wondered if my lipstick was smudged up my nose or something.

Suddenly he pointed at me and said with ever-increasing volume, "It is you isn't it? It really is you!"

I was grateful there was nobody else in the store as his voice rose an octave higher as he commanded me to "Stay there, please don't move! Stay right there, I have to call my mother and tell her you are in my shop."

Feeling a little foolish, I obeyed him, as he shouted into the phone, "The English lady from the movie last night is here! I am talking to her right now!"

I eventually got the top to my gas tank, but he absolutely refused to take the five dollars for it. I tried to leave it on the counter, but he followed me out of the store pushing it back at me with total glee on his face. The thought struck me that it may have been interesting to try and buy a whole new car!

An embarrassing moment occurred that Sabbath, when Douglas and I were walking down the Church steps after morning Service along with the rest of the congregation, when a young teen-ager pointed at me, and said in a very loud voice, "Aren't you the lady who sells pot?"

I had known happier moments!

A few months later I had a phone call from a lady claiming to be the Casting Director for Jerry Lewis. She said he had asked to meet me as he was making a new movie in Miami and was interested in my work.

Convinced this was a silly joke being played on me by one of my fellow actors, I said sarcastically "Oh, sure. When?"

She proceeded to give me directions to an address in Pompano, a town North of Miami, and told me that Mr. Lewis would see me there. Unbelievable though it seemed, I realized that this call was no joke. It was for real!

At the appointed time, clutching my composite of professional photographs and resume, I walked through an open apartment door into a living room crowded with hopeful actors. This was the apartment where Mr. Lewis's Manager was staying, and was being used as a waiting room while the auditions were taking place next door.

One by one, names were called.

After forty-five minutes, I realized that people who had come in *after* me, were being called in to audition *ahead* of me. Finally, I was the only one left in the room.

Then the Casting Director came and got me herself, and took me through the front door of the adjoining apartment.

A voice shouted, "Right in here". It came from a small kitchen where a man with his back to us, was standing at the sink washing up cups.

"Mr. Lewis, this is Angela Bomford," the Casting Director said.

The man turned round, and there next to me, was the big smiling face of the comedy genius Jerry Lewis. As he shook my hand, I remembered standing in long lines outside theatres to see his movies in England.

"Hi Angela. I'm Jerry Lewis. Let's go into the living room and talk," he said.

Over half an hour later we were still chatting. He recounted the time when he had worked in London, and been called 'Govner' by the Cockney crew on the set.

This icon of visual and verbal humor, beloved around the world, shared with me his tremendous admiration of Leonardo da Vinci.

I sat beside Mr. Lewis, while he showed me drawings in a book that resembled a submarine, drawn five hundred years ago by the da Vinci. Centuries passed before man constructed what the great painter and scientist had sketched years before. Mr. Lewis smiled. "Whenever I think I am kind of clever, I get out this book," he said.

In fact Jerry Lewis has an I.Q. of 190, which puts him in the category of a genius– and not just in comedy!

Half an hour later, he announced that the audition was over. "Didn't hurt much did it?" He quipped.

I was open mouthed. I had been expecting to be presented with a script to read, or at least to be asked to show the book all actors carried on an audition back then, with pictures and details of my past experience.

But Mr. Lewis said he already knew a lot about me. Apparently his good friend Dom Deluise, knowing Jerry was coming to Miami to make a movie, had spoken about me. "I can tell that you are an excellent actor, but there really isn't any part for you in my movie," he declared.

My stomach was dropping into my shoes from disappointment, when he added "So I am going to write a scene into it, specially for you."

I floated home to Douglas and told him the good news, and a few weeks later my script arrived.

"Hardly Working" was a comedy gem, pure family fun and exactly the type of character part I love to play.

The premise of the story was that a circus closing puts a clown, Jerry Lewis, out of work. His sister sets up a number of jobs for him, and he of course, makes a hilariously funny hash of them all. In one scene, Jerry enters a building which has the sign "Glass Factory" on it. Moments later, we hear the unbelievably loud and long shattering of broken glass. So his sister is back on the phone trying to get him yet *another* job. The movie is one extremely funny disaster after another.

The scene Mr. Lewis had written for me took place in an antique store. My character was a very upper-class lady, dressed in a fur coat, looking in an antique store for something for a birthday present for her husband, who has "Just bought himself another yacht". She would like to buy him something that would go in "his new toy".

The new assistant in the store, played by Jerry of course, proceeds to show me a mirror set into a circular brass fitting which resembles a porthole. He cannot locate the price of it, so hoping to find the information inside the mirror, proceeds to unscrew the porthole, and open it.

This is where the script said "water comes through the porthole, onto the lady."

I have never been a good swimmer. I cannot bear my head under water, and do a miserable breast stroke with my head bobbing around on top, getting nowhere fast. I tried training myself for the scene, by standing under the shower. I choked and felt awful. I had always shampooed my hair separately, never under the shower head. I didn't worry too much about it however, as obviously it would just be a bucket of water thrown through the porthole anyway.

The first part of the scene was shot in a local antique shop. It was beautiful. But we 'cut' as soon as Jerry started to unscrew the porthole. The second half of the scene would be shot three weeks later at an entirely different location, as obviously water could not be thrown into the antique shop.

My agent finally called me with the address where the rest of the scene would be filmed. It turned out to be a large warehouse where an exact replica of our previous scene in the shop, had been built.

On approaching the location, I was surprised to see an enormous red truck from the Ft. Lauderdale Fire Department parked outside . Nobody was shouting "fire", and all seemed quiet. However, on closer inspection, I realized that a wide hose led from the fire engine into the back of the set. Now alarm bells started going off in my head!

Entering the warehouse, I saw an enormous thick plastic wrapping all the way around the scene area, while outside of it stood the camera and lighting equipment. Obviously, this was in preparation for a whole lot more than a bucket of water!

"Oh me, oh my!" I thought, as I realized that I was in for a "drowning" experience, and wondered how in the world I would survive this day! However, any artist will attest to the fact that when it comes to a performance, all such fears are put aside. For the show must go on!!

In the continuation of a scene, the costume, hair, and make-up must be identical to the previous shoot. I reported to wardrobe, where two identical dresses and fur coats were hanging. The one I had worn before, plus another in case anything went wrong with the first take, and we had to do it again.

Two hours went by, till finally they were ready for my scene.

The great man greeted me with his enormous smile, and the question "Well Angela, are you ready for this?"

I told him I supposed I was, but asked if I might get some idea of the force with which the water would hit my face.

He gave instructions for the water hose to be turned on very briefly, had his stand-in stand in *my* position in front of the "porthole mirror" and gave it a few seconds of flood action. The stand-in was almost blown away by the force!

"Don't worry, I will be holding your arm down low off camera so you won't be blown over," Mr. Lewis assured me. Then he asked me to be certain I closed my eyes just as the water was about to hit my face. "Absolutely nothing is worth risking your eyes for," he added.

I swallowed hard.

My job now was to "time" my reaction perfectly. A fraction of a second too early and I would telegraph to the camera that I was expecting the water. That would ruin the comedy impact. Too late, and I could hurt my eyes. "Nobody ever warns you about this in Drama School," I thought to myself, as I waited for the commands that in those days, always preceded a movie scene take.

Finally they came.

"Quiet on the set!"

I heard the clapboard sound, and then "Speed --- Rolling---- Action!"

Jerry started to unscrew the large brass holdings around the circular porthole mirror, just as he had three weeks before. As he opened it, I saw an enormous tongue of water aiming itself squarely at my face. On and on the water pounded me.

I felt my body being pushed back. The firm grip of the star's hand on my elbow kept me upright, as the now soaking wet fur coat seemed to weigh a ton, pulling me down.

I knew I had to stay in camera range until the barrage of water finally ceased, and I stood there choking, my beautifully dressed hair style, now a soaking, stringy mess. "You fool, you absolute fool," I cried helplessly at the star. It was the perfect reaction from the character I was playing.

Finally Mr. Lewis shouted "Cut".

There followed long seconds of silence, till the camera man gave a thumbs up and through my soaking eardrums, I heard a round of applause from the crew.

Instead of the costly, time-wasting business of having my hair redone, the water cleared, and setting up again, we had done it in one take.

Of course all those applauding were nice and dry, on the other side of the plastic!

Angela rehearsing with Jerry Lewis

It would be two years before the film was released.

Douglas was at work, and I was alone in the house when I read in the paper that "Hardly Working" was showing at the local movie theatre.

I had planned on cleaning out the refrigerator, but instead, I grabbed a fast sandwich, and left in time to catch the two o'clock show.

Showing the photograph of myself with the star at the box-office, I was ushered into the theatre by the Manager, who gave me a large grin and a free pass.

I sat alone, half way back.

It was a school holiday, and the place was packed with children, all obviously enjoying the antics on the screen.

Suddenly, I heard my voice and saw myself walking into the antique store, with Jerry as the shop assistant.

Without a doubt, the most wonderful sound in the world is the laughter of children. As the water almost "drowned" the lady in the fur coat, the movie house was filled with that glorious sound. I found myself laughing out loud too. It was an incredibly superb experience.

When it was over, still smiling, and thanking God for the sheer joy in my heart, I headed to the parking lot.

On placing the key in the lock of my car door, I overheard a slight argument going on between two youths. "Yes it is!" "No it isn't. Don't be stupid. It *can't be her!*" "Look at her! I bet you it is!" cried a third boy.

I walked over to the small group, and said "Yes it is."

Never before or since, have I ever seen so many young mouths hanging open without a sound coming out of them.

A mother appeared with their ride home. She obviously didn't believe a word her children told her about "That lady over there" having been in the movie.

I smiled to myself, drove home, and cleaned out the refrigerator.

Jerry Lewis

April 7, 1979

Ms. Angela Bomford

Dear Angela:

Yes, of course, you may use my name as a
recommendation of your work.

You were a joy to work with and with much of the
thanks going to you, the scene worked beautifully.
I hope you enjoy seeing it as much as I have.

I am pleased to have your composite for my files,
but I had already made a mental note of your fine
work.

Thank you for your kind thoughts.

I wish you continued success.

Always,

Jerry

dab

Letter to Angela from Jerry Lewis

Weeks later, there was another phone call requesting me to meet with Mr. Lewis again in the same place where I had "auditioned" two years before.

There was a small group of actors from the cast in the room when he walked in. After greeting us, he said how pleased he had been with the production.

"I sent for Angela because I think the scene with her is the funniest in the whole movie," he announced, and gave me a big hug in front of everyone.

Later, he told me that he had a super three part script about a Senior Citizen's home, and he was forming a basic repertory company of actors who would appear in all three movies, "And I want you to be one of them," he said.

Finally, after years of training, teaching, auditioning and performing, the proverbial "big chance" had arrived! I drove home on wings, and leapt into Doug's arms as I told him the great news.

A few weeks later, I received the script, and learnt my lines.

The night before my first shoot day, we had an early dinner, as I would be leaving before six the next morning.

Then the telephone rang.

It was the Screen Actor's Guild. My Trade Union was calling to tell me that I was forbidden to report for work on the set.

Apparently one of the backers of the production had changed his mind, and withdrawn his funds. There was not enough in the escrow account to meet the rules of the union.

The problem was never resolved, and as my hand slid off the brass ring, I fell to the floor of disappointment.

CHAPTER 40

Small Screens & Big Hopes

BEING CAST IN an episode of the T.V. series, "B.L.Stryker" starring Burt Reynolds was fun. I played the part of an upper class Palm Beach matron, full of stories of what she believed to be the "Good old days, when Palm Beach really was Palm Beach." At the audition, I had made her a real snob, and apparently the Director liked my interpretation.

It was filmed in a magnificent mansion on the East coast of Palm Beach County, and after the usual make-up and hair session I left wardrobe and made my way into the house. The scene was taking place after a dinner party, so at ten o'clock in the morning, dressed in a long formal gown of blue beaded chiffon over satin, I entered the enormous formal living room.

A beautiful grand piano stood to the right of sliding glass doors which stretched the height and width of the entire room. Through them could be seen white pillars framing a large patio, with marble steps leading down to a manicured lawn. Fifty yards beyond the perfect blanket of green, was a large white yacht moored to a dock, a helicopter parked like a crown on her top deck.

The living room was empty, except for a handsome gentleman standing by the marble mantelpiece. He wore a black tie and dinner jacket. I recognized his rugged good looks immediately after seeing him countless times on both large and small screens. Remembered for his role in the television series "The Virginian" he had been a major actor in a myriad of films and television plays. Giving me an enormous smile, he extended his hand to me. "Hi. I'm Doug McClure" he said.

One by one the rest of the cast emerged in their formal attire. An actor dressed as a waiter was hanging around with the rest of us, waiting for our scene to start. There was also a young woman dressed as a maid. She was obviously nervous, so I tried to make her feel more comfortable by talking to her. However, my smiling efforts were met with stony silence, and it seemed that I was making her even more nervous than before. Later I found out that she had *not* been a fellow actor, but was indeed a *real* maid who worked at the house.

Later, I was cast in a very different role in a movie called "The Maddening" again with Burt Reynolds.

His co-star was one of my favorite female actors, Angie Dickenson. It was a complete departure from the fun loving parts the public had enjoyed seeing Mr. Reynolds play before, and the only lighter scene in the production was the one I played with Josh Mostel, son of Zero Mostel, the original Teyve in " Fiddler On the Roof ".

In another scene, I was supposed to be calling the police from a blood splattered kitchen. However, for my last scene in "The Maddening" I hung about in my costume, which was a robe and slippers. After three hours we had lost the daylight and as it was the last day of shooting, it was never filmed. I had heard of actor's whose carefully rehearsed scenes had landed on the cutting room floor, but I had one that was never even filmed! Such is show business.

Without a doubt, one of the most worthwhile television productions of all time was "America's Most Wanted" which aired for over twenty-three years.

The series was hosted by John Walsh, whose little boy had been abducted and murdered some years before. The program featured the re-enactment of true crimes. Viewers called with information, which over the years, led to the capture of more than eleven hundred felons and located over 59 missing persons.

My agent sent me to audition for a part in an episode dealing with a con artist in Palm Beach who had cheated a wealthy young widow and her child out of all their money, and then disappeared. I was thrilled to be in the cast.

The evening my episode was to air was the same as my husband's retirement party, to be held in a restaurant located in a shopping mall. A television store was located very close to the entrance. The timing was perfect as after the dinner and speeches, there was a break in the program, and I slipped out to the mall just in time to see myself on ten different T.V. screens in the store window.

A middle-aged couple stood next to me, watching my scene. The lady kept glancing at me, then back at the window. Finally as they turned to leave, I couldn't resist giving them a big smile. They looked puzzled, walked away, then came back, then walked away again, obviously thinking "Naw-----it's just someone who looks like her."

Within an hour of the episode airing, the crook was recognized by a viewer who called it in. The felon was arrested. Amazingly, he was working as a chef in a restaurant only two hundred miles away from Palm Beach.

Being in the cast of that wonderful television program was a particularly rewarding experience, knowing that because of our work as actors, we had contributed to punishing a despicable con artist.

By now, our Panamanian born son Malcolm was a Sergeant in the United States Marine Corps serving in Okinawa.

One night he was at the movies with his buddies watching "Hardly Working". When my scene came on with the famous Jerry Lewis, Malcolm informed them that the blonde lady in the fur coat was his mom. It brought guffaws of laughter at the thought of him expecting them to fall for a story like that! I received an S.O.S. asking for a picture of me from the scene with Jerry, to prove he wasn't lying to them! Malcolm also mentioned in his letter that I had spoken pretty good Japanese! It was dubbed, with English sub-titles.

In 1980, we had moved from Miami to live in the Town of Davie, a beautiful suburb of Fort Lauderdale where we still reside.

Fourteen years had passed since we had vacationed in Florida with the children, and on the flight back to Panama, asked each other where we would choose to live if we had any choice. We had both said "Ft. Lauderdale".

From our limited vision at that time, it appeared to be a total impossibility. Doug's shipping career tied us irrevocably to England where we would obviously retire. Yet against all odds, the Lord had opened totally unexpected doors to us, and put us here, living the impossible dream.

To this day, every morning, I step outside our home, lift my hands up to God's glorious sky, and thank Him for bringing me to this beautiful spot on His earth.

Instead of riling against my circumstances while living in Panama, with no air-conditioning, poor health and unsettling circumstances, my life for that nine years could have been much easier if I had truly *lived* my faith, and acted on my favorite Bible verse.

Proverbs ch.3 verses 5 & 6

"Trust in the lord with all your heart, and lean not unto thine own understanding. In all thy ways acknowledge Him, and He shall direct thy paths."

I had a phone call from the Public Broadcasting Station in Miami. They needed an announcer with an English accent for the very popular British Comedies that were airing every weeknight, and asked me to come in for an audition. Apparently I had been recommended by a Casting Director who knew my work.

Remembering my training and subsequent work with the British Broadcasting Corporation when I was fourteen years old, I took a deep breath, and entered the sound booth. A voice I recognized immediately, greeted me. Hal Smith had been the signature voice of the station for many years. Now he smilingly put me at my ease while handing me a copy of introductions.

For the next sixteen years, my voice announced "Are You Being Served" "Keeping Up Appearances" "As Time Goes By" and a host of others. Hal and his wife became very dear friends of Douglas and I. Indeed, without Hal's generous help in sorting out the many problems that faced my computer - challenged mind while writing this book, it would never have made it to the publisher!

Commercial television stations receive their income from advertising. But in order to pay for the excellent programs Public Broadcasting stations air, viewers have to contribute to their purchase. Therefore, Pledge Drives have to be run. This means going on camera, and asking the viewers to send in contributions to keep their favorite shows on the air.

It was decided that professional actors should be used for the task, and after auditioning along with a number of my fellow actors, I was hired to go "on camera" at each pledge drive. This I did for the following five years. The pledge breaks were produced live with no script or teleprompter. Whatever came out of my mouth would be heard in living rooms all over South Florida. A nerve - wracking task at first, but one which I learned to thoroughly enjoy in spite of numerous negative remarks from some of my "friends" . Of course *nobody* likes to be asked for money, particularly if they can get the goods free anyway, and a PBS Pledge Drive does just that.

I would spend hours writing ideas down on small cards, memorizing them to keep the information on each program interesting. Constantly looking for new ways to convince the audience of the importance of funding to keep their favorite programs available, I sometimes used light comedy to keep their attention. Commercial

T.V. was becoming less family friendly every year, while PBS had much better content. I believed fervently in what I was doing.

Sometimes it would be particular fun when the star of the show we were introducing would visit the studio. One day, we were broadcasting the first PBS special of a lovely Viennese Orchestra. It was called "From Holland, With Love". A tall, slim gentleman walked in just before we went on the air. I recognized him from the cover of the tapes we were offering as gifts to those who sent their financial support to the station. Anxious that I should pronounce his name correctly, I asked him how it should be done.

There was no way to know that I was helping to introduce to the United States, an artist whose beautiful orchestral concerts would one day play to capacity stadium audiences, on both sides of the Atlantic. His name was Andre Rieu.

Appearing as a "talking head" some thirty times a year had some drawbacks.

One day, in the middle of making a cake, I realized there weren't enough eggs for the receipt. Leaving the sifted flour in the bowl, I grabbed my car keys to set off for the supermarket. Of course that *just had* to be the day someone recognized me. The lady was very kind, leaning on her overflowing trolley reciting a litany of her favorite programs on our channel. I wanted the earth to open up and swallow me whole, as I stood in my old shorts, hair awry, horribly aware that the only make-up on my face consisted of small bits of flour.

Being recognized in the Library wasn't too bad, but one day in the Doctor's office it was positively embarrassing when a gentleman darted over to the empty seat beside me, exclaiming loudly that he had seen me the night before introducing "The Three Tenors". My face burned red, as it had been a particularly nerve wracking night; in fact one that I would *never* forget!

It had been the first concert tour of Carreras, Domingo and Pavarotti, so the pledge drive presenters were dressed in formal wear. I had on a dark pink sequin skirt with a matching hip length top. We all knew that a record breaking number of viewers would be watching that night.

Half way through one of my live pledge breaks, I heard a loud "psst- psst" noise behind me. It was horribly distracting, as I was trying to keep up my smiling dialogue on track and making sense. It was the lady manning one of the bank of telephones ready to answer the viewers pledge calls. "Surely she doesn't expect me to turn my back to the camera!" I thought. I was at a delicate point in my presentation about the concert, intending to segue into the plug for pledges. It was a good thing I didn't turn round, even slightly, for as soon as I had "thrown" the talk over to my colleague and the red light was off on my camera, the whispering phone operator from behind informed me that the long zip at my back, which stretched from below my waist up the sequin covered top, had parted company! Subconsciously, I had thought the top of my outfit seemed a bit loose. But now it was getting much worse!

I would be on camera again in less than two minutes. There was nothing to be done beyond my issuing a loud stage whisper round the room begging for large safety pins. My partner, totally unaware of any problem, "threw" the pledge talk back to me, and all I could do was smile and hope that what I was saying made sense! The rest of that pledge break was presented with my shoulders lifted as far back as I could, hoping the whole top wouldn't slide off my arms in front of a few hundred thousand viewers.

Thankfully, television was not yet available in 3-D!

Cell phones were still a thing of the future when, returning from a visit to the dentist one day, I noticed the red light blinking on my answering device. It was a message from the television station.

Apparently a man claiming to be the manager of a big star in Great Britain had called asking for my telephone number. In keeping with company policy, the studio operator had not given it to him, but had taken his number to pass on to me. I was sure it was a bogus call, but with my mouth still numb from the dental injection, I dialed it anyway.

A lady answered, and gave me her husband's name. I did not recognize it, but she assured me that he was very well known on British television.

Along with his manager, the three of them had apparently seen me presenting the pledge drive the night before, and were anxious to meet me. Explaining that the men were due back from playing golf shortly, she assured me that someone would call me back. I gave her my number, but remained very skeptical.

Computers were not yet the norm, so I could not look up the name. However, after hanging up the phone, I immediately called our daughter Suzanne in England, and told her the name the lady had claimed as her husband, and very well known in Britain.

I waited for Suzie to say "Never heard of him" and was totally stunned when she told me he was a famous game show host and entertainer, and had at least two of his own television shows running in the U.K. Everything he did was family oriented, and he had been the headline performer at the Royal Command Performance at the London Palladium, as he was beloved by *everyone* in Great Britain!

An hour later, the phone rang. It was the manager of the star calling me back.

"We are producing a new television show in New York. We saw you last night, and agreed that you are exactly the person we will need to introduce our program every week," he said.

He named a Palm Beach restaurant. " We are flying back to the U.K. tomorrow, so could you meet me there this afternoon?" He asked.

Could I just!!

Praying for wisdom, I shampooed my hair, sifted through my wardrobe, and dressed in my favorite television jacket and skirt.

Checking my watch, I barely had enough time to apply some make-up, before setting off on the fifty mile drive North, to what I realized could be *the* most important interview of my life.

Parking on an avenue of beautiful palm trees, thankful the dentist's "numbing stuff" had worn off, I crossed the road, walked up a small flight of steps and entered the restaurant.

"You are Angela Bomford," a charming gentleman with a broad smile declared. He introduced himself taking my hand in a warm clasp. "Let's sit out on the balcony," he suggested. We followed the waiter through the almost empty room. It was mid-afternoon, that gentle time in restaurants after the lunch-bunch are gone, and early diners have not yet arrived.

The waiter led us to a small table on the balcony, and took our order for English tea and muffins. The heavy humidity of summer was gone, replaced by gentle sunshine and a light breeze. Beneath us on the boulevard, Stately Royal palm trees reached to the azure sky, their flowing branches swaying slightly in the breeze.

My host smiled at me as he pushed a VCR tape across the table to me. "This is for you," he said. "It is a copy of some of the shows we have running in England right now. We will be doing something similar in New York later this year, and we want *you* to introduce it on camera every week."

I could hardly believe my ears! He named the network station, explaining that my on-camera introductions would be taped in New York, and seen on network television all over the United States. It would only entail my flying up once a month for a couple of days. An hour later, he gave me his home telephone number in England, with the promise that I would be hearing from him as soon as everything was settled with the network in New York.

After viewing the VCR tapes I was truly impressed. This was a star whose endearing personality drew out the best in children and adults alike. It was easy to see how he had become so admired by people from every walk of life!

By now both Michael, who was living in Spain, and Suzanne in England, were married and had young children while our youngest,

Malcolm was still in the Marines. I walked on air, as it was now feasible that I could one day help the two older children to pay off their mortgages, and help the youngest also, when his time came to marry. It was a wonderful feeling.

Ten days later, the phone rang.

It was a our good friend from England, Peter McSalley who had been the Purser on the "Reina del Mar", informing us that a scandal involving the beloved star of the family T.V. shows had just hit the British headlines. Apparently the famous gentleman had been arrested for a drunken brawl. Within days, further evidence was unearthed proving that he was definitely *not* the family- style man everyone had believed him to be. Immorality so sullied his name that all his shows were immediately cancelled in England, and the American networks stopped all negotiations.

Once again, I hit the floor as my hand slipped from the brass ring.

CHAPTER 40

Part 2

EVERYONE WHO HAS suffered a major disappointment knows it can be physically and mentally draining. However, remembering things which are truly tragic, sometimes puts things into perspective.

Some years before, on October 22nd, 1983 two hundred and forty-one American Marines on a peace keeping mission in Beirut had been killed, most of them sleeping in their bunks. This would prove to be the first of many suicide terrorist attacks on Americans.

My heart had bled for loved ones belonging to the young men, and along with most other people, my nerves were raw imagining the desperate sorrow of the families.

As far as I knew, our Marine son was still safely in Camp Lejeune. However e-mails and cell phones were not yet in use, and being unable to contact Malcolm, I found it impossible to concentrate on anything.

Douglas was at work, and alone in the house, my anger at the atrocity was tearing at my very soul. I had to get out of the house.

My heart was breaking, as I drove aimlessly around town. Fear for my own son's future safety, clutched at my heart.

All flags were at half staff. All but one, that flew above a fast food restaurant. Pulling into the parking lot, I was amazed at the anger which was building in my soul. I asked the manager to do something about lowering the flag over the business as soon as possible, feeling a desperate sense of outrage that the grief of those families was being ignored. It didn't help matters when it became obvious to me that neither he nor anyone else seemed to know what I was talking about. This first "wake up" call would not be enough for the civilized world to understand what was happening.

It was probably a useless thing to do. But as anyone in a hopeless situation knows, one sometimes experiences an overwhelming urge to not only pray, but to *do something,* even if it is only to draw attention to the plight of others.

That night the television news showed Marines from Camp Lejeune piling into trucks, en route to the planes that would fly them to Beirut to replace their fallen comrades. We craned our necks towards the set, trying desperately to see if our Marine was among them.

It was two anxious filled days before Malcolm was able to contact us. He was, for the moment anyway, still safely in the United States. I thanked God, and prayed for the safety of those other young lives that had now been put in harms way.

After four years serving in the Marine Corps, Malcolm decided against re-enlisting, and began studying at a College in Central Florida. We were so very happy to know he was now safely home on American soil. I cherished the thought of what would now be his very frequent visits home.

Two months later, the telephone rang. Douglas was at work and I was alone in the house. It was Malcolm.

"I have good news, and I have bad news," he announced. I could not imagine what it could be. "The bad news is I am dropping out of College because I am bored stiff doing stuff I learned in High School, and the good news is that I am going back into the Marines."

He had left with the rank of Sergeant, and had only three months to re-enlist with the same rank. Longer than that, and he would have to go back to square one, including Boot Camp again.

I told Malcolm that it was his life, and he must do what he felt was right for him. I knew beyond a shadow of a doubt that it was the right reaction. However, the phone call over, a dreadful noise filled the house. It was a cross between a scream and a horrible wailing

261

sound, like an animal being torn from her offspring. Seconds later, I realized the sound was coming from me.

Self pity needs to get on with being occupied.

There had been no audition calls for months. I took the grocery list off the frig door, and went to the supermarket.

Carting my purchases back to the car, I saw a "Help Wanted" sign in a ladies hand-bag store. I noted the phone number, and went home. Discovering they needed a part-time shop assistant, I showered and changed then went right back and got the job.

It was a year later that I found out how I got it. The owner and her manager were both very small ladies, and subsequently had a hard time reaching the top shelves. It was neither my interviewing skills, nor my scintillating personality that had got me the job--- I had got it because I was tall! It was a real ego squasher!

Although I was fortunate enough to be cast in a few television commercials and movies, parts for a middle-aged English lady were painfully few. The very small payment from my part-time job wasn't doing much for the family budget, but show business was my first love and the idea of settling into any other world was abhorrent to me.

In spite of all my British training and education, and all my years as a professional actor, without a United States degree, I would not be allowed to teach Drama in the U.S. school system. A brilliant pianist I knew had gone back to college and studied hard so she could teach music in schools. She had no choice but to study subjects totally unrelated to music including astronomy, in her effort to gain the degree needed. She had finally given up in disgust, thus depriving local students of a fantastic teacher. While I knew I had a lot to contribute to a Drama Department in a High School or College, I decided I could not waste my time and money to be frustrated in such a manner.

So while working in the hand-bag store, I tried various evening classes in Hotel Management and later, in Personnel training, later called "Human Resources".

Months passed, as I prayed for guidance, but nothing seemed to fit. Until one evening, I was on a coffee break from my class."Hi there!

What are you doing here?" a voice shouted. A cheery Afro-American lady I had sold a handbag to a few days earlier was calling me. She was the Head of the Adult Night School, and asked me what classes I was taking. "Word Processing" I replied with a bored expression. "You should be in the Travel Agent classes girl" she admonished me with a grin. " You would be a *great* Travel Agent!" She exclaimed.

Doug and I had visited a beautiful cruise ship the year before. The chandeliers had sparkled, and I had fallen in love once again with the idea of life at sea. I had told Douglas we would cruise on a ship like that one day, but he had picked up a brochure at the Purser's desk, taken one look at the prices, and said "No. We won't!" But now a tingle of excitement went through me. As a Travel Agent, surely I would get a break on prices on the cruises? Wouldn't I?

After a few classes, I marveled at my feeling of contentment. It wasn't my first choice of profession but it was a wonderful second best. Out of sixteen who began the course, only four of us would finish it.

It was a bright January morning in 1986 when I was driving to my Airline Computer class. Suddenly, through the wind screen of my car, I saw the vapor trail of an enormous size coming up into the sky just slightly to the left of me. We had seen manned rocket launches quite clearly in the past, being located only a hundred and seventy miles from Cape Kennedy, and now I remembered that the Challenger was to go up that day.

At a stop light, I watched as the trail continued its climb into the sky. Suddenly, the leading mass exploded, shooting enormous clouds and pieces across my line of vision I knew about a part of the booster separating after a certain time into the launch, but this looked too big for that. "Surely nothing could have gone wrong?" I thought. However, it proved to be a scene that I would see a dozen times over on my television screen, for seconds later my car radio confirmed the horror of what my eyes had beheld. I had just witnessed the tragic deaths of seven brave people, including six astronauts and a school teacher. Five men and two women. Their families and nation were so very proud of them. But now they were gone.

"We will never forget them, nor the last time we saw them this morning, as they prepared for their journey and waved goodbye, and slipped the surly bonds of earth to touch the face of God."

President Ronald Reagan. January 28th, 1986

I followed up every Travel Agent wanted advertisement, but without at least two years of experience, nobody would grant me an interview.

Over thirty years had passed since I had waved my newly acquired acting credentials around trying to get hired. Then I was told I was "too young". Now when I finally managed to get an interview, the pitying look on the interviewers face said , "too old". I was just in my fifties, but they wanted someone in their twenties, with at least two years experience on airline computers. Starting out a new career is rarely easy, but setting out to conquer new horizons in middle age, as many have discovered, is a downright scary experience!

One day I walked into a Travel agency ten minutes from my home, and asked for a job. The owner gave me a written test then she asked me to return the next day. I told the Lord that starting my new career as a Travel Agent with that very nice lady, in that office so very close to my home would be perfect.

The next day, convinced of my success, I walked cheerily into the agency. However, the owner had decided I would not be able to handle the job due to my lack of airline computer experience. Once again I walked out disappointed in the owner, myself, and the Lord for not fixing things exactly as I had wanted them! It would have been *just perfect,* -----wouldn't it?

Ten years later, that owner had closed her business, and was a colleague of mine in a different Travel Agency. When she learned how successful I had been at booking groups on cruises and tours all over the world, all business that could have been hers, she graciously admitted regretting the day she had turned my application down!

Meanwhile, it was soon apparent why my other interviews had come to nothing. The Lord had different plans for me, placing me in a small two person office, with a wonderful Christian manager. Rebecca Davidson had a super sense of humor, teaching me the travel business from top to bottom and helping me with the many Airline computer challenges. As I was paid by the hour, she made certain I had the time off needed to work on the few T.V. commercials and movie parts that came my way.

Helping people to realize their dreams of travelling to far away places thrilled me! Dear Square Dance and Church friends booked their vacations with me and recommended my service to others, resulting in business growth for the office. At night I was sometimes doing Pledge Drive for PBS and it was kind of was fun when a client came into the office and realized they had just seen their Travel Agent on television the night before.

My career as a Travel Agent would span twenty-seven happy years.

CHAPTER 41

A Time To Learn

MICHAEL HAD BEEN ten years old at our wedding, his sister had been seven. Now Mike lived on the Costa del Sol, Spain, with his beautiful wife Patricia and two sons, while he worked in Real Estate.

During her nursing career, Suzanne had fallen in love and married Miles, who was now a successful surgeon. They had three fine boys.

Meanwhile, our Panamanian baby, after serving seven years in the United States Marine Corps, had married a delightful American girl, and given us our sixth grandson. Sean would grow up to be a wonderful light in our lives.

While boys are lots of fun, my heart yearned to have a little girl dancing in a tutu. I asked the Lord if it could possibly be in His will to give us a grand-daughter one day, then promptly went to the mall and bought a pink bed-spread for the spare room. There was no way for me to know that when she finally arrived, our dear Shelby Bomford would one day win scholarship money for college, due not only to her scholastic achievements, but with her talent as a beautiful ballet dancer.

Meanwhile, it had been difficult to be involved in any meaningful way with our overseas grandchildren, but we did the best we could, with alternating visits between England and Spain each year, and watching them all grow from babyhood to young men.

It was at the end of one of these trips in March 1997, that I learned a valuable lesson, albeit, the hard way!

Our seven day visit to Spain was at an end, and Michael had dropped us off at Malaga airport and said goodbye. I had a lump in my throat, realizing that as usual, it would be two long years before we would see him or his family again.

We stood at the airline check-in counter, wondering what was taking the young lady so long to process our tickets. I knew everything was in order, as I had called and confirmed our flights the previous day. Finally the ticket agent told us that the connection from Madrid to Miami shown on our tickets was non- existent. The Trans-Atlantic flight would take off to Miami before our flight to Madrid had arrived.

I was in shock.

Electronic ticketing was still a thing of the future, and I held the hard copy of the tickets in my hand which I had printed myself at the Travel Agency. I had been doing this for ten years now, and knew it was a physical impossibility for any computer to print a ticket for a flight that was not available. It just could not happen! Much later, we learned that the airline had changed to a summer schedule, and failed to change it in their computers!

"The next flight from Madrid to Miami is tomorrow, and it is full. We cannot help you here. Get to Madrid, and they will help you," was the only advice the ticket agent would give us. We knew we were being told to move on, as there was a long line waiting behind us. Then she added in a serious tone, "You should really take this up with your Travel Agent when you get home." "I *am* my Travel Agent," I hissed in frustration. It wasn't her fault, but it was annoying to discover once again that no matter what went wrong during a trip, shifting blame to the Travel Agent thousands of miles away was the usual reaction.

In Madrid we discovered the only available flight would leave two days later, with a five hour layover in San Juan. "We may have a couple of cancellations in the morning if you can get in line early" the agent advised. You bet we would!

Along with all the other "displaced passengers" from the flight that did not exist, we were dispatched to a Madrid Hotel, armed with room and meal vouchers.

After dinner, we struck up a conversation with another stranded passenger. He too was a Travel Agent who had printed out his own ticket in his Miami agency.

In hushed tones, he boasted to me that he had been assured of two seats on the direct flight home the following day, as he had lied to the airline saying his wife had very bad heart problems. "They will give us first class if they can't do anything else," he added with a smirk.

Dishonesty in any form is abhorrent to me, and lying about an illness to "get a jump ahead" on others, I found particularly obnoxious. Instead of quietly praying about the situation, I allowed my blood to boil all night long.

The next morning, the airline provided mini-buses to take us back to the airport. I knew that those who made it to the front of the line at the counter would have the best chance of getting any "no show" seats on the one and only flight that day to Miami.

The bus stopped at the airport, and I felt anger surge through me, as the "lying" Travel Agent and his wife pushed through to get ahead of us off the bus. I was to learn the hard way, (literally!) that one should never allow anger to dictate one's actions!

Hurrying down the steep steps off the bus, my purse in one hand, and my carry-on bag in the other, my foot hit something solid, knocking me badly off balance. I felt my body literally fly through the air, only to slam down hard on the cement airport pavement.

The pain was excruciating.

I knew that two things were certain. I had definitely broken something, and I would not be flying anywhere for many days to come!

I am not sure whether it was my initial screams or the wail of the ambulance sirens that attracted them, but a large crowd of curious onlookers gathered round us. Without a doubt, our two large suitcases would have disappeared, if Douglas had not been smart enough to put them in the care of the Airport Police who had arrived quickly on the scene. They promised to take care of them till Doug could come back later, thus freeing my husband to accompany me in the ambulance.

However, it would be some time before I saw the Madrid Airport again.

With ambulance sirens screaming and the rapid Spanish language buzzing in my ears, I thought of our Fire Fighter/Paramedic son Malcolm, wishing he was with me, not thousands of miles away, doubtless taking care of someone else!

We finally arrived at a hospital somewhere in Madrid.

It was a good thing that my pain was so acute, as there was no room in my psyche to register either embarrassment or humiliation, when a team of young people of both sexes, all shouting at once in their native tongue, proceeded to strip me naked. Finally, a thin sheet was unceremoniously thrown over me and I was wheeled through endless corridors, to the X-ray room.

Finally, situated in a semi-private room, the doctor brought the results to us. My femur was not only broken, but badly shattered.

In no condition to conjure up even the basic "kitchen Spanish" I had used in Panama a quarter of a century earlier, I thanked God for a husband who had spoken perfect Spanish every day on his job at the Port of Miami.

The surgeon gave me the option of either flying nine hours home in agony, or let him operate. There was really no choice. I knew the Captain of the plane would refuse to have a screaming woman on his nine hour flight!

I knew that Spanish doctors had saved the lives of both our daughter-in-law and our baby grandson years before. Taking a deep breath I said "Let's get on with it." I did a lot of praying while waiting forty-eight ours for the big moment.

Coming out of the anesthetic, I saw the doctor leaning over me. "Gracias doctor, gracias," I said, relieved that the whole thing was apparently over. However the Doctor was most apologetic. "No, no, Senora," he said. He was obviously upset. Apparently they had not been able to insert the endotracheal tube, which breathes for the patient with a ventilator, and without which it was too dangerous to operate. I had woken up in the same condition I had been in before.

I looked up from the gurney. Corridor lights flashed by, as I was wheeled back to the unfamiliar room. Probably they were much the same as any lights in a hospital back home, but the foreign chatter around me made everything seem so much worse.

The doctors told Douglas they could not operate, but neither could I be flown across the Atlantic Ocean.

Stranded as we were, it was a horrible dilemma, and Douglas counts that as one of the worst days of his life.

"Dear Lord," I prayed, "Whatever now?"

I had told the doctor of my concern for Doug whose face had taken on an ashen hue. The hospital served the most wonderful food, and from then on, included a tray of the same for Douglas every meal time. Eating became the highlight of our day.

Anyone who has experienced pain knows how difficult it is to concentrate on anything else, and as the television only spoke in Spanish, and no books or magazines were available in English, it was hard to occupy my thoughts with much else!

The next day, Douglas explored the immediate area outside the hospital, and found the entire area was the "hospital center" of Madrid. Not a store, restaurant or hotel was in sight. Douglas would sleep on two chairs next to my bed, as the hospital would be our home. But for how long, we did not know.

Meanwhile, we had been warned that security was a major problem. It was so bad, that patients were not allowed to take anything into hospital with them but a robe, slippers and a tooth brush.

Douglas took a cab back to the airport, and picked up our luggage from the Police. At the suggestion of a smart staff member, Douglas hid them both behind the door, covered in blankets. I asked for big safety pins, and used them to secure our Passports in Doug's hip pocket, along with a warning not to let the pants out of his sight while he was in the showers, which were in a room down the hall, and was used by all the male patients.

Our sense of security was not improved by the knowledge that a felon was in the next room, in spite of the constant noise from his guard's "squawk box".

I was in a semi-private room. It was a government run hospital, part of the Socialized Health scheme of Spain. My American daughter-in-law Deborah, a Nurse in Palm Beach County, voiced horror at hearing there was no telephone in the room, and probably almost fainted when Doug told her there was no bathroom either!

Cell phones were still a thing of the future, and Douglas had to use a public corridor phone to call our three children in three different countries, giving them our news.

A great highlight was when an enormous bouquet of flowers arrived. It was from Michael, who had taken his annual two weeks off while we were with him, so could not take any more time from his job, to drive the three hundred and fifty miles to Madrid. But with virtually zero accommodations available, it would have been impossible for him to stay near us anyway.

We were impressed by the cleanliness of the hospital. It seemed that someone was in sweeping and cleaning every couple of hours.

A routine of sorts evolved, as each morning Douglas brought a cup coffee for me from the corridor machine, just before two Nurses came to give me a bed bath. There was nothing unusual about this, except that the chief Nurse was a male.

Both he and his female assistant insisted that my husband should leave the room during their extremely thorough ministrations. The next day, at my request Douglas carefully explained that we had been married for thirty-five years, and that he would *not* be leaving the room. When one is truly ill and in pain, nothing matters! It always makes for a laugh now, when I remember that the male Nurse's name was "Modesto". He spoke no English. However, when I screamed at the pain of being turned on my side with a still shattered hip, he quoted from Queen Elizabeth's Christmas speech a few years earlier. Her two sons had broken marriages, and Windsor Castle had caught fire. So Her Majesty had quoted a Latin phrase, which Modesto now quoted, apparently sympathizing with me. " Eso es un annus horribilis" he said, sploshing the sponge back into the bowl of water.

Finally, a different surgeon agreed to attempt an operation on my shattered femur. I didn't want to think what might happen if they couldn't get the wretched gadget down my throat again. There was no choice but to pray hard, and trust it would go well.

Douglas was, as ever, a tower of strength. "We'll get through this together, and dance the Cha Cha again!" he assured me. Praying this would be so, and repeating the last verse from Isaiah chapter forty in my head, I was wheeled away from him once gain, and into an operating room.

"But they that wait upon the Lord shall renew their strength. They shall mount up with wings as eagles; they shall run and not be weary; and they shall walk, and not faint." Isaiah 40: v.31

This time it was different. This time I was wide awake, and could hear the incredibly loud voices of the team all talking at once.

I remember thinking they might be discussing the latest football results, as I lay naked on a hard steel "bed", void of even a sheet. It was useless to feel insulted. I was trying to shout over the racket in my kitchen Spanish, but nobody noticed. Indeed, nobody was even looking at me. I wondered if there were other folks around in the same room, waiting to be operated on, and that I was but one body on an assembly line of patients waiting for surgery to be performed.

Someone stuck something down my throat. I started to gag. Again, nobody seemed to be looking my way. I prayed "Lord, I am choking to death. Help me." Suddenly a thought came to me very clearly "Breathe through your nose".

I woke in my bed, with two pins holding the shattered bones together, and only a band-aid over the site of the incision.

On my return to the states, two orthopedic surgeons said they did not yet perform that surgery in America. While the operating room might have been noisy, they had obviously known exactly what they were doing. Those pins are still serving me well sixteen years later.

We were still not out of the woods however, as more challenges lay ahead.

After the usual fasting and denial of any liquids for nine hours before the surgery, I craved what every true child of England needs to have when under stress --- a good cup of tea!

With so little to look forward to, this was a big deal to me, and as tea-time approached, I got very excited at the prospect. I ordered "Te caliente con leche frio por favor," which for my ten years living in Latin America, had always meant, "Hot tea with cold milk please."

I watched the minute hand crawl round to four o'clock, until finally, the door opened and the "tea" lady came in. She carried a cup the size of a soup bowl, with a tea bag dangling from a pint of ice-cold milk. "You asked for hot tea with cold milk, and that is what you've got," she told me in Spanish.

I guess when one is just not well, one's emotions get out of control, because feeling like a total fool, I burst into tears.

Ten days had to elapse after the surgery before I would be allowed to fly. All invalids quickly become a pain in the neck to their caregivers, and I knew that my mind needed to be occupied with more than pain and discomfort. I decided that a game of cards with Douglas would be a good distraction. But with no shops around the area, where would we get a pack ?

I thought it trite to pray for something so unimportant. However, knowing that no sort of gambling was to take place, and that the fun provided would help me enormously, I asked the Lord to forgive me for asking for something so trivial, and asked for a pack of cards.

The lady on the other side of the dividing curtain of our semi-private room, always had a lot of visitors. With his impeccable Spanish, Douglas got into conversation with one of them, and a pack of cards was promised. A few hours later we played our first game. The distraction made an enormous difference. While physically the same, mentally I felt a hundred percent better.

Finally a day was set for my release. Grateful that I had taken my own advice to clients and taken Trip Insurance, the wheels were set in motion for our flight home. Knowing I would need to keep one leg straight out in front, I prayed for a first class seat, closest to the bathroom, with a flight attendant whose first language would be English .

However, there was yet another big hurdle before us.

We had to pay the hospital for thirteen nights, food for two, and surgery before I could be released.

It was a National Health hospital. Nobody *paid* any bills! They had no way to handle a credit card. They would only accept payment in Spain's currency (pesetas at that time) before they would release me. The fact that our Insurance company would reimburse us *after* we got home did not help us right now!

"What about contacting Peter Graham?" I asked, remembering the first person I had met in Panama thirty-five years before. Peter had retired to Madrid with his family years before, but Douglas had always kept in touch with him. Now Douglas looked up his telephone number, and departed to the public phone in the corridor, while I prayed that Peter would be able to help us.

After an interminable amount of time, Douglas came back to my room looking very depressed. "There is no reply. They must have gone to their fruit farm in the hills for the Easter week" he informed me dismally.

Three more attempts were made that day, but without success. It became obvious that Peter and his wife had gone to their "getaway" in the country outside Madrid and we had no way to contact them.

"Oh dear Lord, what in the living world are we to do" I asked in reverent prayer.

No money could be "wired" to us at the hospital from anyone including the credit card company. Spanish cash was what the hospital needed, and Spanish cash was what we must pay with.

Then I did something folks would call very foolish. I prayed long and hard, that somehow, *something* would bring Peter and his wife back to Madrid.

The next afternoon I urged Douglas to phone them again.

My husband reappeared with a victorious grin on his face. "It was pouring with rain at their country place, so they decided to come back to Madrid. I told Peter I needed half a million pesetas by Friday. He is bringing it Thursday," Douglas ended with total relief written on his face.

As he had to travel by train to get to the hospital, Peter arrived with the cash strapped around him in a large body-belt. Of course he knew that Douglas would wire him the money as soon as we got back to Florida, but it was a kindness we would never forget.

We paid the hospital bill in cash, and were given permission to leave.

It still amazes me the way the Lord provided an answer to each and every one of the myriad details we had to cope with during that stressful time.

But there was more to come.

Spanish hospitals like a patient to have a family member or friend with them twenty-four seven. It helps the staff, and the patient. When my father had been in hospital in England years before, the family had been confined to a couple of "visiting hours" three days a week.

The moment the bell rang announcing the end of the hour, a huffy nurse would shoo us away if we didn't move fast enough. I found the Spanish hospital's attitude to family and friends refreshing and quite wonderful. Here, parents, spouse, and sometimes numerous children along with aunts and uncles would visit the patient. It made it a bit crowded and noisy on occasion, but I enjoyed the atmosphere of love that surrounded the three different room-mates I had during my stay.

The Insurance company gave us excellent service, and once a date was set for us to travel, we were assured that first class tickets on a direct flight to Miami would be waiting for us at the airport. It should be plain sailing from now on.

However, there was yet *another* problem in store for us.

Easter week is a very major holiday in Catholic countries, and our flight was leaving on Good Friday.

The hospital warned us that, apart from a skeleton staff, the hospital would be closed. Also although the Insurance company would cover an ambulance to the airport for us, there would not be any available, as they had to keep them for dire emergencies only.

We tried to book a cab, but none of the companies would be working. They said the roads would be blocked off for religious parades. There was no way to get to the airport.

Everything had been going so well. Now this!

I often wonder why we worry so much?

I should have known that I was in the Lord's care, and he would provide the means to get to our flight. But how? The hospital could offer no solution, and no cab company would take our booking. All I could do was pray.

That evening, the father of my room-mate was visiting her. Douglas chatted with him, and mentioned our dilemma. He was a self-employed cab driver! He would pick us up any time we wanted, and drive us on Good Friday round the back streets to the airport.

That patient whose father "just happened" to be a cab driver, could have been put in any of dozens of wards. She just "happened" to be put in my room.

Coincidence? Never in a million years!

The doctor issued a dire warning; I must not allow my left toe to even touch the ground. Attempts to use crutches all ended in my almost falling down. Eventually, it was deemed not an option. To this day, seeing a person on crutches evokes the deepest admiration in me.

I spent much of the last few days visualizing every stage of the journey, and planning strategy for overcoming every hazard between the hospital bed in Madrid, and my own bed four and a half thousand miles away.

Finally the big day arrived. It had been only two weeks since I had inhaled fresh air, but it seemed like months. Stowed onto the back seat of the tiny cab, we commenced our winding journey through the back streets of Madrid, avoiding the Good Friday procession routes. Finally the airport came into view, and Doug and I breathed a deep sigh of relief and thanksgiving.

The airport wheel-chair was pushed by a small chattering man, with all the enthusiasm of a race car driver. My heart was in my mouth as he narrowly missed slamming my stuck out leg into other people's baggage, and elevator doors. He finally gave up the job to Douglas, who was obliged to bear the yelps and stares of the other ladies in the rest room, as he had no other option but to accompany me there!

I had always seen wheel-chair passengers boarded first. However, it became obvious that there was no such thing as a departure lounge for our Trans-Atlantic flight, as we were directed outdoors. With the aid of a hydraulic lift, my wheel-chair and I were lifted onto a small bus and we set off across the tarmac. Alarm bells started to clang in my head as we approached an enormous American Airlines jumbo jet. The sun shone brilliantly on the chrome of a stairway that went straight up for miles, like the stairway to paradise! I soothed myself with the thought that here too, there would be another hydraulic device for my wheel-chair, while the other passengers would negotiate the steep steps.

But I was in for a nasty shock.

Douglas wheeled me from my gentle decent from the bus, to the foot of the aircraft steps. I looked up at the passenger door of the plane. That twenty foot height looked further away than ever, and no special equipment was appearing. Instead, there stood two very tall Basque gentlemen who proceeded to take me out of the airport wheel-chair, and sit me on an incredibly narrow wooden chair with a high back. My left leg was still sticking straight out, as they fastened two seat belts criss-crossing my shoulders. It was then that I realized what was to happen. With one either side of me, they were going to haul me up the steep steps. "Just like a Disneyworld ride," my ever optimistic husband shouted, as my body lurched higher and higher straight up twenty feet to the passenger door. I was facing forward, the space between my body and the ground growing ever larger as I was jerked up each steep step. Shivering with both cold and fear, I clutched onto my skirt which the cold wind threatened to blow up over my head.

It was then that I learned there is something very disconcerting about a total lack of control over one's safety, and when the distance between my body and the ground became sickeningly large, I closed my eyes and prayed "Lord, I know you would not bring me this far, to have me fall to my death on a Madrid tarmac. Please give these men strength, and let me get onto this plane safely." My nerves were so shattered that moments later, when I heard an American accent saying "Welcome aboard," I burst into tears with relief. I had not heard that wonderful sound in many weeks, and it was music to my ears. That lovely stewardess led us into the front row first class seats by the window. But even more importantly when facing a nine hour flight, unable to take a step without pain, in front of me was the most welcome view of all. The door to the rest room!

"Thank you Lord" I breathed.

Malcolm met us at Miami airport, our two year old grandson in his arms, and his beautifully pregnant wife Deborah, at his side. Tears of joy ran down my cheeks, for it was the most welcome sight I had ever encountered in my life.

Days later, the bone specialist told me that if I was very lucky, I would only spend three months in a wheel chair, warning me however, that forty percent of people with my type of injury, with the bone so badly shattered, never recovered.

It was during those difficult weeks that I truly learned about prayer, patience, good friends, the depth of my husband's love, and the scope of God's grace.

My wonderful Douglas, had fortunately retired a few years before, as he cooked and cleaned, did laundry, carried me into the shower, and faithfully wheeled me round the neighborhood every day. Good friends sat with me on the evenings he had his Royal British Legion meetings and his choir practice. I wanted to shout from the roof tops, that true love has little to do with youth, good looks or moonlight, and everything to do with caring for the beloved "In sickness and in health". One of the greatest achievements was that at no time did Douglas ever make me feel I was a nuisance to him. Which of course I often was, like the day I tried to help load the clothes washer (which I could not really reach,) and succeeded only in throwing underwear down the back of the wretched thing. Another time I tried to do the dusting, and got my wheel-chair jammed between the stereo and the dining table.

Finally the big day came when I was able to transfer into the supermarket handicapped electric chair. The highlight of my week was to tear around from the produce to the canned fruit section. Not able to drive a real car, it still helped my sense of well-being, as a dashing driver of Davie!

Fortunately, our Church at that time had a ramp up to the choir loft. It was a joy to be able to sing from my wheel-chair. Months passed as I graduated first to a walking frame, then a cane.

One year after the incredible surgery in Spain, thanks be to God and a brilliant surgeon, Douglas and I were dancing the cha-cha again.

CHAPTER 42

A Time To Mourn

THE JOB OF a Travel Agent was sometimes satisfying, but very often frustrating. Along with the armchair travelers who talk about going, plan on going, but never go anywhere, are the "book, change and cancel" folk. Not a dime is earned for the dozens of hours of work put in by the Travel Agent on these people.

However, the upside was the many satisfied clients who booked their trips every year with me, and I particularly enjoyed planning our small Group Trips.

Douglas was a huge asset every year, for along with his delightful disposition and sense of humor, the fact that he was a superb ballroom dancer was not lost on the ladies without partners, as he steered them smilingly round the cruise ship dance floors. In fact, soon after Douglas had retired, we had travelled as the Ballroom Dance teachers for some of the cruise lines.

At the end of every trip, the question was asked "Where to next year Angela?" So instead of just sailing the Caribbean, we ventured further afield.

When the group included Square Dance friends I stowed my tape-recorder in the bottom of my suitcase, thus taking great "callers" with us.

One summer, after we had Square Danced till late in a hotel in Anchorage, we all went for a walk. In a park nearby, we saw parents pushing their children on swings at midnight in broad daylight. Later in that trip, arriving at a beautiful new hotel in Fairbanks, we heard a great Western Band performing. They were out on a huge white terrace overlooking a river. Within minutes, our group was Line Dancing and inhaling pristine air, while in the distance, seaplanes skimmed to a halt on the water.

Days later, we stood on the top deck of our ship, surrounded by glaciers so white that they looked blue, and heard the gasp of delight on seeing the classic picture before us - the tail of a whale reaching up, and waving upon the icy waters .

On a Hawaiian Cruise, we had the chance to swim in the surf on Waikiki beach, Diamond Head reaching up nearby. I will never forget looking down from the Pearl Harbor Memorial at the submerged USS Arizona beneath.

It had been Sunday December 7th 1941, when eleven hundred and seventy seven sailors, many still asleep in their bunks, died without warning. Japanese planes had attacked the fleet of the United States, while the Japanese Ambassador was at that moment speaking with the United States Secretary of State in Washington. It was indeed, as predicted by President Roosevelt, a day that "would live in infamy."

The magnificent Canadian Rockies tour, ending with two days at the Calgary Stampede was a huge hit, as was a fifteen day cruise on a new ship from Barcelona. We went ashore and visited Monte Carlo, Rome, Florence and Lisbon before sailing home across the Atlantic Ocean to Fort Lauderdale.

Some of our greatest travel memories were formed while taking a group on an incredible Greek Island cruise.

Walking across the raised boards of an ongoing archaeological dig on the island of Santorini, we saw a three thousand year old bed which had been discovered beneath the ash of a volcano. Staircases could still be seen where three storied buildings had once stood. This ancient town had been buried in volcanic ash until 1967 when excavations began. While the ash had preserved pitchers and storage vessels and incredible frescos, the population had evidently abandoned the area in the 17th Century B.C. due to so many earthquakes. A small, perfectly preserved goblet was jammed in the corner of one structure. Perhaps it was a special vessel a young wife wanted to protect, hoping to return one day, as she evacuated from her home with her family, friends, and neighbors.

Unlike Pompeii, there had been no evidence of any human remains.

The greatest thrill of my travelling experiences took place on the island of Patmos. I stood in the cave where John the Divine wrote the Book of Revelation as he stated in Chapter 1 verse 9

" *I, John, who also am your brother and companion in tribulation, and in the kingdom and patience of Jesus Christ, was in the isle that is called Patmos for the word of God and for the testimony of Jesus Christ.*

Standing in that cave, my spiritual breath was almost taken away at the realization of where I was.

Above the cave there is still a working monastery where carefully preserved copies of parts of our Bible can be seen through thick glass. It was awesome indeed to see a copy of the Book of Job, which had been written on parchment in the Seventh Century.

Parts of the Bible dated from the year 941, and pages of the Gospel of Mark from the Fifth Century had the names of God and Jesus written in gold. While other parts of our Bible are preserved in other parts of the world, here I was with my husband, friends and clients, seeing these wonders with our own eyes. I felt blessed all over.

It is very doubtful that I would have had the opportunity to travel so extensively and seen so many wondrous things, if I had not become a Travel Agent.

The New Millennium had been greeted with incredible fireworks around the globe just a year earlier. Now the group wanted me to organize a trip across Europe, and after months of planning and preparation, finally the big day arrived. Douglas and I flew to England first for a few days with family including Suzanne and my brother Norman, before meeting the group in a Munich hotel. From there, all twenty-two of us would travel through Germany, Switzerland, Italy and Austria.

There is something very special about a train ride with panoramic views of snow-clad mountains, or strolling through picturesque Swiss villages awash in cuckoo clocks, while looking up at the splendor of the Jungfrau.

While some may laugh at the touristy things one does travelling, I found it a joy to share a gondola in Venice with Douglas and some of our group. While the Gondolier steered us through the famous canals, his companion, while not one of the Three Tenors, serenaded us quite beautifully with "O Solo Mio".

Vienna held a special thrill for me, as we attended a Viennese Waltz concert in the hall where Johann Strauss had first conducted his famous music. Listening to that wonderful three- four rhythm, I could almost see the long-gloved ladies twirling about the floor in their crinoline gowns. The next day, we actually sailed down "The Blue Danube" itself, to the strains of that lilting melody played on the boat's public address system.

The group had bonded well. We laughed and enjoyed ourselves.

We had no idea that at that same moment, evil men were making their final preparations to inflict an act of terror so vile, that the world would never be the same again.

With only two more days left of our European tour, our bus stopped at a village high in the Austrian Alps, for a mid-afternoon break.

Spotting a large display of picture post cards outside a little shop I headed in that direction. We were to take the "Sound of Music" tour the following day in Salzburg. I plucked out a card showing Julie Andrews with the Von Trapp children, smiling as I recollected my own performance in the show in the Panama Canal Zone over thirty years before.

At that moment a lady came out from the shop shouting "They've hit the World Trade Center again."

It was September 11th, 2001.

That night in a hotel high in the Austrian Alps, I sat at dinner with my deeply distressed group of passengers.

Up in our rooms, we had all watched the television coverage of the terrorist attack.

The Chairman of our Church Board was with us, and led us in prayer before our meal.

In deep shock, unable to grasp the reality of such an inhuman act, we picked at the food on our plates in silence. But soon my dear friends and travelling companions began to demand the impossible from me. "Get us home Angela," they pleaded, "Just get us home."

Every airport in the United States had been closed. We could do nothing but follow the itinerary taking the Salzburg tour the next day, and pray we may be allowed to board our flights home as planned on the thirteenth of September.

The next day, we reached Salzburg, where the Austrian people had draped wide black bands of ribbon down the buildings in Mozart Square. The location had been used in the movie after Maria's wedding, when the Nazis had been shown marching in.

"The Sound of Music" tour had been the one I had particularly looked forward to for months.

Like most people I had seen the brilliant movie numerous times, and wanted to see all the locations where the shots had been filmed. In keeping with the mood of that moment however, it was pouring with rain as our tour bus passed the fountain Julie Andrews and the children had marched around.

The local tour guide tried valiantly to keep up the string of patter no doubt usually received well by his audience. But today, he met nothing but red eyes and vacant looks. "Poor chap," I thought.

Then news came of the continued closure of all U.S. airports. All efforts to contact the airlines were met by a busy signal. Meanwhile the round of tour groups immediately behind us continued to arrive from other parts of the continent, and they needed our rooms.

We had to move out of the hotel. But where to? Every hotel was packed with Americans unable to get home.

While we realized how fortunate we were to be safe and well, far from the suffering in New York, it was nerve-wracking for my passengers, as we all had to split up into any hotel with a room in the vicinity that could accommodate us.

The tour company did an excellent job, eventually finding accommodation for my group, as all of them had booked their flights through me, with the tour company. Ironically however, as Doug and I had visited England first, we had booked our flights independently *not* through the tour company. Although we were the leaders, and I was the Travel Agent, the tour company could not help us. We were on our own.

Thinking of the horror and sadness enveloping the families of the victims of the attack, my prayer for a room seemed very trite. But we were homeless with our suitcases in a foreign country.

We took a cab to Munich airport in the hope we may learn something. It was eerily empty. Only one couple stood at the Swissair counter.

They had just had the news confirmed that all U.S. airports were still closed "Till further notice." When that would be, nobody knew. They were begging the attendant to phone the hotel where they had just given up their room, to ask if they would let them back in. Quickly I called out "Please ask if they have another room available!" I held my breath, praying hard. Finally the answer came back. "Yes."

We carried our luggage out to the curb and shared a cab with the only other two passengers we had seen in the entire airport.

It was a small hotel set outside a Medieval German village, and most of the guests appeared to be from the U.S.

The Manager, complete in lederhosen, could not have been kinder. About twenty Americans had lingered in the dining room after breakfast, when he addressed the group, expressing his deep sadness at the terrible loss of life in New York.

"Your country is suffering badly. You are our guests here in Germany and for now this is your home," he declared. "This dining room will remain open continuously, with a supply of tea, coffee and snacks supplied for you all. It is the least we can do." This kind German gentleman realized the need for those of us from the United States to draw together at this tragic time.

Since the German bombs had dropped in England when I was a child, I had always felt a shiver of fear when I heard a German accent. But now I knew that from that day onwards, it would always be a welcome sound to my ears. That Manager had no way of knowing that not only was he lending succor to a frightened group of people during their moment of crisis, but he was also healing a very old, very deep wound. Now I am in regular contact with German friends, and always look forward to their annual visit to our home for a meal when they are in Florida.

There was nothing but a busy signal from the airline. There was nothing we could do but wait, so Douglas and I decided to explore the area.

A short walk from the little hotel was an enormously thick wall surrounding a Medieval village. There, every shop window displayed black ribbons. Some were draped around a Statue of Liberty or the U.S. flag, along with signs of sympathy written in English.

We came across what was obviously a centuries old Protestant Parish Church. We walked in, and were amazed to see so many people kneeling in prayer. Without understanding the language, the familiar cadence told us we were hearing The Lord's Prayer being recited. It was obviously a special gathering to pray for the victims of the tragedy that had happened thousands of miles away.

On the ancient stone wall of the church were two enormous plaques. Names of the village men who had lost their lives during the two World Wars were inscribed on them. One was from the First World War of 1914 to 1918, and the other from the Second World War that lasted in Europe from 1939 to 1945.

I thought of all the Memorials I had seen across Great Britain, and the men my father had seen killed beside him in the trenches of France in the First World War. A generation later, Douglas had lost his brother Harry, in the Second World War. It seemed as if all the tears of all the mothers and fathers, wives and sweethearts, brothers, sisters and children of all those killed in war on both sides, were streaming down. For on that day, the world was facing yet another enemy of freedom and love.

My heart rebelled. "Why Lord? Why did anyone bother fighting? It just isn't worth the sacrifice!" my spirit cried.

Then I remembered all my precious Jewish friends. And suddenly I knew that sometimes, some things are truly worth fighting for.

It was five days later when the last of our group finally landed safely back home in the United States.

The ordeal has never deterred any of us from travelling overseas again, for to allow that to happen, would mean that those who would terrorize us, had won. And that must *never* happen.

CHAPTER 43

Truly A Time To Dance

I HAD NEVER LIED to my husband. But now I had to.

It had taken five months to arrange a surprise eightieth Birthday party for Douglas. Every precaution had been taken to keep the secret. A local golf club restaurant had been paid in cash so that no paper trail would exist in my check-book or on a credit card statement. Invitations were mailed out from a friend's house, with their return address.

The biggest secret of all however, had to be *very* carefully concealed.

I was determined that Douglas would have all three of his children with him for his big celebration. But how could I get Michael from Spain, and Suzanne from England without Douglas knowing anything about them being in the United States until the party was under way? It took a lot of prayer. I asked the Lord for ideas that would make my wonderful husband's special day, one that would give him true joy and happy memories.

At that time, we had to pay for overseas phone calls, and tell-tale conversation minutes could not show up on the monthly phone bill. Doug's eagle eye would wonder why only *I* had been talking to the children, and not him! So phoning them was "out".

Fortunately, Douglas had not yet mastered e-mail, so the complicated arrangements to get Michael and Suzanne to Florida were done on-line.

After months of careful organization, flights were finally arranged. Michael was bringing his son Sebastian, now thirteen, along with him. They would fly from Spain to England, overnight with Suzanne, then all three would fly from London arriving in Florida the day before the party, which was a Saturday.

After booking two rooms at a hotel near the party venue, it was arranged that I would meet them there at four o'clock in the afternoon, an hour after their aircraft was due to land. I wracked my brain for a week, trying to think of a valid excuse to be gone from four to six o'clock on a Saturday afternoon. Douglas knew I never shopped at week-ends, so where was I going?

Then I had an idea. A wedding shower! Men are never invited to wedding showers! I approached Maritza, a colleague at the Travel Agency who I knew had a daughter of marriageable age, and asked her if she would pretend to invite me to a wedding shower. I had no clue that in fact her daughter *was* getting married, and *was* indeed, having her bridal shower *that very Saturday!*

The invitation duly arrived, and I showed it to Douglas. My cover story was perfect!

After months of secret preparation, the plan was complete.

Finally the day of the secret arrival of Michael, Suzanne and Sebastian, arrived. Taking my cell phone into the bathroom to be sure Douglas could not hear my conversation, I dialed the airline desk for "arrival times".

Then I got a shock. Their flight from London was over three hours late. They would not be at the hotel before seven o'clock in the evening! "So much for my cover story", I thought.

Now there was a new problem. What excuse could I find to leave the house and stay out alone on a Saturday night? I had never chosen to be away from Douglas on a Saturday night. In our marriage, except for work, it would never happen!

Once again locked in the bathroom with my cell phone, I made a call to a good friend who was on the guest list. I whispered my problem into the cell phone to Eunice. "Please call me tonight at exactly seven o'clock. Don't worry about anything I say, just listen to me, and then hang up," I begged. She agreed.

Then, drawing on all my acting skills, I feigned weariness, and told Douglas I would call Maritza with my regrets at missing her shower, and spend the afternoon resting.

To be certain the birthday boy would be dressed in jacket and tie at the appointed time, I had told him that arrangements had been made for a special lunch for his birthday, with just two tables; the family on one and eight ballroom dancing friends on the other. But I kept the location a secret.

That evening, pretending to be engrossed in our umpteenth viewing of "Doctor Zhivago", I gripped the arm-rest of my recliner, while watching the hands of the clock out of the corner of my eye.

Omar Sharif was shoving his way across our television screen thigh high in snow, when at exactly seven o'clock, the telephone rang.

"Hi there Eunice. What's up?" I asked. I let a few seconds elapse, apparently listening to her. "Oh no!" I exclaimed loudly, "Can't *you* sign for it?"

I could see Douglas looking at me from his armchair with a quizzed expression. I let more silent seconds pass by, then after more phony complaints, I continued. "Oh I suppose I can come now if I really *have* to. I'll see you soon". I hung up on a very good, but totally confused friend!

"Sorry love," I said to Douglas. "Eunice had gone to the restaurant to finish something off for me with the caterer, and they have got something wrong. Eunice wanted to change it, but they say the instruction has to come from me. They won't take her signature for it."

By now it was dark, and ever solicitous of my safety, Douglas offered to drive me there. "Oh no thanks, that would spoil the surprise!" I answered quickly. "Oh boy would it ever!" I thought, grabbing my purse, and heading for the door.

The receptionist at the hotel called their rooms. It had been almost two years since I had seen Suzanne, and three since seeing Michael and Sebastian.

Suddenly they appeared.

The little boy who had so enthusiastically mopped up his gravy with his bread when he was ten years old, was now a handsome man in his fifties, while his younger son thirteen year old Sebastian on his first trip outside Spain, walked beside him. Both had ear to ear grins as they hugged me.

The little seven year old who had been my bridesmaid, little Suzie, had matured into a beautiful woman. She had been a Nurse and raised three sons, but looked twenty years younger than her half century.

In order to explain my longer-than-expected absence from home, I phoned Douglas telling him that the manager of the party venue had invited me to have dinner "on the house", as they had "messed up" on the table arrangements. "But I won't be long," I finished. More lies and deceit, while I was dining with his children! Horrible!!

While Sebastian enthused over eating his first, real American hamburger, I went over the modus operandi for the next day. The three of them would arrive at the Golf Club before the guests, and hide in the Manager's office until their planned appearance. Only four guests knew about them being in the country.

The big day arrived.

Soon after noon, we left the house, Douglas having no idea where he was driving to, but just following my navigation info, "Right here, left there" etc., It was hot in the car, and he kept urging me to take off the jacket I was wearing, but it was hiding my dressy glitter top, and I didn't want to blow my cover!

Explaining we were having our celebration in the small side room, we walked up the steps and opened the big door to the Club-house.

Seeing tables covered with beautiful linen and glassware, balloons high over each chair, Douglas said, "Oh look. They must be expecting a wedding party". At that moment the entire Square Dance Club along with Ballroom Dancing friends and guests hiding around the corner of the room, jumped out with a huge shout of "surprise" and the D.J. struck up with "He's a Jolly Good Fellow."

It was a great moment. But my stomach was doing leap-frogs, knowing the *biggest* surprise for Douglas was yet to come!

After everyone was settled down at their tables, I took the microphone and announced that because our family was so scattered, they had never been able to attend special celebrations. Therefore, Malcolm, our youngest child, had arranged for a conference call on his cell phone with Spain and England.

Moments later, Malcolm's cell phone rang. There was total silence in the room as Malcolm handed the phone to his father, who started talking to Michael, who he believed to be in Spain.

After a sentence or two, Michael walked out of the Manager's Office onto the dance floor still talking on his cell phone, followed by his sister and his son.

The guests, suddenly realizing what was happening, gave a gasp. Douglas was facing the other way, talking into the phone. I asked him to turn around.

Douglas could obviously not believe his eyes, as he saw his two children and one grandchild supposedly thousands of miles away, standing in front of him.

That was the first time all three of the children had been in the same room together with us in thirty-two years.

The Manager remarked later that the emotion in the room was so potent, her servers had a problem doing their job, as they along with her, had tears of joy running down their faces.

After the meal, I sang "You Light Up My Life," to Douglas, then after Square and Ballroom dancing, games and cake, the party was over. The family gathered at our home. We would only have three days together, as Mike and Suzie had to return to their jobs and Sebastian to his Spanish school.

Our Children L to R – Malcolm, Suzanne, Michael

Douglas played tennis with them while I, (still never having mastered the art of getting my racket to meet the ball,) wielded my camera to record the unique event.

I was so very thankful to the Lord for those magical moments, and for a husband who could still run around a tennis court at eighty!

Ecclesiastes Ch 3. v. 4 "A time to weep, and a time to laugh; a time to mourn, and a time to dance.

EPILOGUE

IN 2008, WE took the Panama Canal cruise, and spent a day in Panama City.

There we met with some of the men Douglas had mentored into the shipping business almost fifty years earlier. I looked around the table, remembering them as the young fellows who worked for Doug's company when they were in their early twenties. They had all become successful business men, some already retired.

Over lunch, Juan Price told the story of his interview with Douglas when, as a sixteen year old Panamanian boy, he had applied for the job of messenger.

"Mr. Bomford, after all these years I have a confession to make to you," Juan announced across the table. He had everyone's attention. "At the interview for the job of a messenger, you asked me if I could ride a motor- bike, and I said yes." Juan cleared his throat and continued. "It has taken me forty-five years, but now I must confess to you that at that time, I had never been on a motor -cycle in my life. But my friend had one, and I spent all that night practicing on his!" he ended.

Howls of laughter went round the table. The young man of so many years before, had obviously been very desperate to get the job! Juan went on to say that when Douglas promoted him to the Mail Room, he carefully studied Doug's superbly worded business letters. This had helped him considerably when he eventually opened his own Insurance Agency.

After more such stories from round the table, a big vote of thanks to Douglas was offered. His positive influence had obviously made a huge difference to all their lives. It was a very proud moment for me, as I saw and felt the total respect and love these business men had for my husband.

I remembered all the Sundays we had driven straight from Church to the Panama office, pre-teen Suzanne and toddler Malcolm in tow, so that Douglas could check the telex messages. As area Manager for the whole of Central America and the Caribbean, as well as handling some twenty-five ships a week transiting the Canal, Doug's job had been almost a seven day week saga!

The gentleman who had met us off our cruise ship and organized the day for us, was Tony Conte, who I remembered from the days we lived in Panama, as a fresh-faced, extremely polite young man.

Today Tony took us first to the Ancon Theatre Guild, where as a lonely bride forty-seven years before, I had made friends and appeared in plays. Arrangements had been made for us to get into the building, and I was thrilled to see photographs of both Doug's sister Vera (who had passed away some years before) and myself displayed in the lobby.

Later Tony drove us to the home of my King from "The King and I", Adolfo Arias. Adolfo's beautiful home is situated on the Panama Bay, next door to the Panamanian Presidential Palace.

A servant answered the door and escorted us to the balcony. I remembered the times I had stood here at the cast parties which Adolfo had kindly hosted after the shows. Now I was once again looking at the stupendous view of the bay. The last time I had looked at that view there had been nothing on the other side of the bay but a white beach. Now there were dozens of tall white buildings, a sure sign of the prosperity of this new Panama City.

Suddenly I heard the voice that had rung out over the auditorium years before "Mrs. Anna!" I was enfolded in a warm embrace by a smiling King of Siam. Adolfo was now ninety years young, and while we did not polka round his living room to "Shall We Dance" our hearts and minds were back on a stage, in the previous century.

All too soon, Tony had to remind us that our ship would sail without us if we did not leave. It was time to say farewell to dear friends from the past, Panama City, and the memories of the first nine years of our married life.

In March of 2012, by decree of President Sarkozy of France, Douglas was appointed a Chavalier of the Legion of Honor, the highest decoration possible from France, in recognition of his part in the liberation of that country during the Second World War. The medal had been created by Napoleon in 1802, to acknowledge services rendered to France by persons of exceptional merit.

Once again, geography made it possible for only one of Doug's three children, and two of his seven grand-children to attend the ceremony, and take part in our very proud moment. But that night, television news coverage included a close-up of Douglas as the medal was pinned on his jacket by the French Consul.

Douglas Bomford, with the Medal of the French Legion of Honor. Pictured with his proud son, Malcolm

Two weeks later, we celebrated our Golden Wedding Anniversary.

Had it really been fifty years since I had walked up the aisle of my Church in England and seen Douglas turn to me with his huge smile?

Our vows had been taken before family and friends who thought we were both quite insane. Douglas was taking a terrible risk marrying a girl he had courted only six weeks, chancing that as an instant wife and mother, she would fit into the life of his family in a foreign land. Dark predictions of the bride being "Back here in six months" had circulated, while she had just smiled and smiled.

The Lord has blessed all three of our children with good spouses, and successful marriages.

The little boy Michael gave us two fine grandsons, Christopher and Sebastian Bomford, now both in their twenties whose pictures have been seen in advertisements from Spain to the United States.

Little Suzie, who had shyly asked to be my bridesmaid, is now Suzanne Dickson, mother of three young men. Iain Dickson is a Marine Biologist using his skills in Medical Research, hoping to contribute to a cure for debilitating diseases. Graham Dickson is a successful actor in England while his younger brother, Simon Dickson is studying for his Masters degree in film journalism. He has already been published in a well known American film journal.

Our Panamanian born child, Malcolm recently retired as a Battalion Chief of West Palm Beach fire department, but continues to train Paramedics at Palm Beach State College. His wife Deborah Bomford, is a Nurse Practitioner, and won the title of Mrs. Florida Continental 2012 and Mrs. U.S. Continental 2013. Their son Sean is heading for College studies in Computer Science while sister Shelby Bomford, just fifteen, is winning beauty pageants to raise scholarship money for her education as a Child's Advocate Attorney. Meanwhile, she is raising funds and donating to the needs of "The Place of Hope," a faith-based family style foster care organization. Shelby is a very beautiful dancer. How her great-aunts Olive and Vera, would have enjoyed her!

Now when I sit in a theatre holding my husband's hand, I smile, remembering the desperate fear that haunted me of ever having to sit "down there in the audience" instead of being up on the stage as a performer. For not only do I delight at seeing all the new young talent on display, but in my heart, I would not change places with them for all the gold in the world. Singing with Douglas in the Church choir, narrating the Bible, or using my hands in sign language during Worship Services, keeps me totally content.

Only the Lord could have worked such a miracle.

Choir Members of Plantation Community Church
Angela and Douglas Bomford 2013

We had been visiting England for my brother Norman's eighty-ninth birthday in 2009. The day before our flight home to Florida, it was suggested we might like to see the new "Floral Pavilion Theatre" in New Brighton.

The original building had been torn down.

It had been where my father had talked the band leader into letting me sing when I was three years old; where as a fourteen year old, I had sung with Carol Gatley, and developed a crush on the handsome twenty-three year old Director of the show, Mr. Bomford.

The Floral Pavilion, the same place where fourteen years later, after singing again with Carol, I had gone round to the front of the auditorium and met Douglas Bomford again.

Now my nephew drove the family to the spot where so many of our memories lay.

The new building was magnificent. The lobby consisted of a full size lounge with couches and easy chairs.

While waiting for tea to be served, I walked down the carpeted steps, anxious to see the new auditorium. A lady on guard at the entrance explained that there was a private meeting taking place, and I was not allowed even a brief look-see inside. I explained my history with the theatre, and begged to have a tiny peek as I was flying home the next day, four thousand miles away, and would probably never return. But to no avail. I did not see the inside of the auditorium then, and I probably never will.

Turning away in disappointment, I saw Douglas approaching me, a big smile on his face. "You will never guess who has just walked in!" He exclaimed. "Carol Gatley!"

Carol had no idea we were even in England. She just "happened" to have driven there for a cup of tea with a friend. Now both in our seventies, we were like school girls as we hugged and laughed. Carol looked fantastic. I would have recognized her anywhere.

Out of 58,000 people living in Wallasey, Carol and her friend had chosen to visit at exactly the same time as us. Had she arrived an hour earlier or later, or on any other day, we would never have met.

Carol Gatley Elifson & Angela Bomford at the Floral Pavilion, New Brighton, 2009

I don't believe in coincidence or fate. But I do believe in a wonderful, loving God, Who knows our hearts, for He made us.

I breathed a prayer of thanksgiving. The Lord had so very graciously added this special little bit of serendipity, placing icing on the cake of our last day, on our last trip to the land of our birth, dear England.

Psalm 24. V 10 *"Who is He, this King of glory? The Lord of hosts – He is the King of glory."*

THE END

CPSIA information can be obtained at www.ICGtesting.com
Printed in the USA
LVOW13s1739310813

350248LV00003B/10/P